The Big Oak at Big Oak Flat about 1870.

The

BIG OAK FLAT ROAD

an account of freighting from Stockton to

Yosemite Valley

MARGARET E. SCHLICHTMANN

AND

IRENE D. PADEN

AWANI PRESS

FREDERICKSBURG, TEXAS

©1986 The Awani Press
Fredericksburg, Texas 78624
ISBN 0-915266-17-2
Fifth Printing

Contents

Illustrations

Foreword

As you read these pages, be you hiker-explorer, armchair historian, librarian or researcher, you will understand and appreciate the fact that a lot of California history—events, places, and especially people, extending from Stockton to Yosemite Valley—would have been lost and forgotten had it not been for the perseverance and meticulous note-keeping of people like Margaret Schlichtmann and Irene Paden, and their patient husbands, Emil and Bill, who drove them over hundreds of miles of dusty foothill and mountain roads to interview and record the stories of pioneers—cattlemen, inn-keepers, miners and housewives—and present them in this book.

The prestigious Commonwealth Club Award for the best contribution to California history was presented to the authors when this book was published in 1955. Except for the addition of this forword and a number of historic photographs no changes have been made to the first edition. The librarian and research historian will be pleased with the careful documentation of the authors, their Notes, Appendix, Bibliography and Index.

Many of the once-lively settlements such as Boneyard, Noisy Flat, and Keystone, have disappeared, and much of the old Big Oak Flat Road has been replaced by modern, high-speed highway, but many of the places described on these pages may be located without too much difficulty. Some sections may be walked on foot. For a delightful all-day down-hill hike in Yosemite National Park have a driver drop you at Gin Flat on the Tioga Road. There you can explore the ruins of the Curtain cow camp (see page 229), then go on to Tamarack Flat (p. 234) and down past the beautiful dry-rock masonry of the zig-zags, built by Italian stone masons (p. 251), for a breath-taking first view of Yosemite Valley shown on the cover of this book. (Be sure to check with the rangers at National Park Service Headquarters in Yosemite Valley before starting, to be sure the route is clear.)

However you travel this delightful segment of California history, have fun!

Douglass Hubbard
Editor

Preface

The story of the freight route from Stockton through the Southern Mines to Yosemite has been a cooperative effort and was begun by Margaret E. Schlichtmann some fifteen years ago. Her project took the form of interviews with old residents of the road many of which were written down at the time and signed by the persons interviewed. A natural outgrowth of these visits is a splendid collection of old photographs or of reproductions when an original was impossible to obtain.

In time her objective changed from the simple gathering of human interest stories to a determination that they should contain nothing but unimpeachable facts. The scope of the undertaking as it then stood was the Big Oak Flat Road, proper, beginning at Chinese Camp and extending into Yosemite Valley.

Mrs. Schlichtmann did not wish to prepare her own findings for publication. She knew that my husband and I were interested in historic roads; that he had done the field work and I the writing in the production of two books on the Oregon-California Trail. She asked me if I would undertake to read and compile her facts and from them write a book which would serve as a history of the famous old freight route.

But my husband and I were also interested in the little town of Knight's Ferry where both his grandfather and mine had lived and worked. Almost everything freighted over the Big Oak Flat Road or used by its families came by boat to Stockton and was there loaded onto pack mules or stowed into the great wagons for the journey by way of Knight's Ferry to the mines or to Yosemite. So we had no difficulty in persuading her to enlarge the scope of her interest to take in the freight route and to start at the logical beginning—the "loading levee" at Stockton. This suggested a natural division of

i

research problems. Mrs. Schlichtmann became responsible for the research entailed by ten chapters of the main body of the book with only casual contributions from me. Her field lay from Knights Ferry eastward into Yosemite, with the addition of many human interest stories within the National Park boundaries. My husband and I located the historic sites in Yosemite and assembled the facts presented in the first two chapters, on Stockton and Knights Ferry — some of which have just come to light. For good measure he added a field study of the "mysterious" route of Joseph Reddeford Walker over the Sierra Nevada in the year 1833.

The chapter on Yosemite Valley, although scrupulously tested for accuracy and presumably correct, does not attempt any scientific explanations of its stupendous beginnings and lets the scenic master-piece come unaided through its first two billion years. Neither does it deal in detail with its "discovery" by the Mariposa Battalion in 1851 and the conquest of the Yosemite tribe. For these data one cannot do better than to read *One Hundred Years in Yosemite* by Carl Parcher Russell.

Our story tells of the early white families of the valley, of their lives elbow to elbow with the three or four local Indian villages. Deals with the nerve-wracking experiences of the first year-around settlers in the great granite gorge which was rumored to choke with snow every winter; tells of the world travelers who came to see the wonder of its 2500-foot falls in much the same frame of mind that would have spurred them through the jungle for a sight-seeing jaunt along the Amazon.

Mrs. Schlichtmann's material is out of the ordinary and almost completely original. It has been gathered from letters and questionnaires as well as from the countless interviews mentioned and each detail has been presented to several informants of whom she has had about ten who remember the '60s and some fourteen of the second generation. If they cannot reach an agreement (which is amazingly seldom) and the detail is unimportant we have dropped the matter. Otherwise we present both sides and leave the reader to make his own decision. In everything we have let the facts speak.

The old freight route was the life line of the country we write about. Its families lived "along the road." Its history was their history and the converse was equally true. Mrs. Schlichtmann collected such a bottomless fund of unhackneyed incidents and stories of this fascinating section of the Southern Mines of California that we could not use them all.

The two appendices contain related material, too detailed to place in the text.

Mrs. Schlichtmann's original maps are accurate and helpful.

The volume covers much that is a comparatively unworked field.

IRENE D. PADEN

Acknowledgments

To those noble men and women who pioneered the road and to their descendants, most of whom were born in the Southern Mines and who have been so generous with their time and so gracious in giving us the information we needed. Especially are we grateful to a small group of friends who, for love of the Old Road, have answered innumerable questions, written countless letters, given days of their time, the hospitality of their homes, the use of pictures, scrapbooks, documents, private letters and everything that might be of service: Celia Crocker Thompson of Lodi, Robert A. Curtin of San Rafael, the late Saul Morris of Stockton, Edwin and Charles Harper of Big Oak Flat, Helen Cutting Stratton of Chinese Camp and George Egling of San Jose.

We also acknowledge with deep appreciation extremely valuable contributions and help from Helen Weber Kennedy, Inez Henderson Pond, Ellen Deering and Dr. Rockwell D. Hunt in Stockton; from Virginia Best Adams, Grace Sovulewski Ewing, Lawrence Degnan, John C. Preston, Donald E. McHenry, Douglass H. Hubbard and Wayne Bryant at Yosemite National Park; Ralph Anderson and Homer W. Robinson formerly at Yosemite National Park; Dr. Carl P. Russell in Berkeley; William Sell at Ahwahnee, Madera County; Harold C. Holmes, John P. Ryan and Judge A. T. Shine in Oakland; Ruth Ann Newport, W. F. Speer, Lewis Bach, John Newman, Don Hineman and John O'Hara of Sonora; Lynn Owen·and Edith Brabazon of Moccasin; Catherine Munn Phelan of San Mateo; Dr. Duane Deakins of Murphys; John H. Lawrence in San Francisco; Mrs. Raymond Willms, Mrs. Tina Williams and Mrs. Samuel Baugh of Knight's Ferry; Charles Leidig of Hayward; Clotilda De Paoli and Sylvia Vail of Big Oak Flat; David Tulloch, Mrs. Daniel Nolan Brennan and Mrs.

v

Lucile Tulloch of Oakdale; Ed Whitmore of Modesto and Howard Egling of Le Grand.

We wish also to express special appreciation to the staffs of the Bancroft Library at Berkeley, the State Library at Sacramento, the California Historical Society Library at San Francisco, the College of the Pacific Library and the Haggin Museum at Stockton; the San Leandro and Oakland Public Libraries.

In particular we wish to thank Mrs. J. B. Lanktree of Alameda for supplying a quiet apartment in which to write.

We also gratefully acknowledge indebtedness to our husbands: to Emil P. Schlichtmann for driving the family car literally thousands of miles up and down the Big Oak Flat Road from Stockton to Yosemite Valley; for doing a superlative job of copying such old photographs and daguerreotypes as we were not able to acquire and for compiling our mileage charts, which are as accurate as the slight variations of modern speedometers permit them to be; to the late William G. Paden whose last piece of field research was working out the 1833 route of Joseph Reddeford Walker and his mountain men over the Sierra Nevada, a "mystery trail" not previously located but which is described in the last chapter of this volume.

We also thank the many other friends who have assisted us in countless ways. Without their measureless help there could have been no beginning and certainly no adequate end to this book.

CHAPTER I

FROM BOAT TO BEAST

Surely a road never had a more definite starting point than did the old freight route to the Southern Mines and Yosemite. It began at the loading levee in Stockton where the river boats dropped their cargo; began in full vigor and pride of achievement from the first year of its existence and from the first hundred yards of its journey.

To ascertain why there should be river boats or a levee, or why, indeed, there should be a Stockton we must go back more than a century.

It is likely that the first white visitor to the fertile lower San Joaquin Valley was Lieutenant José Joaquin Moraga, commanding a small group of men from the Expedition of Juan Bautista de Anza. They saw the river, which Anza had named Rio de San Francisco, and actually camped near the site of Stockton. This was in 1776. Later his son, Ensign Gabriel Moraga, began a more or less systematic exploration of the unknown waterways of California. While on the expedition of 1805 he found and named El Rio de los Reyes (Kings River) and it is believed that he named the San Joaquin at that time as he is known to have done so before the explorations of the succeeding year. It was bestowed in memory of Saint Joachim who is honored by the Catholic Church as the father of the Virgin Mary. Moraga, naturally, used the Spanish version of the name which was also his father's.[1]

A few years passed and Jedediah Smith, the first American to come overland from the United States to California, arrived, late in 1826, at Mission San Gabriel with his party of trappers and his Bible. Travelling northward, he finally made camp on the Stanislaus River and, leaving his trappers there to wait for him, set out in

May for the east over one of the Indian trails. He immediately returned and, in 1828, trekked north the length of California and Oregon. On the Umpqua River the party was attacked by Indians and all killed but Smith and three others who then made their way to Fort Vancouver on the Columbia where they were befriended by the Hudson's Bay Company. Smith's journal, found in Maurice S. Sullivan's "Travels of Jedediah Smith," tells us that Smith then continued his journey eastward. The next year the Hudson's Bay Company's French trappers branched out toward California to find the beaver country of which the men had told them.[2]

At this time the San Joaquin Valley was peppered with Indian villages containing fifty to one hundred dwellings each. Most of the inhabitants appear to have been contented with their easy existence but one tribe, in pursuance of a grudge against the missions, had the unpleasant habit of leading raids into their holdings and running off to the mountains large herds of cattle and horses. In 1829 the Spanish forces from San Jose and San Francisco followed them into their own territory, east of the San Joaquin, prepared to corner the Indians and administer a much-needed lesson in manners. Twice the Siyakumna entrenched themselves and, under their wily chief Estanislao, managed to hold their position although badly cut up. The white soldiers, this time under the command of General Mariano Guadalupe Vallejo, finally ran out of ammunition. The Indians then disappeared under cover of darkness. This happened on the river now called Stanislaus in memory of the grim-faced brown leader. Their village was at the place now called Knight's Ferry.

Three years later the Ewing Young Expedition went north through the central river valleys and reported the many villages of which, they said, the most hostile were near the Calaveras River. There was no soil cultivation. The Indians lived on dried fish and on the products of the country. There were no white inhabitants, they stated positively, in either the valley of the San Joaquin or of the Sacramento River nor on any of their tributaries. The Expedition returned south on the following year, 1833, and found the villages practically wiped out by an epidemic of some type of intermittent fever and with many of the dead lying unburied.[3]

In this same year another party of experienced pathfinders swept their eyes over the almost limitless vista of the great central valley. They were the mountain men under the leadership of Joseph Reddeford Walker. They came over the mountains from the east and headed for the coast.[4] It was an important expedition but not particularly so to the future city of Stockton.

Quite different was the arrival in the San Joaquin Valley of the Bidwell-Bartleson Party in 1841—the first settlers to cross the central Sierra Nevada. The deserts and rugged mountains had caused them terrible privations and they were hurrying as best they could to reach the succor of the settlements. They crossed the river, passing almost within eye-span of the future Stockton, and with them traveled its founder-to-be, Charles Marie Weber.[5]

Weber's birthplace was that trouble-filled country which became Bavaria[6] and he spent his first winter in California happily speaking German with the genial proprietor of Fort Sutter.[7]

John August Sutter's domain, a spreading grant from the Mexican Government which he called New Helvetia, and whose headquarters the Americans termed Fort Sutter, was on the navigable Sacramento. The new arrival decided to emulate Sutter's procedure and to obtain a similar grant. Weber's mind, far more acute and business-like than that of Sutter, was filled with plans. Without doubt he recalled the vista of flat land, mountain-bounded to the east and west, that he had seen when crossing the great sister stream, the San Joaquin. If nothing better offered, this had possibilities.

He took up residence in the Mexican pueblo of San Jose, one of three in Alta California[8] and applied for Mexican citizenship which was the first step in acquiring a grant. Here he discovered that time was important. Land was being apportioned rapidly. Under Spanish rule only a few grants had been assigned. W. W. Robinson, in his book, *Land in California*, sums it as in the neighborhood of twenty-five. The Mexican period began in 1822; popular pressure resulted in the secularization of the missions in 1833 and the release of their enormous holdings for distribution to individuals. The period of the ranchos had begun. By the time of the Bear Flag episode in '46 the Mexican governors had given away, freely and apparently gladly, over 500 grants. Even three years earlier, when Weber applied for Mexican citizenship, it was apparent that suitable unoccupied land could not last forever. So he formed a partnership with one William Gulnac, who had married a Mexican girl and had already attained the necessary citizenship.

William, now called by the Spanish equivalent, Guillermo, made application for and received eleven square leagues of land, or nearly 50,000 acres. The grant lay near the junction of the San Joaquin with its small tributary, Calaveras River.

Meanwhile the Hudson's Bay Company's French trappers had set up a base of operations on a location very slightly higher than its surroundings and a few miles south of the same junction. There is a modern town on the site named, logically, French Camp. Every year during the trapping season the camp became populous; the Indians who prepared the pelts moved in and, for a time, there might be as many as three or four hundred souls.[9] Gulnac's grant included miles of waterways along which the Hudson's Bay men laid their traps. It was given the name Rancho del Campo de los Franceses, or Ranch of the French Camp. Gulnac received it in January of 1844, and it was understood that Weber was to be a full partner.

Not many of the native Californians asked for grants so far from the coastal communities. Most of the ranchos along the Sacramento, Feather and other inland rivers were held by men of non-Latin origin. An exception was El Rancho del Rio Estanislaus (including modern Knight's Ferry),[10] granted to Francisco Rico and Jose Antonio Castro on December 29, 1843—just a few days before Gulnac received his grant; but, for the most part, the Mexican Californians did not care to trust themselves to the mercies of the Sierra foothill Indians. So it happened that this rich river bottom land, now counted as fertile as any in the state, was still unclaimed.

Weber did not stumble ignorantly into a dangerous situation. He felt that he could cope with it. While at Fort Sutter he had met a tall and personable individual, José Jesús (pronounced Hosáy Hasoóse), chief of the Siyakumna tribe and successor to Estanislao. The name was reminiscent of his early upbringing at the mission but he had fallen from grace and was now extremely unrepentant and a leader of the "Horsethief Indians." He hated the Mexican Californians and his tribe was dreaded for unprovoked raids on outlying ranchos but Weber felt that he might be persuaded to act reasonably in the case of a man of other nationality.

Springtime was flood season in the tule lands of the San Joaquin Valley so there may have been good reason why Guillermo Gulnac could not settle on the grant at once. We are told that it was summer when he arrived and that he was accompanied by his son, Jose, and the well-known pioneer, Peter Lassen. Weber was involved in several types of business in San Jose and in the management of a cattle ranch nearby, so remained behind.[11]

The short account given in Mason's History of Amador County best fits the facts evidenced by old documents in California History: The three men arrived at the French Camp only to find that the trappers had left for the season. Gulnac was uneasy about the Indians and continued on with Lassen who was headed north. On the Consumnes River they bivouacked in a rude hut to be closer to Fort Sutter and John Sutter gave a swivel gun to Gulnac for protection.

From another source come a few more data: Lassen and Jose were seen at this hut prior to April 23, 1844, by one, W. L. Wiggins, who wrote to Thomas O. Larkin (U. S. consul to Mexican California) on that date claiming that Lassen had stolen his horse and that Sutter had then augmented the offence by sneering at him. He said that Lassen ". . . was on the eve of departing and going to his farm up on the Sacramento. . . ."[12]

When Weber discovered that Gulnac had not fulfilled the terms of the grant by continuing to live there he obtained a passport to visit Fort Sutter. He hoped to settle the Indian problem by making a treaty with José Jesús. A runner was sent to bring in the chief and the two men met with ceremony, making a friendship pact which they kept faithfully as long as they lived. When Weber left his grant to command a company of volunteers in the revolt against the rule from Mexico City, José Jesús with a group of his braves went along to show their willingness to act as reinforcements. When José Jesús, many years later, was wounded in a rousing good fight Weber paid his hospital bill.

Tradition in Stockton suggests that José Jesús recommended the site where Weber later built his home, facing a large navigable slough east of the main river and now called Stockton Channel. If so the wily chief was responsible for locating the headquarters of the new rancho practically next to the village of the Yachekos of whom he was not fond.[13]

The first settlers to arrive were Thomas Lindsay of the Workman-Rowland Party of 1841 and his companion, James Williams, of the Chiles-Walker Party of 1843. They built a shelter of slender poles cut from the clustering oak trees and thatched it with tules. It stood on Lindsay Point, at the west end of present Lindsay Street projecting into an enlargement of the slough which had been christened McLeod Lake for the leader of one of the fur trapping parties. By August several other similar buildings had mushroomed on the tule-fringed bank.

At the same time Gulnac offered a parcel of land to one, David Kelsey, if he and his family would agree to live on it for a year.[14] As a potent reminder for the Indians to treat them with respect Gulnac gave Kelsey the "swivel," or small cannon, which Captain Sutter had presented to him. Every evening as the red sun sank into the marshes, the Kelsey family solemnly fired the tiny cannon over the flats to impress the invisible, but always portentous Indians.

All went well until Kelsey made a trip to San Jose and contracted smallpox. He completed the journey home and, as he began to feel ill, the entire family started for Sutter's Fort to get help. They arrived at Lindsay's on the point and could go no farther. The men moved away and left them the house for shelter. David Kelsey died there and the eleven-year-old daughter, America, nursed her mother and brother through the horrible disease. As they improved it became evident that the mother would be blind. Two men, happening on the scene after the worst was over, conquered their dread sufficiently to bury Kelsey at what is now the southwest corner of El Dorado and Fremont Streets. One of them, George F. Wyman, in due time married America.[15] Willard J. Buzzell wed an indefinitely described sister, Frances.[16]

If the founder of Stockton had hoped to trade with the men of Hudson's Bay Company he was destined for disappointment. The company felt that the California expedition had better be discontinued. The supply of beaver was diminishing and no longer justified so great a trek. Trouble with Mexico threatened and the English wished to watch from a distance without danger of premature involvement. Indeed the mere approach of permanent settlers caused the nomadic fur trappers to retreat.[17] In 1845 Ermatinger, the leader of the last party, supposedly cached some of their weapons and broke camp apparently intending to return but they never came back.

Miss Henrietta Reynolds of Stockton was told by her uncle, James Andrew Reynolds, that he and two of his brothers were playing one day in 1856 near their home in "Sand Plains" as the country around French Camp was called during that period. A man beckoned to them. It was Mr. Noble, the first settler, who told them that if they would dig under a certain oak on a nearby knoll they would find the weapons. They did so and turned up some muskets and swords in scabbords which they divided among themselves. As they grew older they became aware that the weapons were not what trappers might have been expected to use. A perfect answer has yet to be divulged. The knoll was leveled and is part of a school yard. The oak is gone. But some of the weapons were placed by Miss Reynolds in the Haggin Memorial Museum in Stockton and may be seen there.

Sometime after 1845 Gulnac, who had preferred the life in the settlements and had spent most of his time there, sold out to his more optimistic partner and returned to the coast.[18] In 1847 Weber arrived to stay.

After that the grant was his—sink or swim.

A paper in the hands of his descendants has come down to the present day, surviving in some miraculous fashion the floods and the fires that overwhelmed the early settlement. It fits nicely into the mosaic of the state's history and seems to indicate that a movement was on foot to unite all persons of foreign blood, whether or

Home of Charles Marie Weber, Stockton.

Knight's Ferry probably in the 1870's. The original bridge was destroyed by the flood of 1862 and rebuilt in 1863.

State of California,

ss

County of Tuolumne,

Certificate of the Yo Semite Turnpike Road Company, issued in 1869.

not they had been naturalized Mexican citizens. The document was dated March 27, 1845, and set the time for meeting at San Jose on July 4th to which it was requested that delegates be sent. From this meeting it was hoped would come harmony and the advancement of the best interests of such foreigners. Meanwhile, the document suggested bluntly that they refrain from taking part in political maneuvers. It was signed by John "Marshe," William "Gulnack." Charles M. Weber and twenty more. One of its intentions, so Weber's descendants feel, was to prevent others from emulating John August Sutter's ill-advised campaign in support of Micheltorena and the government from Mexico City. Another was to circumvent, if within their power, England's possible bid for possession.[19]

Charles Weber had learned, during his first four years in California, that there was a definite leaning to establish an American-governed section on the west coast similar to that of Texas. Thompson and West's History of San Joaquin County, published in 1879, tells us that the boundaries had been tentatively mentioned as following the edge of San Francisco Bay and up the San Joaquin River, the Americans proposing to remain north and east of the line where but few of the Mexican Californians had located. If, in the unsettled condition of California, the division had been made the east bank of the San Joaquin would have been in the American portion.[20]

Needless to say the division did not come, but the idea may have had the effect of locating Stockton on the east bank of the river.

During the trouble between the States and Mexico, Weber was an independent thinker. He was for Californians, both native-born, Mexican Californians and the permanent settlers from the States. He was against the rule from Mexico City. He went into such energetic action as seemed best to him heedless, as was his habit,

of how it appeared to others. He commanded a company of volunteers. At the cessation of hostilities he was commended by his
government; retired from service and proceeded shortly to the
business of building a house on his Rancho del Campo de los
Franceses.

A small peninsula projected from the east bank of what is now
Stockton Channel and, about 1847, Weber erected a house on it of
which a portion was adobe. Because of its situation on the slough
most of the supplies and visitors came by boat. The Indians of
the vicinity used rafts—long, narrow and pointed at both ends,
cleverly fashioned of tules tied together. The Americans came in
whaleboats or whatever they could command. A sailing vessel
might take two weeks to come upstream from San Francisco.

Behind the rough, picturesque house a moat was dug. It ran the
full width of the peninsula about where Center Street was later
surveyed. A sturdy stockade supplemented the moat. Behind them
the horses were safe. Although friendly the nearby Indians were
apt to be opportunists.

This location became the nucleus of the city of Stockton and is
still known as Weber's Point.

The plan had been to construct a wharf and warehouse near
Weber's home but, when the boat arrived with the lumber, it was
mistakenly unloaded across Stockton Channel. There was no easy
way to re-deliver a disjointed warehouse over a wide waterway
so it was erected where the lumber lay. Due to this accident building began early on the mainland instead of being temporarily con-
stricted on the peninsula.

Lindsay and Williams also returned to the grant, but the Indians
ran off all the stock belonging to Lindsay and he, himself, was
killed. The little cluster of tule huts (all standing between present
Main and Center Streets, Fourth and Wall), were burned. In

November of 1847 there was only one wooden house in the settlement, then appropriately known as Tuleburgh. This was Buzzell's Tavern, a resting place between Sutter's Fort and San Jose, which stood where 28 West Weber Avenue now is. However there were possibly a dozen more settlers. While Nicholas Gann was camping on his way through the village, his wife gave birth to a son, William—probably the first child born of American parents in what is now San Joaquin County.[21]

Discovery of gold in the spring of 1848 again upset the balance of affairs in California. Men, only home a few months from the Mexican campaigns, set out again, this time for the Sierra Nevada and the golden river beds. Charles Weber trimmed his sails to the prevailing wind, collected his settlers and a number of Indians and set out for Sutter's Mill, prospecting as they went and finding their first color on the Mokelumne River. They selected a spot near the mill and started mining operations on Weber's Creek where Weber presently brought more recruits, including twenty-five of José Jesús braves. Several other prominent pioneers of California accumulated quick wealth by means of the assistance of friendly Indians; John Bidwell at Bidwell's Bar, Pierson B. Reading at Clear Creek, James Savage in the Southern Mines, William Knight at Knight's Ferry although the latter did not live to profit by it, and others.

When the Indians had learned how to prospect Weber sent them back to the Stanislaus River to see what they could dig out near the rancheria. The results were so impressive that Weber returned and organized a group which he called the Stockton Mining Company. With him, into the new diggings, went men whose names are well known: Dr. I. S. Isbel,[22] John Murphy of Murphy's Camp, Sullivan of Sullivan's Creek, Woods of Woods Creek, Angel of Angel's Camp and a motley crew of Indians.

As these were joined by newcomers and the Southern Mines grew in fame, Weber decided to devote his energies to furnishing supplies. He went back to Tuleburgh, dissolved the mining company and started a store on Weber Avenue west of El Dorado and about 100 feet west of the old What Cheer House.

In 1847 the founder had the tiny village surveyed by Jasper O'Farrell and laid out symmetrically but apparently no map or plan of this undertaking remains in existence.

Affairs now moved with frightening and unbelievable speed. The acquisition of California by the States at the end of the Mexican War terminated all talk of a separate republic. Some of the Mexican Californians were angry and uneasy; some thought it would be better in the long run to be a part of the United States than of Mexico, as long as the Treaty of Guadalupe Hidalgo guaranteed the continued ownership of their land-grants. It was intended that all rights should be protected, but Weber's was too great a prize to go unchallenged. The Rancho of the French Camp was in litigation for so many years that, when the Supreme Court of the United States finally decided in his favor, it was "A. Lincoln" who signed the patent.

Meanwhile the men of California, of whatever racial extraction, had their hands full. Here they were, just having exchanged allegiance from one nation to another, with no organized government and the gold stampede (which all recognized as a tremendous westward movement) in full swing. The amazing Constitutional Convention resulting in statehood for California was put under way, in August 1849, assisted by a few of the leading Mexican Californians. Highly influential General Mariano Guadalupe Vallejo was a member of the Convention. It is true that he was handicapped by a limited knowledge of technical English expressions and thought for some hours that the "freeholders" in which all Americans seemed so interested were Mexican beans (frijoles), but laughed as heartily as the rest when his mistake was explained.

As the spring of 1849 walked up the mountain, the more adventurous spirits walked with her, sometimes making but sticky progress. These hardy gold-seekers most frequently came as far as Tuleburgh by boat and were all too likely to abandon the vessel just where she lay—in front of Weber's front door. Finally, measures had to be taken to clear out the waterway.

William Redmond Ryan visited "Stocton" rather early in '49 and wrote: "I counted eight tents, some spiral, others walled-in with canvass, one of which, about fifty feet long, served for a store. There were several bulrush huts, and one immense wooden house in course of erection, some sixty feet square, and promising two stories. It was intended for trading purposes, and had been long required by the proprietor, Mr. Weaver [undoubtedly Weber], whose business was very extensive, considering the appearance of the place, and who was the owner of the chief portion of the land about there. He was endeavoring to attract settlers to the spot, by offering them locations at nominal rents or land for nothing, provided they would build upon it. In this enterprise he had not as yet been very successful." Ryan went on to say that the location was a low, flat plain near a swamp and that fever and ague rage in summer while, in the winter "... the fierce winds sweep with unbroken fury ..." Fuel and fodder were scarce and he considered a residence there "miserable to the last degree."[23]

James H. Carson, who had been in the mines in '48, passed again through the town on May 1, 1849, which must have been a beautiful spring day. He was inspired to write: "... Stockton, that I had last seen graced only by Joe Buzzel's log house with a tule roof, was now a vast linen city. The tall masts of barques, brigs and schooners were seen high pointed in the blue vault above—while the merry 'yo ho!' of the sailor could be heard, as box, bale and barrel were landed on the banks of the slough. A rush and whirl of noisy human beings were continually before the eye. The magic wand of gold had been shaken over a desolate place, and on it a vast city had arisen in the bidding."[24] It was, however, not as yet a comfortable city and the crossing of any street, although the side-walks were spread with wet hay and brush,[25] was attended with the danger of losing one's boots. Men grew in the habit of walking bent double with fingers thrust through their boot straps to keep them from sucking off in the deep, sticky mud.[26]

The newcomers passing through on their way to the mines might have supplied themselves with necessities for the rugged life they faced. Again they might have arrived empty-handed. Such an opportunity for business comes but once in several generations. Stores and hotels sprang up in tents. The United States Hotel, owned by one Tyseen, had its beginnings in a tent in 1849 and was Stockton's first public house.[27] The Rev. James Corwin, a Method-ist, held services by the fall of 1849. The first Presbyterian Church built in California was dedicated on May 5, 1850. It was financed by public subscription headed by Rev. James Woods.[28] The town grew until Weber decided to enlarge its boundaries. In 1849 Major Richard P. Hammond re-surveyed it in a one mile square of which the boundary streets were Flora on the north, Aurora on the east, Twigg on the south with Bragg and Tule Streets on the west.[29] The newly laid out town was named for Commodore Robert F. Stock-ton whom Weber had met and admired during the time he was away with the troops.

Weber did not forget French Camp. He had the same man sur-vey the old trappers' headquarters, giving it the title "Castoria" in honor of the beaver—sometimes termed "castor." The name was practically never used.[30]

In 1850 the first stage line started business between Stockton and Mokelumne Hill; the first newspaper, the *Stockton Times,* printed on foolscap, appeared March 16th of that year, and in November of the same year, Charles Weber married Ellen, the daughter of Martin Murphy of the Stevens, Murphy, Townsend Party of 1844. She was a personality in her own right and was one of the first two women to reach the settlements of California by way of the canyon of the Truckee River, later used by railroad and highway. The impressive white mansion built for the bride was constructed of lumber brought around the Horn and of native adobe. The second house was erected near the old one. Here the founder lived for the rest of his life; the house, outlasting him by a year, was destroyed by fire in 1881. It was replaced and both the new house and two heavily timbered rooms from the dwelling used by Weber and his vacqueros have been moved outside the city and are in constant use by his descendants.

Supplies of all kinds came up the river and everything was stacked on the loading levee—seemingly in confused heaps, but sooner or later they were sorted out and went trundling off to their destinations. Pack trains had begun to be surplanted by freight wagons as early as 1849 and, due to the flatness of the country for miles around, the latter achieved a quick popularity. By 1851 it is estimated that 500 wagons and 1500 pack animals were shuttling back and forth along the freight route to the Southern Mines.[31] Efficient stage lines were running and a mail contract had been let. Goods for the mines went out the "miner's road," where tents, open camps and cooking fires made a lively scene for about two miles. It is now Miner Avenue.

Of course the town was flooded every few years. In January of 1862 the worst flood in its history inundated the growing community. For a month the *Alta California* in distant San Francisco headlined, day by day, the progress of the destroying waters and chronicled the fact that Charles Weber's house, constructed partially of adobe, was settling and crumbling. In spite of the founder's efforts through the years to promote an effective flood control at his own expense,[32] he could not cope with the excessive growth of the community.

In 1862 Weber had another survey made—this time by Duncan Beaumont. It was two miles square. The boundary streets were North, East, South and Tule Streets. North is now Harding Way; East is Wilson Way; South is Charter Way. Tule was Edison and was the boundary because at that time the land west of it was marsh. Later the city filled in to complete the full two miles and Pershing Avenue became the west boundary.

Space for parks, sites for churches and schools were always given freely. Anything which he considered for the good of the city could be had from Charles Weber, but the responsibility was great and the load too heavy. His health failed. He grew crotchety; misunderstandings arose and he became unpopular in a city that had outgrown the personal touch.

Between floods the place burned up with a regularity worthy of a better cause. Hard times came along in 1854 and occasionally afterward;[33] but neither fire nor flood nor pestilence, which struck violently now and then, were able permanently to retard progress in this strategically located center. It has always been a land of opportunity.

CHAPTER II

THE FIRST LAP—RIVER TO FOOTHILLS

In 1849 a miners' trail led from the loading levee straight to the gold camps at Sonora, Chinese Camp, Big Oak Flat and other diggings whose names became household words. For the first two miles it was lined with tents. At night, for the entire distance, its lights were camp fires. An almost continuous procession of men and pack animals plodded its rough miles, glad of any kind of thoroughfare that would take them to their destination.

Before the dry season of '49 had soddened into winter mud, David Morrell Locke traveled in the first wheeled vehicle ever to pass along this sketchy road as far as Knight's Ferry;[1] the change from pack mule to freight wagon had begun and, from then on, was never allowed to lapse. Soon the goods transported yearly to the Ferry amounted to thousands of tons.

When, in the '50s, the clattering wagons with their six to sixteen mules or horses came down the miners' trail they were empty. After hours of back-breaking work at the loading levee the teamsters coaxed and swore until the animals lay into their collars and the heavily inert wagons were started. Lurching and groaning, they moved slowly out of town along what is now Weber Avenue, Pilgrim Street, Main Street and Wilson Way and was then the beginning of the Mariposa Military Road to Fort Millerton and Fort Tejon.[2] After about a mile they completed the townward loop and met the oncoming empty wagons and trotting pack trains. Passing these from time to time they moved on laboriously toward the mountains. The pack animals carried an average of 300 pounds each. In summer each freight animal could pull some 2000 pounds; in winter only 1500.

The teamsters leaving Stockton dreaded wet weather. The soil immediately around the town was a rich gumbo and the first rains turned roads into quagmires. At such times the drivers started in the afternoon; fought their way through the mud, yard by yard, and spent the night at "The Nightingale."

For the first three miles the military road was coincidental with the beginnings of the route to the mines, called at first the Sonora Trail and later the Sonora Road; then the latter separated and turned eastward toward Farmington. In the morning they had a firmer road and a rested team. This satisfactorily solves the problem of why Nightingale Station, in the intersection of the Mariposa and the Farmington roads, is listed as the first night's stop.

Another solution of the mud difficulty was to drive from the levee to French Camp from whence a firm, sandy roadway could be found to what is now Manteca; thence to the Stanislaus River opposite Oakdale. This is near the spot still known as Fremont's Crossing.[3] Across from Oakdale the freighters struck the sandy north bank of the Stanislaus River and followed it to Knight's Ferry. This was known as the river road or the winter route. The going was very bad between Stockton and French Camp; in fact, freight was sometimes sent that far by boat and reloaded in wagons.[4] Eventually the townspeople connected them with a plank road.

The Nightingale still stands on the east side of Highway 4. It is known that John Nightingale bought a ranch near Linden in 1854 so it is possible that he opened his station at about the same time. The present building, however, is probably not so old. It has real dignity and charm, with heavy white pillars in front and a wrought iron railing around the small upper balcony. Each of its large upstairs bedrooms held four occupants and the gathering room downstairs was utilized for dances.

A few yards beyond John and Sarah Nightingale's old station

the freight route turned left into the Farmington Road and started for the mountains.

Four Mile House and Eight Mile House stood on the Sonora Road beyond its point of severance from the Military Road. Twelve Mile House catered to the stages, serving breakfasts to the passengers at fifty cents each. Fourteen Mile House was a favorite with the teamsters, but there was not a home nor a ranch on the entire route that would not supply a meal or a bed when necessary. When Ulysses S. Grant passed this way on mule-back in the summer of 1852 there was a house every few miles and the traffic was considered as heavy as any place in the United States.[5]

The little settlement of Farmington grew and improved quickly. In 1858 D. B. Stamper erected a hotel; a blacksmith shop and saloon followed soon and, after a few years, the J. A. Campbell family kept a popular roadside stopping place known as Farmington Hotel.

At 3.3 miles beyond Farmington the modern traveler is forced to leave the old freight road and to detour to the right around an unseen dam through country where beef cattle fatten in fenced fields; then to turn left on the road to Milton and to cross the line into Stanislaus County. Presently one comes to a dead-end against a crossroad and must turn left again toward Eugene. In springtime these green rolling hills are beautiful. Littlejohn Creek meanders here and there. Hundreds of red cattle brighten the landscape and scores of graceful white egrets. Beyond the bridge over Littlejohn Creek one comes again to a dead-end against a crossroad. An empty house faces its thistle-thicketed barns across the road; a forsaken home almost hidden under matted elms. In their deep shade lurk the stumps of oaks cut long ago for timber. The five mile detour is complete, for this was a well known landmark on the Sonora Road and was the beginning of a settlement strung eastward along its course and known tersely as "Twenty Six Mile" or simply "Twenty Six."

Here, at one time and another, was the residence of the sons, James and Patrick, of the pioneer Patrick Ford whose original home was the rear of the building.

The first comers were squatters named Dillon and M. J. Dooly. When stages began to run they maintained a barn and kept the stage horses.[6] Later Dooly ran one of the first stage lines. The four young Irishmen who became the permanent settlers of Twenty Six Mile all worked for Dillon and Dooly at first, as hostlers or in some such capacity; then they obtained land from them and presumably from the government also, and built their homes. They were Patrick Ford and the three brothers, James, Daniel and Luke Nolan.

Next to the Ford home came the land of James Nolan. It was he who kept the store, bar and post office officially known as Twenty Six Mile and now obliterated. Beyond it and still on the north side of the road, is a fenced enclosure often utilized as a corral. It used to be the neat garden surrounding the James Nolan home and the flower beds were outlined with stone ale bottles. They are still there but trampled solidly into the hard earth. They were imported from Ireland packed in barrels and were sold at the bar. Several ranches of the vicinity had their landscaping emphasized with these containers giving a remarkably chaste effect; but the brew that came out of them (which, presumably, was not wasted) was the color and almost the consistency of molasses and was not a beverage for weaklings.

Across from this home site was the stage barn of Dillon and Dooly. Next, on the north, is pretty little St. Joseph's church, with its white altar and pointed windows, for which Daniel Nolan donated the land in 1886. His ranch is just beyond it. Daniel had but one child, Hannah. She married T. D. Brennan and secured the succession with eleven children. Their home, standing a quarter mile south of the road, is the third building to be erected on the site and one family has lived there continuously since gold rush days.

The Milton Road presently turns north. In the angle is Twenty Eight Mile House boasting two false fronts and a "drive-under." At one time it was a store, post office and bar. Patrick Ford's daughter Kate inherited this portion of the land and, marrying Daniel Kelliher, came here to live. Although, after the fashion of the time, the teamsters dubbed it Twenty Eight Mile, the Kellihers called it Eugene for their son. In due time fire destroyed the bar furnishings which they then replaced with the ones formerly used at the earlier Twenty Six Mile. They have been presented intact to the Haggin Memorial Museum in Stockton by the daughters of the family and portray an excellent picture of the interior of the old roadhouse bars characteristic of the day.

At Eugene the Sonora Road parts company with the road to Milton which starts off to the north taking the paving with it. The former, curving and whimsical, keeps on toward Knight's Ferry past the land of the fourth early settler, Luke Nolan.

At 4.8 miles beyond Eugene there is an unmarked fork in the road. The left branch, crossing a little slough, approximates the old road. In spring these rolling knolls are velvety green. In summer wild oats fur their smoothly molded sides in all shades of beige and silvery grey like the flanks of a Siamese cat.

A good black-topped highway (successor to the old river route) swings along opportunely from the southwest and, gathering in the meandering little hill-road, proceeds to the left. It then immediately pours itself into a canyon leading toward the Stanislaus River.

Over a gateway a sign reads: "Rancheria del Rio Estanislaus."

Beyond it spread the opulent valleys and grass-covered hills of the old Mexican grant. Ignoring its invitation one comes at once to Knight's Ferry.

In the days before detours and modern complications it was considered an even forty miles from the loading levee. The road did not curve to the left in town as at present but went straight down the hill to the ferry.

When in 1849 D. M. Locke rode the first wagon into the settlement he found a trading post of the simplest kind presided over by William Knight, a decisive and rather hard-bitten pioneer who was said to have been educated in Baltimore as a doctor. Available data tells us that, after his graduation at the age of 24, Knight some years later adventurously settled in Santa Fe, became naturalized as a Mexican citizen and married Carmel, daughter of José Tapia, a former governor of New Mexico. In 1841 he came into California with the Workman-Rowland Party. Apparently he approved of the new country, as he soon returned for his family, leaving them at Los Angeles while he went north and, in some fashion, obtained a renewal of his naturalization documents. Again he returned for his wife and children and settled them on the Sacramento River at a spot now known as Knight's Landing. This was in 1843. An Indian mound rose safely above flood waters and on it Knight built a cabin of poles held with rawhide thongs and sporting a roof of tules. This was burned in 1845 and replaced by a log house, the first built in the county, the timbers of which were hauled one at a time by a riata fastened to a saddle horse. In '46 he obtained a land grant of ten square leagues in the vicinity and called it Rancho Carmel for his wife.[7] Margaret Ruppel quotes that he was in appearance ". . . tall and knarled as a mountain pine, ageless with a long white beard which seemed transplanted, some how, from his bald and shiny head."[8] He was a choleric individual and is said at different times to have challenged both General Vallejo and John Sutter to a duel with pistols.[9] In 1846 he enlisted in the California Battalion, serving as a private in Company A. under Lieut. Colonel John Charles Fremont who wrote of him in his Memoirs: "He was one of the settlers and one of the best. . . . I had engaged him as scout, for which he proved excellently well qualified. His specialty was hunting. . . ."

During the first month or two after the discovery of gold Knight left Carmel and his children at the Landing and set out. He took five Indians with him and headed for the first big river crossing between the boat landing at Stockton and the mountains. Here he set the Indians to panning gold and set himself to the task of running a trading post and a small row-boat ferry over the Stanislaus River. This was soon known by the name of Knight's Ferry. And, so the story goes, the diggings nearby, worked by Knight's Indians and probably by those of Charles Weber, opened operations in the fabulous Southern Mines.

D. M. Locke wrote in his journal on August 16, 1849: "We reached Knight's at 10 o'clock A.M. Took breakfast pork & beans, hard bread & coffee $1.50 each. Went and saw them digging gold for the first time. The Indians only dug enough to get liquor 50c a glass."

H. E. Dudley, later the first citizen of Dudley Station on the Coulterville Road, arrived at Knight's trading post on the very same day. He wrote in his diary: "On Thursday the 16th we arrived at the Stanislaus river at what is called Knights Crossing, here we stopped two nights on one of which the kyotes or Indians carried off our frypan, for which I gave them credit. Didn't old Knight's coffee & beans suffer some, and faith that was about everything he had in the provision line."

Jacob Wright Harlan had occasion to cross the river in the spring of '49. "The ferry boat," he wrote, "was a little skiff that would hold about five or six persons, and our wagon had to be taken apart and carried over piecemeal." He described their attempt to tow the wagon bed which resulted in swamping it just above the "rapids." A young man named Brannon nearly lost his life in the flooded river.

Ferrying this party took the entire day and they paid the ferryman $200.00.[10]

Knight planned an adequate wagon ferry but did not live to construct it. He was dead within a few months after this incident and rumor says that, like so many of the early pioneers, his death was caused by a gunshot wound. His widow, Carmel, married John Wolfskill, a neighbor, twenty miles distant.[11] The firm of Dent and Vantine, in which there is some evidence that John R. Willms should be included,[12] were probably Knight's partners in the trading post. They seem to have taken over his affairs. The Dents wrote to Major S. Cooper at Benicia and asked him to come and take care of Knight's effects but he never made the trip.[13] The proposed ferry was soon built—a fine scow, well railed in, one of the best in the country. They also established a combined restaurant and boarding house.[14] The ferry was managed by two persons who maneuvered it across the 150 foot river with ropes. The crossing took only a minute or two and the fare settled down to a moderate two dollars.[15]

There were three Dent brothers. John and Lewis came by ox-team from St. Louis in '49.[16] George is said to have arrived with his pretty wife in 1851. She was then, it is supposed, the only white woman in the settlement.[17] The family soon owned a ranch well-stocked with cattle and horses, and by the year 1855 George was postmaster. In the same year that George arrived the government took over the trading post for an Indian reservation store and eventually John Dent was appointed Indian Agent by President Buchanan. They had the town surveyed and registered under the name "Dentville" but the title was not destined to be much used and was soon forgotten.[18]

An interesting sidelight on one of the Dent brothers comes to us from William Redmond Ryan in his Personal Adventures in Upper and Lower California. He had been at the upper crossing of the Stanislaus River and was on his way to Stockton when the meeting occurred. The brother may have been Lewis who is known to have been a lawyer. Ryan wrote: "In the morning the Doctor came up with us, accompanied by another gentleman, a lawyer named Dent, and an intimate friend of his. He had left the States a considerable time previously to this, and shortly after the discovery of the gold countries, and had been trading with the Indians and the Americans in various parts of the mines, with unusual success. He was now on his way to Stocton, to procure a large supply of champagne brandy and dry goods, his partner meanwhile remaining at the 'diggins,' to attend to the trading post. I found him to be a highly intelligent, well-informed gentleman, and learned that he stood in excellent repute as a professional man. His character and habits were of a practical stamp, and well adapted to the half-venturous, half-civilized life of California, during this interesting and bustling period of its history. He was looking forward to the settlement of the country, and appeared sanguine as to the position it would eventually, and at no distant period, occupy as one of the States."[19]

In 1852 the spring freshets were high and owners of ferries up and down the Stanislaus were caught unaware. Evidently Dent and Vantine were able to save theirs as, for a time, they seem to have had the only ferry in operation on the entire river.

The settlement grew steadily and was in a favorable location to catch trade. Miners wishing to reach the mountains trudged along the well-beaten Indian trails and several of these converged on the rancheria of José Jesús where the tribe maintained a river crossing with native boats just below the present bridge site. A footbridge was constructed. All memory of it is erased but there is evidence that one at least, and possibly more, existed.[20] It connected the town with Pentland's vineyard downstream from the present bridge and on the south side of the river-bottom-land.

The river had endless potentialities for generating power and always fascinated the busy brain of D. M. Locke. Although he had taught school to obtain the money to come west he soon gained experience in business in the growing town of San Francisco. His diary told that, on August 31, 1850, he began to dig wells in that place and soon was peddling water from barrels on a cart. In the fall of '51 he laid pipes along the Market Street and the California Street wharves and took a contract to supply water to shipping. Meanwhile he returned at odd times to Knight's Ferry and, forming a partnership with the Dent brothers, planned the first dam on the Stanislaus—an affair solidly constructed of logs upriver from the present bridge. In 1853 Elbridge Gerry Locke, brother of D. M., arrived from the east coast and, according to his diary, commenced work on the dam in August of that year. Next he undertook the building of a wing-dam and the erection of a saw mill and a grist mill. The saw mill was in operation by June, 1854, and probably, according to Mr. David Tulloch, stood on the south bank near the present bridge terminus. It was completed first and one of E. G. Locke's brief entries reads: "Tended saw mill." Four months later it is supposed that the grist mill went into operation. E. G. Locke's diary is succinct and deals mostly with the tally of working days of each carpenter, but it is evident that the grist mill was in running order at least as early as January 19,

1855, when an entry states that it started "on Richardson wheat." A daguerrotype in the possession of Mrs. J. F. Tulloch of Oakdale shows that the mill was a frame structure set far down in the river bottom. The bridge was not yet built and does not, of course, appear in the picture. After the grist mill was finished Locke and Company built a passable wagon road as an approach to it.[21]

The Miners' and Business Mens' Directory for the year commencing January 1, 1856, bore, under the caption, "Knight's Ferry," this item: "Some 300 yards above the Ferry is located the Flouring and Saw Mills of Messrs Locke and Company...." If Mr. Tulloch's opinion that the saw mill was on the south bank is correct, this blanket distance of 300 yards would indicate that it was very nearly opposite the flour mill. The Directory also included this advertisement: "Stanislaus Mills, Knight's Ferry, San Joaquin County. Locke and Co. Proprietors. The Mill was built in 1853-54. By 1856 it has a fireproof warehouse capable of storing 2000 tons of wheat. Mills and warehouse cost the proprietor over $50,000. Stanislaus Mills supply flour to all points of the Southern Mines, Stockton and San Francisco."

All this time heavy wagon traffic at Knight's Ferry was being ferried across the river. A Stockton paper noted that on one day in 1850 more than one hundred heavily loaded freighters passed through the town on their way to the mining camps beyond,[22] and for the next two decades the town was a freighting center. According to Robert A. Curtin there was a bridge at Two Mile Bar which, as the name suggests, was about two miles upstream and he supplied information as to the existence of an early road, north of the river and connecting the two settlements, where for a few years it was customary for freight wagons to travel on their way to cross the bridge at that place. There has been a dearth of exact information concerning the dates and ownership of the various bridges and

ferries in the neighborhood so we are truly indebted to the scrapbook of Mr. Curtin for the foregoing item. This first bridge, which
antedated the one at Knight's Ferry by at least five years, was "an
arched bridge," an uncovered wooden structure built by one, E. C.
Frisbee, who kept a trading post at Two Mile Bar. Frisbee, short,
stout and suspicious, had a glass eye which never closed and which
in the unpredictable early fifties was something of an asset, permitting him to sit comfortably in his store and take short naps with
impunity.

The name "Dent Bar" on a map of 1853 would seem to indicate
that the Dent family had interests upstream either at or near Six
Mile Bar.[23] An article in the *San Francisco Bulletin* intimates that
there was either a bridge or a better ferry farther up the Stanislaus
by 1856, and that travel was being deflected to that route because
of the lack of a bridge at Knight's Ferry.[24]

To Mr. Ed Whitmore of Modesto we are also grateful beyond
measure for the following data, backed up by the appropriate legal
documents to prove them: The Dents were in the middle '50s at
the height of their influence in Knight's Ferry and the neighboring region. Beside the property, of whatever nature, near Six Mile
Bar and the Knight's Ferry boat they owned and operated Keeler's
ferry, downstream from Knight's near the junction of Edwards'
Creek with the Stanislaus River. It was just below the cliff now
known as Lovers' Leap and then referred to quite seriously as
"The Jumping Off Place."[25] By 1856 there were rumors that the
Dents were about to abandon the ferry franchises for the purpose
of building a bridge a half mile or more above the Knight's ferry
crossing. This did not set well with the business men of the town
and a petition was started, dated August 1, 1856, praying that
Thomas W. Lane and others might be issued a license to build a
toll bridge or a suitable ferry at the (then) present crossing. Signed
by Palmer & Allen, merchants, and seventy other citizens.

It was then that the Dents commenced to bow out and get ready for more spectacular careers in other places. On October 11, 1856, a document was signed stating that D. M. Locke was a partner in both ferries. Two days later the petition was filed. At some indefinite time Locke sold Stanislaus Mills to Hestres & Magendie. On November 1st of '56 the Dents sold both ferries to Locke who then gave notice of intention to build a bridge immediately above the Stanislaus Mills where he already owned land on both sides of the river. Locke also acquired the bridge at Two Mile Bar. Fortunately the necessary legal papers were filed and are now at the Court House in Modesto, California. They are written in longhand, of course, but have all the necessary whereas's.[26]

Meanwhile the town grew. The present general store is said to have been built in '52 and residences even then climbed the steep and narrow streets. Lots brought as much as $2000 apiece. Business flourished. Beside his share in the ferry Vantine had an excellent winery. Dakin and McLauflin ran a smithy and wheelwright shop and made wagons that faithfully came to market on Saturdays for fifty years. Young Lewis McLauflin and Hugh Edwards, visioning a quick fortune, ran away to San Francisco intending to sell sea-gulls' eggs from the Farallone Islands. They found their prospective poultry business surrounded by far too much salt water but the inner drive that started McLauflin on this novel venture led him later, as the broker for Fair and Mackay, to several fortunes won and lost in the stock market. It was he who attempted to negotiate their famous corner in wheat.[27] Abraham Schell was the lawyer and banker for Knight's Ferry.[28] The Lewis Voyle family ran first a public house in "Buena Vista" on the south side of the river and then a livery stable on the Canyon Road. Ranchers, heedless of the quest for gold, built homes near the trading center. John R. Willms, one of the first, founded his ranch in 1852 and the family has lived there a full century. He registered the first cattle brand in Stanislaus County. The second brand belonged to Lewis Williams, another '49er, who built his home three miles outside the town where the establishment is still in view from the Sonora Road. Mr. Williams married in succession two sisters; a third died at his home while on a visit; so that these three daughters of far-off Wales lie side by side in the Knight's Ferry cemetery. Mr. Williams bought the property of Thomas Edwards who had run an early hostelry called Owens House but who moved into town about 1860 and purchased the house belonging to John Dent. Lewis moved to Stockton in 1858 to practice law. John and George had left Knight's Ferry by 1860.[29]

Early in the history of the settlement the Chinese arrived. Their wierd shacks looked flimsy but were exceedingly adhesive. Every successive house had but three walls and was added on the side wall of its predecessor. As a Chinese builder was accustomed to put in ten nails where an American would use one, Chinatown was a solid unit almost a block long made up of cubicles. Once in awhile a fire would sweep away the whole odd-smelling affair for, the minute a blaze started, the entire Chinese colony rushed for the river—pigtails and shirt tails flying—and stayed there, chattering noisily in their shrill singsong, until it was over. Because their houses could not be pulled apart with grappling hooks they were the bane of the volunteer fire department. None, however, questioned their frugality or industry. During the persistently wet season of 1851-52, when wagon traffic was hopelessly bogged, the Chinese, weighted with fantastically heavy burdens swung from poles and neck yokes kept the supply line moving between Stockton and the Ferry.[30] And finally, at the end of the phenomenal era of prosperity, for more years than the old-timers can remember, a small square adobe was the home of the last Chinese, Oh Kow.

* * *

By August, 1858, the substantial Locke bridge was in operation and at the end of five months a formal report showed the net profits of the Stanislaus Bridge and Ferry Company for that period as something over $4700. The bridge was a great boost to business and, in the year 1859, a newspaper, *The Ferry Bee,* edited by W. J. Collier, appeared but lasted only a little over a year. It was a four-page, twenty-column affair; its final editor being J. B. Kennedy. Later the *Stanislaus Index* took over its assets and was published by Garrison & Whicher until 1862 when it gave up the ghost.[31]

The town was prosperous and contented. All these citizens and many others served their community, each in his own way.

And then came the deluge.

In the Southern Mines time is reckoned from the flood of '62.

The Stanislaus rose and roared. Two Mile Bar was devastated. A house owned first by Lewis Williams and later purchased by William Göbel was chained to two large trees. The chain broke but the dwelling became lodged and was saved. Very little else survived. Mr. Proctor, engaged in removing the goods from Flower and Proctor's store, floated down stream with the building and was drowned.[32] The bridge at Two Mile recently acquired by Locke was propelled down the river like a battering ram, sweeping away a tremendous chain used as a log boom and crashing through the log dam. An indefinitely described "wire" suspension foot bridge was entangled and disappeared into the tossing wreckage. The mass hit the Knight's Ferry bridge squarely, hurling it downstream. The bank below it crumbled and washed away. The foundations of the frame flour mill caved in and it was tossed to total destruction. The sacked flour, however, washed into a cove where it was afterward salvaged. The water had penetrated about an inch, forming when dried, a hard crust beneath which the remainder of the flour was perfect. With the bridges and the mill went the homes of Oscar Bouckou and several others and the wheelwright and blacksmith shops of Isaac Dakin and Lewis McLauflin. The two young housewives, Mary Jameson Locke and Laura Jameson Dakin, who were sisters and writers for Godey's Ladies' Book and current magazines, must have felt that they had had more than their share of calamity.

Bancroft's Hand Book Almanac for 1863 says: "About one-half of the town of Knight's Ferry, an enterprising place in the foothills, was literally swept away by the impetuous current of the swollen stream. The river rose twelve feet higher at this place than the highest previous water-mark and the current was sufficiently strong to propel millstones, iron safes, and huge boulders."

The townspeople started to rebuild at once, hardly waiting until the waters subsided. The topography of the place had changed though, and it never again looked the same. A road (whether or not the main freight route is not known) which had run along the edge of the river bluff was obliterated and there never since has been a road between Main Street and the water.

Hestres & Magendie decided not to rebuild the flour mill and the noble stone building so familiar for the better part of a century was then erected by David W. Tulloch whose family has remained a factor in the town history ever since. The bridge was a different matter. Locke rebuilt that at once, selecting each massive timber himself as it stood in the forest. As he grew old it was a matter of pride to him that it remained so sturdy. 1863 was a dry year and it was difficult to float the logs down from the mountains through the shallows of the river but it made the construction of the bridge piers easier. They were eight feet higher than those of the unfortunate first venture and the span, completed by May 30th of 1863, as noted by Brewer in his pocket journal, still stands in daily use as one of the longest covered bridges in the west.

It was the drought of this year that caused Mr. Edwards to take his family and his cattle across the Sierra and to settle in Owens Valley, later founding the town of Independence and, still later, after moving west again, that of Crockett, California.[33]

In 1863 Abraham Schell acquired over 15,000 acres of the Rancheria del Rio Estanislaus and established the vineyard and winery of which the large, cave-like cellars remain.[34] These were the days of the Civil War. Men drilled in the armory, captained by Mr. Schell. A cannon, probably from the militia post of 1849, was mounted and fired on all suitable occasions, but the horror and tragedy of war were far away and did not touch the mountain communities.

Knight's Ferry, in the days of its most intense activity, served the hurrying procession of miners. With the end of placer mining these intinerant, rootless men settled down somewhere and ceased to move. The town then served the freighters that rumbled and boomed across the bridge. Eventually it became a trading center for the families of cattlemen and ranchers.

By the end of the '60s the transcontinental railroad made certain luxuries accessible in the west and the mountain towns claimed their full share. Silks and imported foodstuffs from the Orient they had always enjoyed. Now they could buy American manufactured and canned goods and order various trade magazines and periodicals for their own pleasure and betterment. Post office records[35] show that in 1869 Isaac Dakin subscribed for and received *Harper's Weekly Magazine, Harper's Bazaar,* the *New York Tribune,* the *Wagon Builder's Journal,* the *Rural Press,* the *Stockton Daily Independent, Godey's Ladies' Magazine,* the *Horticulturalists' Monthly* and the *Christian Union.* Goods of fine quality crowded the crude shelves of the stores. Life was a queer blend of privation and ease.

But the peak days of growth were over for the town on the Stanislaus. The highway, when at last it appeared, "passed by on the other side." The town is unspoiled and is a must for those who are interested in the settlements founded as a direct result of the discovery of gold.

* * *

Of the happenings of the first decade in the town's history the visits of Ulysses S. Grant are probably the ones most discussed. They were uneventful and almost unnoticed at the time but his later greatness focussed attention on them and, because of much misunderstanding and incorrect conclusions, they warrant an attempt at explanation. Grant, a brother-in-law of the Dents, had come with heroism through the Mexican War and arrived in California where, after an assignment at Fort Vancouver in the Oregon country, he was given a captaincy and an extremely dull post at Fort Humboldt near what is now Eureka, California. He was lonely, homesick and bored. He was not paid enough to send for his wife, the former Julia Dent, and his small son, to say nothing of the baby he had never seen. He saw no chance for betterment. He was given a chance to resign and did so, afterward leaving for home as soon as seemed practical[36] but, between 1852 and '54 he had made three visits to Knight's Ferry.[37]

There is a tradition in the town that Grant drew the plans for the first covered bridge during one of his visits. As such stories usually have some basis in fact the authors made a determined effort to trace it down. The late George S. Voyle was interviewed at his home in Visalia and told this story: An amusing character in Knight's Ferry, Mark B. Brown the sexton, was locally known as "Doggie Brown" from the amazing number of canines that trailed

him wherever he went. His home was northwest of town near the
cemetery and, when his lonely death made it necessary for the
neighbors to clear out the house, very little was found that they
cared to keep. Some verse was saved which has since been printed
for the interest of his fellow townspeople and, when Mr. Voyle's
father returned home from this act of neighborliness, he took with
him a workmanlike drawing in ink of one set of braces for a bridge.
It was signed "Ulysses S. Grant." When the Voyles moved to
Visalia the drawing went along packed with other papers in a trunk
which was then stored in a tank house. The wet winter of 1951-52
caused the tank to overflow and reduced the stored papers to pulp
—completely beyond restoration. Mr. Voyle's description of the
drawing was, however, clear and concise. It was clean, he said, and
showed no sign of use. He knew of no way that comparison could
have been made between the drawing and any bridge that existed
before the flood of 1862, as no pictures have been found showing
detail of the bracing. D. M. Locke, to the end of a long and upright
life, denied that Grant had anything to do with the planning. His
son, Alex, denied it in a formal interview[38] and no one has been
found who can connect the drawing with the bridge in any more
definite way. Mr. Elias, in *Stories of the Stanislaus,* states that the
Dents were about to build a bridge in the summer of 1854 and that
Captain Grant was able to give them assistance through his knowledge of engineering and that he made a trip to Sonora especially
to select timber for the structure. This might have been a first
operation toward the building of the rumored bridge mentioned on
page 28 of this volume, or the Dents may have planned one at
another site. No data has been available to us showing that they
actually erected one.

Another tradition concerning Grant came from usually accurate
sources: He was said to have commanded a military post at Knight's

Ferry, and the very spot where his camp was supposedly pitched was pointed out. This, unless he commanded by remote control, appeared impossible. An inquiring letter sent to Washington, D. C., elicited answers from the office of the Adjutant General and from the Chief Archivist of War Records to the effect that no such post had been held by him. Luckily, Jacob Wright Harlan, in his book, *California '46 to '88,* gave the key to the situation. He wrote:

". . . we went on to Knight's Ferry on the Stanislaus river, where Captain Grant was stationed, although what good was accomplished by him or any soldiers being at such a place was not very apparent to us. The captain was absent and did not make his appearance while we were there."[39]

This item was dated April, 1849.

Undoubtedly there was another Captain Grant whose presence in Knight's Ferry preceded that of the future president. The site of the 1849 encampment of militia is given as the south bank of the river below the bridge at the point where the James Stone home was later erected. It was marked with an oak tree larger than the rest of the river bank growth.

Further proof of a predecessor was furnished by Grant himself: In the year 1879 he and his party were in California on their way home from a trip around the world. They wished to include a visit to Yosemite and, at Stockton while en route, Grant was evidently accosted by a stranger who claimed to have seen him before. Grant then addressed the citizens in a speech including the following terse sentences:

"Among many gentlemen I met today was one who was sure he knew me at Knight's Ferry in 1849. While I could not dispute the gentleman's word, I was never on this side of the Rockies previous to 1852. I was only three times at Knight's Ferry in 1852 and in 1854 and I think some one must have been personating me there.

However I am glad to meet you to-day and can never henceforth deny being in Stockton in 1879."[40]

Grant's blunt statement leaves no doubt as to the main point at issue: it was another man whom the stranger had met. In the light of Jacob Wright Harlan's statement it was almost certainly the Captain Grant who commanded the encampment of soldiers in 1849. Through the years the identity of this pioneer figure has become vague and any anecdote or story concerning either Captain Grant unfortunately is apt to be attributed to the more famous of the two.

U. S. Grant's visits to the town were few and short. His last sojourn was in the spring of '54. He was unhappy, drifting, putting in the days until it would be advisable to start for home. The years have set an aureole about the moody, silent visitor that was not visible at the time. He loved to ride but, when not on a horse, spent many aloof hours whittling. Some of his biographers seem to believe that it was his withdrawal from the regular army that cleared his path to greatness; that it was because he, a West Point graduate, later served among the untrained forces that he had a chance to rise to Commander-in-Chief of the Union forces and to hold the nation undivided. But during the last days he spent at Knight's Ferry he had reached a low level of discouragement and had not yet begun to climb. The citizens of the town had no conception that the unresponsive young man of whom they had heard rumors of "too much liquor" would be hailed in less than a dozen years as the savior of the nation.

In a short time he made his few and brief farewells and started on his predestined road to the White House.

* * *

The homes and families of Knight's Ferry have remained as nearly undisturbed through a century as those of any town of comparable size we can call to mind. It is amazing that so many of the old wooden structures are left.

To see and understand the town enter it from the west by the canyon road but do not make the curve into Main Street. Continue straight across a grassy down-slope to the river where, in a large piling of boulders, are some cable fastenings said by those who should know to indicate the old landing. Here was Knight's row-boat crossing and later Dent and Vantine's railed wagon ferry. There was a ferry toll house on the south bank.

Above the road and facing the river the first building is the Masonic Hall housing Summit Lodge, No. 112, F. & A. M. It first met on February 7, 1857, using the same furnishings still utilized there today.

Outside the fence, a few feet up the hill to the west and back of the building is supposed to be the grave of the town's founder, William Knight. It is toward the brow of the slope up from the canyon road to the fence. The spot was shown to us by Robert A. Curtin who had it pointed out to him years ago by the late George Voyle of Knight's Ferry. Mr. Voyle told the authors that he was uncertain just where the grave lies but that, as a little boy, he was frightened by the thought of it and would never go up the stairs and into the hall unless his mother walked on that side of him. Mr. Curtin went unhesitatingly to the spot and we have never found his phenomenal memory to be at fault nor the data contained in his many scrapbooks and written remembrances of the country-side. The site of the grave is controversial, however, as Sol P. Elias states that a tradition in town places it off the northeast corner of the hall.

Immediately back of the Masonic Hall is the home of Mrs. Samuel Baugh. At one time it was octagonal with a small cupola in the center of the roof and was occupied by Mr. and Mrs. George

Dent, but it has been remodeled until little trace of its former shape remains. Mrs. Baugh's father, William Göbel, came from St. Louis in '49 with the Dent brothers. Samuel Baugh owned the blacksmith and wheelwright shop in town about the turn of the century.

The yellow house next to the Masonic Hall was the home of Abraham Schell. In 1861 he started a lending library of some 900 volumes. The safe where he handled the banking business of the community is let into the wall of the big front room. The substantial dwelling is now the property of Mr. Schell's heirs.

Up the canyon road a hundred yards or so is a small bridge over a rivulet which comes down the hill at an angle to the highway. David Tulloch and George Voyle are authorities for the statement that John Dent's home where Ulysses S. Grant visited was on a flat just above the branch ravine west of the highway. The house, which they describe as a two-room adobe, might have been on the level where "Robuck's Roost" now stands, or possibly on the tiny flat below it and just above the stream. The ravine appears on old maps as "Dent's Gulch" and runs into the river. It was set out to grapes for its full length. Later the property was sold to Mr. Lodtmann and was used as a winery. The firm of "E. & J. Lodtmann" had a brewery as well. The canyon road appears on old maps as "Grant Street."

Directly across Main Street from the Schell residence is the vine-covered fire house with its bell tower. As far as is known it is the original building and is just big enough to hold the spindling, rackety hook and ladder wagon. The record of the organization of the volunteer fire department in 1871, under the chairmanship of A. T. Bartlett, is among the documents carefully preserved by Mr. and Mrs. Roy De Graffenreid at the Red and White Store.

West of the Masonic Hall and across the canyon road was the

site of Major Lane's Hotel which flourished when the town was young and which burned in 1864. Later the Voyle livery stable was built near the site.

Before the flood of '62 the old freight road was closer to the river than Main Street is today and the space sloping up from it to the Masonic Hall and the Schell home was used as a plaza. In the southeast corner of the latter was a pretentious, two-story brick building erected as the Fisher Hotel but taken over as a courthouse during the ten years, from '62 to '72, that Knight's Ferry was the county seat of Stanislaus County. Two stories was more than sufficient for the county's not-too-staggering quota of business so the county officers frugally rented the upper story back to the hotel which then proceeded as usual.

The ancient store building, once owned and operated by O. C. Drew, is under a group of cottonwood trees on the northeast corner of Main and Dean Streets. It contains some of the original Wells Fargo & Company's wooden pigeon-holes for letters and packages. Opposite the store and backed up to the always unpredictable Stanislaus River was Dakin's second wheelwright shop.

Up the hill one block the gracious shady-porched house on the northwest corner of Dean and Ellen Streets was the home of Lewis Dent, long occupied by the Charles T. Kennedys. The name "L. Dent" is scratched with a diamond on a window pane at the rear of the house. The gnarled fig tree in the yard is said to be 107 years old, having priority over any in the great central valleys.[41]

Another block up the hill, on the northeast corner of Dean and Vantine Streets, is the home built and occupied by Isaac Dakin and his family in the late '50s and now the home of Mr. Guy Tandy. The eldest son, Wilbur Dakin, remembered that it had a spring in the cellar and could have withstood a siege. Younger children Henry and Alice were also born here.

The property above it on the north was the site of the McLauflin residence. The northwest corner of the intersection is owned by John Grohl whose family still holds the property at Green Springs where they lived three generations ago. On the southeast corner the Voyles made their home.

On Shurl Street the church was erected on the foundations of the original place of worship. On Main Street, opposite the end of Shurl, was the Barnes Hotel, famous because of Mother Barnes, its proprietress. She was quite able to run all departments under her power; was both cook and waitress and always cut her own hair off short at the back of her neck. She wore carpet slippers and brought the baked potatoes to the table in her apron where she slapped them out by hand. She was also her own bouncer and promptly evicted any person who didn't measure up to her standards. Probably for that very reason her place was popular.

Chinatown ran from this point to the old mill, clustering on both sides of Main Street. Here China Mary hung caged mocking birds in the windows of her delapidated cabin and here, where one sees an abrupt little mound on the south side of the road, the last Oriental, Oh Kow, dwelt on like a winter fly in his adobe under the locusts. The presence of the "tree of heaven" bears witness to their one-time residence for the Chinese were fond of its feathery leaves and comfortable shade and spread it wherever they went.

The metal jail is said to have been built after 1900.

The ruins of the fine old flour mill are a mixture of the first and second structures. The brick storage warehouse and Locke's little stone cottage across the road remained intact when the rest toppled into the river and were lost. The ill-fated first mill was a frame building standing close to the water. When the second mill was built of stone it was placed higher and Mr. Tulloch added the stone warehouse which stands between the brick structure and the bridge.

Both the Locke and the Tulloch mills were in turn connected with the road by a pedestrian bridge jutting out from a second story entrance.

The long masonry wall running along the roadside from the west end of the mill and ending under a luxuriance of blackberry vines is all that is left of a proposed woolen mill that was promoted in 1885 but never made the grade. Across on the hillside is a blossoming oleander which David Tulloch says was planted by his grandmother in 1855.

From the north end of the bridge a very dim road may be seen leading eastward into the hills. This was the road to Copperopolis sixteen miles away, built by Mr. Tulloch and traveled every second day during its peak by teams hauling flour and barley. It is now impassable.

Up the river and just below the last bend Locke swung a tremendous chain to form a log boom which held back debris. It was broken at the time of the flood. A few links were salvaged from it, of which three are hanging in the I.O.O.F. Hall, the property of Stanislaus Lodge, No. 170, instituted in 1870. Much of it still lies in the river bed. Nearer the bridge, at the smooth water, was the later Tulloch Dam. Old irons are imbedded in the rocks and some cement work is visible.

The Locke Dam, of logs, was just above it. The wing dam came down the north side of the river and ended at the island under the bridge. The concrete wing dam, still visible, was built by Mr. Tulloch right over the original log wing dam built by Elbridge Locke as recorded, day by day, in his diary. The door-like opening in the wing dam was where the great mill wheel hung, no change in location being made by Mr. Tulloch.

The saw mill was indefinitely near the bridge and on the south bank.[42]

The covered bridge used to have foot walks elevated about eighteen inches on either side; between them was only room for the wheels of a wagon to turn comfortably and the depressed road-bed was filled with sand. The walks have been removed to give more space although it is still a tight squeeze for two-way traffic. In 1869 the bridge was sold to Thomas Roberts who in turn sold to the county in 1884. Since then it has been toll free.

Old pictures show the later Locke residence, or toll house, at the southern end of the present bridge west of the road. The house now owned and occupied by R. G. Hunter is just beyond the original toll house site. Most of the historical landmarks including mill, bridge, rancheria and Grayson Hotel are on Mr. Hunter's property.

Across the road from Mr. Hunter's home was the rancheria of José Jesús. During the winter huts occupied the meadow; the tribal burial ground was just beyond them to the east. Written opinions of the habits and living conditions of any Indian tribe run an amazing gamut—from something akin to admiration, down through tolerance to absolute disgust. The residents of Knight's Ferry seem to have taken their adjacent rancheria in their stride. It was a big one—about two hundred in population, and, due to its powerful chiefs, was of the socially elect among the nearby tribes. Other villages trekked miles to take part in their powwows. Its dugout and sod-roofed sweat house held an amazing number; one authority said a thousand. The huts were made of straw and small sticks and looked like baskets turned upside down. Into these the families crawled through small holes in the front. There seems never to have been a clash between the original citizens of the rancheria and the white newcomers.

Years passed. The basket-like huts gave way to shacks of un-painted boards of which but one remains, blackened and weather-beaten. Their habits changed also and the indigenous Knight's Ferrians grew to acknowledge their white neighbors as friends. Luis was the last of the tribe, a simple, sweet-natured man. When, after a long absence, Mrs. Tulloch returned for a final visit both the pioneer woman and the Indian wept at parting.

At the height of the freighting industry, when many of the teamsters were driving one wagon and trailing another, it was customary to leave the trailer, or "back-action," near the toll house while the team pulled the first wagon up the hill. The mules then ambled down again with great clanking of chain harness and picked up the trailer. This, the first real hill of the journey, was a serious obstacle in muddy weather and provided to the small boys of the town a fund of profanity which they considered useful. Girls were carefully kept elsewhere.

On the top of the cliff south of the river a settlement came into being which was called Buena Vista. It began to grow just after the flood of 1862 when most of the inhabitants of Two Mile Bar moved down the river and on to the grateful security of higher land. The name is now seldom heard, and, although Highway 120 is (from here well into the mountains) laid along the approximate course of the Old Sonora Road, the latter name is seldom heard either. It turns eastward within the settlement and unrolls its attenuated length toward the Sierra.

A few yards beyond the turn, on the left, was an establishment that began as Dent's Hotel but was better known for a much longer period as Grayson's and was operated by Daniel and his wife Mary. The early building burned but was reconstructed and still stands facing the highway. There were, according to the directories, three adult males in the family—C. W., R. H. and D. (Daniel) Grayson—all from Arkansas. Their hotel was of excellent reputation. Standing, as it did, at the extreme limit of town and backed up against the rancheria of Estanislao and José Jesús, it marked the point of departure from the familiar living conditions of the valley settlements and was the last stop before commencing the pull that exchanged foothills for mountains.

CHAPTER III

FEEDER ROADS AND FORGOTTEN TOWNS

East of Knight's Ferry the freighters, with much swearing and cracking of whips, urged their straining teams over the bulge of the hill and settled down to the job of hating the next five or six miles.

This portion of the road was dreaded at most times of the year. In winter the rolling 1000 foot elevation was blasted by chill winds off the snow while the bottomless mud lasted through the spring months. No freight man ever left a brother teamster stranded so it was not unusual to see several great wagons and trailers with their attendant drivers and animals waiting to assist one another past a particularly obnoxious bog hole.[1] In midsummer the sun shimmered back from silvery dead grasses and heated to stove-top temperature the dull black lava chunks strewn everywhere. On hot days one could cook an egg on any sun-touched rock.

In the mornings the drivers often saw rattlesnakes dusting themselves in the powdery dirt of the road. The frightened teams would not pass so the teamsters went out to battle and became expert at decapitating the snakes with one crack of a bull whip. A portion of this stretch was known as Devil's Flat and it had many atttributes not conducive to the peace of mind of a conscientious driver.

Freighting was one of the big industries of California—the foundation of many a fortune. The mining country was rough and widespread; the settlements often isolated; yet the pioneer families must eat and be clothed. The ponderous wagons must find passage across rocky flats, swampy meadows and through rugged and dangerous canyons. Moreover a freighter never found what would now be considered even a fair road. All such construction must be done by hand. A shelf hewn painfully out of a precipitous

47

canyon-side was made only the width of the lumbering vehicles with a foot or two to spare in case the driver wanted to walk back and inspect the lashing of his load. Passing was sometimes an impossibility and was, at other times, accomplished at the ragged verge of eternity. The drivers prevented such an impasse by keeping informed on the probable time that a given outfit might be expected along the road. Ethics took care of most eventualities. The loaded team pulling up-grade was given the best of the situation; was allowed the inside of the road; was not expected to stop. Such an outfit was noisy—wheels pounding on and off of rocks, whips cracking, men cursing, animals snorting. The team coming down the grade stopped just short of the last turnout before a narrow stretch and listened. If advisable it waited. Many of the lead spans of horses or mules wore above their collars a sort of flattened half hoop strung with jangling bells which served as a warning.

The clangor of the bell-team was a stirring sound that tugged at the heart strings of the old-time teamster as the long drawn whistle of a far locomotive heard in the night brings a sharp nostalgia to the superannuated engineer.

A driver's team was his love, his livelihood and his chief claim to distinction and the teamsters were important people in the '50s, '60s and '70s. Never as dashing as the stage drivers, a few specimens of whom took pleasure in scaring the Yosemite tourists out of their eye-teeth, but very substantial citizens. Many of them owned their valuable outfits and many were sons of the landed proprietors of the region. Some of the best-known of those who drew freight from the loading levee at Stockton out past the Nightingale and into the mountains were G. L. Rodden, Sandy Campbell, George W. Wilbur, Joe Collins, John Curtin and sons, John Probst who drove twelve oxen and was known throughout the

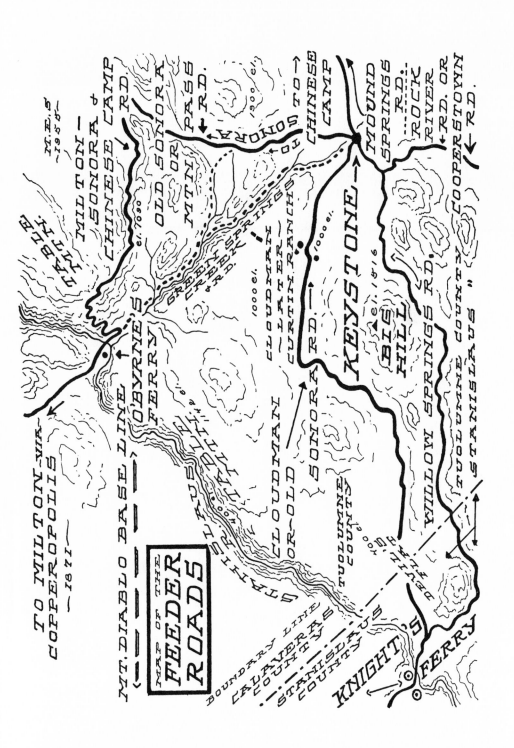

MAP OF THE
FEEDER ROADS

country as "Bull John," Charles Wagner, Al Clifford, Joseph
Mitchell, H. N. Brunson, "Curly" Beith, J. P. Peters, John Fox,
Henry Heckman, Gus Lotman (or possibly Lodtmann), Ira Ladd,
George McQuade and son, David Libby and "Ace" Bartholomew.

Beyond Knight's Ferry miles of ruined rock fences appear. The
magnitude of effort necessary to build them exhausts the imagina-
tion, but they are not confined to this district. They are common
in the rocky foothills up and down the length of the mining area.
Ranchers say that they were originally as much as five feet high
and cattle-proof. Some, less high, were used simply as boundary
fences for lack of any other material as available. Many were built
by Chinese labor.

More than a mile from the intersection of the road from
Knight's Ferry bridge with Highway 120 a road turns south. It is
the modern equivalent of the Willow Springs Road named from
free-flowing springs on the old Hodgdon Ranch from whence
Willow Springs Creek flows into the Stanislaus River. It was
originally the age-old trail of the mountain Indians. During the
seasonal powwow at the rancheria of José Jesús, Indians from
several tribes gathered at what is now Knight's Ferry by means
of this thoroughfare. The trail kept south of "the Big Hill," later
known as Rushing Hill and always used as a landmark.

The first white men who went to the mountains naturally followed this known pathway. The '49ers used it. In that fairly dry
year it worked well. In 1850, which was a wet season, the route
became a swamp and the route now pursued by Highway 120 began
to be evolved, but the Willow Springs Road continued in dry
weather favor until about 1870. In early days the ranches (mentioned in order from the modern highway) were owned by Lewis
Williams, Stone, Hodgdon, Dan Mann, Thorpe, Rushing and (at
its junction with the road from Modesto then known as the Rock

River Road) 3000 acres by Louis D. Gobin. The ruins of Gobin's adobe house have marked the site for years. His large barn was an institution and, as soon as the hay was "fed up," it served as a dance hall for the rest of each winter. The barn was torn down and rebuilt on the Ingall's ranch.

Possibly six miles south of the Rushing Ranch at Big Hill, and on Rock River Road, was the "Rock River Ranch" of William F. Cooper, an officer under General Scott in the Mexican War. Cooperstown came into being along the south end of Cooper's ranch about one-half mile from his house. It was natural that the Rock River Road from this point (even after merging with the Willow Springs Road at the Gobin Ranch) should often be termed "the Cooperstown Road."

At first James Thorpe handled the stage station and eating place for the route in his adobe home. In 1863 William Henry Rushing, at the age of 28, bought out the business and established the famous Rushing Ranch. The Willow Springs School stood in a pasture just northwest of Rushing Hill and faithfully served the children of the far-flung community for years.

So much for the feeder roads from the south.

Considering the Sonora Road for a few miles farther, it is only necessary to say that it stayed very closely to the course of Highway 120.

At 2.7 miles from the Knight's Ferry-bridge-road the old road to Two Mile Bar bridge turned off the Sonora Road toward the north. This was used only prior to the flood of 1862 and was known as Devil's Flat. The land on both sides of the highway was the John Dunlap Ranch. His rock fences were five feet high and cattle-tight.

Beyond him the A. S. Dingley Ranch spread on all sides.

At 4.4 the Mark Crabtree Ranch lay to the north. It was a stopping place for teamsters until about 1900.

Jeremiah Hodgdon's foothill ranch lay to the south of the road. A fruit stand and a small zoo have stood on the highway for many years. Hodgdon was better known for his summer ranch within the present Yosemite National Park boundaries where he took his cattle for summer grazing and maintained a stage stopping place.

At 5.7 John White's ranch lay to the south. The land of his two bachelor brothers, Joseph and Tom was on the north. Rushing Hill is to the south, topped by a modern fire lookout.

To the right of the road was the land of "Bull John" Probst. It is now the Johnson estate and is a quail refuge. John Probst's descendants are still in residence.

The Kessler Ranch, some miles farther on, has its name on the gate. It was originally claimed by Daniel Cloudman, a '49er, then belonged to John Curtin, later still to the Ellinwood family and was recently purchased by Dr. Kessler of San Francisco.

The land extends for more than a mile along the road but a fine spring originally decided the location of the house. Cloudman, on his first plodding journey past the spot, was tired and ill. The spring gushing beside the trail was shaded by a young oak just large enough to afford protection from the sun. He stayed several hours and, as soon as was practical, came back and acquired the land. He and this favorite tree remained together the rest of his life. The spring has since been deepened into a well and a small windmill west of the bunkhouses stands guard over it, companioned by the old oak.

From time unknown it had been a camping place of Indians from the north who came to gather acorns or simply stopped on their way to the big powwows. Daniel Cloudman continued to make them welcome and the rift of rock south of the highway was tacitly considered their property. At that time there was a grove of large oaks near the creek across the highway. Acorns were plenty and the rocks were full of grinding holes. The Indians were Cloud-man's good friends. In fact, after the shock of impact with the rough and often ruthless miners had worn off, there was little trouble between Indians and whites for the entire length of the road to Yosemite.

That Cloudman should keep an eating place for teamsters was considered a matter of course. After all, he lived there and the teamsters had to eat. The newer and drier route leading past his house was known as the Cloudman Road from its junction with the Willow Springs Road clear to Keystone, but actually both of these roads were simply alternate routes (named for purposes of clarity and convenience) on the old Sonora Road.

It was 1879 when John Curtin, a native of Ireland, acquired the ranch and for 23 years he drove a sixteen mule team between Stockton and the Southern Mines. He was assisted by three of his sons, Michael, Robert A. and John B. Curtin. The latter seized the opportunity of long, lonely hours to study law. He carried Black-stone as unfailingly as the blacksnake and, fastening the jerk-line to the saddle of the steady "wheeler" which he rode, let the well-trained animals pick their way. At the age of twenty-two he was District Attorney and later became State Senator from the district, locally known as "Honest John."

A post office officially termed Cloudman was opened in '82 in John Curtin's front room. Daniel C. Cloudman, growing older and deafer, was appointed postmaster. In '95 the first telephone toll station in Tuolumne County was installed in the same room.

John Curtin, Jr., took over the management in 1908, adding by purchase several adjoining ranches. One especially was of interest because of the owner's name. Jack Wade, better known as "Nigger Jack" came to the state as a slave, bought his freedom and settled down as a recluse. His 460 acres were located at the base of Table Mountain, southwest of O'Byrne's Ferry bridge. He was respected for his honesty but was illiterate and suspicious. He lived alone to a great age in a tiny hut squarely in the middle of his property and surrounded by his cattle, hogs and chickens. On present-day maps a mountain of the vicinity bears the caption, "Nigger Jack Peak."

The Curtins were an example of the many ranchers who passed gradually from the freighting to the cattle business, keeping their stock on the home (or foothill) ranch in the winters and pasturing them on their high mountain range in the summers.

The main dwelling now on the property was built during the Curtin regime. It is the fifth house to be used as headquarters; fire—the terror of the foothills—having destroyed the other four.

At 8.4 a clump of trees north of the road once sheltered the ranch house and teamsters' stop operated by Captain Charles Lewis. Reputedly he was one of the many who left their ships in the harbor at San Francisco and made for the diggings. On the death of his wife he had no heart to remain. He buried her near the end of the grove; marked the grave with a pile of white quartz and left the mountains.

Across the highway to the south and over a knoll was the Hugh Mundy Ranch. His summer grazing ground for sheep in early days was Gin Flat. He sold to "French Andre."

When almost two miles past the Kessler ranch house a small dirt thoroughfare leads south. In the words of the time-honored joke "Don't take that one"; for about 100 yards beyond is another similar little road along which the old freight route turned away from the present highway. Both these lanes are at present labeled "Red Hill Road." Along the course of the second one the old Sonora Road proceeded a few hundred yards, or as far as Keystone.

Keystone may be recognized by the tracks of the Sierra Railroad connecting Oakdale with Jamestown and Sonora. It was begun in 1897, completed to Angel's Camp in 1902; gradually became dormant; was given new impetus by the Hetch Hetchy Railroad which operated as a branch of the Sierra; gradually became dormant again at the completion of the Hetch Hetchy dam project and is now used mainly for freight. Where the road crosses the tracks a queer, high-shouldered shelter, open on two sides, served as a depot. Over the arch is the word "Keystone." This was once a prosperous crossroads settlement but was not destined to survive.

The best-known local character was Billy Fields who arrived early in the gold rush and sold liquor and a sparse selection of supplies to passing miners. Scraggly eucalyptus trees shade the rock foundations of his small store directly across the road from the depot. His house was a few yards north near Green Springs Creek.

Keystone was the setting for a good many melodramatic happenings. Robert Curtin remembers that, about 1878, some outlaws invaded the premises and when they rode away, left Billy Fields shot in wrist and breast and unconscious. They also tied young John Grohl, who had come down the Sonora Road from Green Springs for the mail, and left the two together. John managed to grip a sharp kitchen knife in his teeth and commenced sawing at the rope on Fields' wrists. Finally he cut a strand. From that start they succeeded in freeing each other and John rode to Chinese Camp for Dr. Lampson.

In spite of such periodical excitements Billy Fields was in business a long time. It was '92 when he finally died of a gunshot wound. He is buried at the west end of the pasture that parallels the tracks on the north. There is no marker and his grave is frequented mainly by tapping woodpeckers and an occasional rattlesnake. The Horatio Brunson family later acquired his land, added to Fields' structures and operated a large freighter stop for many years.

Keystone is said to have gained its name from the number of roads focussing there. In this chapter we are giving such data as we have accumulated about these feeder roads with the towns, or crossroad stores, that enlivened their otherwise lonely miles. They were important in their day but are lost to memory now except for just such small mentionings as are given here. If they are not of interest skip the next few pages. If they are, by all means use the map.

First—the combined Willow Springs and Rock River Road (often called Cooperstown Road) arrived at Keystone from the south via what is now the railroad track. From here on to within a mile of Chinese Camp the route that evolved from this old Indian trail had another name, the Mound Springs Road.

Second—the Sonora Road, which deviates from the course of Highway 120 to curve through Keystone on a detour of less than one-half mile, leaves by way of the railroad tracks, joins the highway again and makes its way more or less north, through Mountain Pass, to Jamestown and Sonora. At Keystone it ceased to be called the Cloudman Road and became the Mountain Pass Road but that eccentricity was just to make things interesting for future historians. In its entirety it was still the old Sonora Road.

The forgotten community of Green Springs stood north of the highway (Sonora Road) at .6 mile beyond the turnoff into Keystone and is noted as the locale of Bret Harte's "Sappho of Green Springs." There are at least two springs of which one has been cemented and is wreathed thickly in blackberry vines. In the early '50s Thomas Edwards operated a stopping place here and the Joseph Aldridge home also dated back to mining days. The John Grohl family lived at Green Springs very early and the property still remains in their possession.

One-quarter mile west of the springs, but considered as being at the settlement, is the grave of John T. Brasefield. He is buried under a symmetrical oak tree which is often eaten off by cattle to an even distance from the ground. John Brasefield was born in 1830 and died of a gunshot wound in 1855. Further information about him seems to be non-existent. He may have been a stranger who left a waiting and wondering family somewhere in the east or he may have been well rooted in California. Possibly some reader will be able to add extra details to present knowledge of this grave.

The first orange trees in Tuolumne County were planted on the Jules and Jean Reynaud ranch to the right of the highway.

Presently Highway 120 (approximately the old Sonora Road) crosses Green Springs Creek and, a mile farther, the Milton-Chinese Camp Road leading to O'Byrne's Ferry bridge and Copperopolis. Just beyond, on the early Beckwith ranch, stands a ruined stone structure. This was originally about ten feet high, had four embrasures facing the road and was intended for defense against Indians. The Captain Grant who commanded the militia at Knight's Ferry in 1849 had something to do with its construction according to Robert Curtin. Old-timers have referred to it as the fort.

Yosemite Junction was known in trail days as the Goodwin ranch. J. W. Goodwin founded this stopping place in 1854 and ran it twenty-seven years. Beside the regular buildings he erected a winery of stone and adobe of which remnants remain, shaded by century-old but still prolific fig trees. The first of the two "Mountain Passes" through Table Mountain can be seen just ahead but, for the purposes of this account we may end the description of the Sonora Road at the Yosemite Junction corner.

Third—a feeder road of little importance came into Keystone from O'Byrne's Ferry by a route passing the ranch of Ambrose De

Bernardi. In fact he practically constructed it himself for convenience in reaching the foothill towns where he peddled his fruit and vegetables, wine and vinegar. This route was called the Green Springs Road because it remained close to the lower part of Green Springs Creek, a tributary of the Stanislaus River. It was used by neighboring ranchers as a shortcut. It is said that the saddle trail, which was its humble beginning, was a favorite of Joaquín Murieta and his riders on their way from Marsh's Flat and Indian Bar (their hangouts south of Moccasin) to Shaw's Flat and Sawmill Flat near Sonora. Privacy, to them, was more desirable than better travelling conditions. The Green Springs Road was never much used and is now practically obliterated.

Fourth—Cutting across the Mountain Pass Road (Highway 120) near Goodwin's (Yosemite Junction) was the all-important Milton-Chinese Camp Road just mentioned. At the time of the Civil War it siphoned business from Copperopolis, then the main source of copper for the nation. After the year 1870 when the railroad was constructed from Stockton to Milton the supplies came by boat to the former, thence by railway to Milton and from there by stage or freighter to the mountain mining settlements and Yosemite. The Milton-Chinese Camp Road carried this traffic and, although it went through Goodwin's instead of through Keystone, many of the wagons branched off to pass through the congested cross roads of the latter on their way to other places. As the vehicles reached Goodwin's they were confronted with one of the few road signs placed in early mining days: a large slab of wood hanging from a tree depicting a pig-tailed Chinese with a pack on his back. The caption read, "Me go China Camp . . . Three mile one half."

Milton is almost deserted now and has some interesting ruins of stone and adobe buildings. Portions of the railway depot are to be found, forgotten stores and an occasional dwelling. As the town is on the north side of the Stanislaus River the road crossed at O'Byrne's Ferry, a small settlement that made dramatic history during its adolescence. The ferry did not last three years, for in the flood of '52, it was swept downstream and dashed to pieces. Some form of crossing was imperative and Patrick O'Byrne commenced work on a bridge. The San Francisco *Alta California* ran an article on September 12, 1852, which stated: "Mr. Byrne is building a suspension bridge over the Stanislaus River at Byrne's Ferry. It is eight feet above highwater and is made of chain cables."

This was probably the beginning of the controversy as to whether the name of the builder was Patrick O. Byrne or Patrick O'Byrne,[2] with the suitable resultant effect upon the name of the ferry and the subsequent bridge. The same publication, in its issue of January 18, 1853, speaks of the "enterprising projector and chief promoter" as Mr. P. O'Byrne. This is now considered correct. The *Alta California* also made the broad statement that the wire suspension bridge then under construction was "to endure for all time"—an optimism corrected in the issue for November 25th of the same year as follows: "The bridge across the Stanislaus River known as Byrne's Ferry Bridge fell in on Wednesday in consequence of the chains parting at one end. There was on the bridge at the time a six ox-team and two men. The team was lost, but the men succeeded in making their escape. The cause of the chain breaking is thought to be the extra weight caused by the rain. It is estimated that $3000 will repair the damage."

The bridge was repaired or rebuilt and lasted until 1862, the much vaunted flood year of exciting memory, when it went down the roaring river in company with a flume, a house and a miscellany of smaller things. It was replaced at once by a cantilever type with no center piling to annoy winter floods. The third O'Byrne's Ferry

Bridge is said by S. Griswold Morley, in his *The Covered Bridges of California,* to be the longest covered bridge of that particular type in the nation. It is angular and singularly ungraceful but has always carried light traffic competently although the timbers of its massive interior bracing are bent far out of line. Progress has now slated it for removal but, fortunately, it will probably be set up again in some state park as an historic memento.*

On the north side of the Stanislaus at O'Byrne's Ferry the Pardee brothers, George and Joe, operated a trading post in 1850. For years George made it his business to see that the American flag flew from the top of Table Mountain on that portion of the great plateau nearest to their little store. This is reputed to be that section of the mountains of which Bret Harte's "Outcasts of Poker Flat" gives a picture.

Fifth—and most important to this account was the Mound Springs Road connecting Keystone with the Big Oak Flat Road which began at Chinese Camp and took the freight outfits the rest of the way to Yosemite Valley. Mound Springs Road is (excepting the Sonora Road-Highway 120) the only one leaving Keystone which is still fit to travel; it proceeds across the Sierra Railroad tracks and up the hill in plain sight. Although it served as a feeder to the Sonora Road by siphoning in the traffic from La Grange, Coulterville and other points south, it was actually a sort of detour. It diverged, only to connect again higher in the mountains after a decided swing to the south and east. Because of its many good road houses and stopping places it was more popular with the drivers than the Mountain Pass section which it by-passed. On the long slow up-haul they usually took it. Coming back empty they were apt to clatter and bounce through Mountain Pass.

The first landmark, only a few yards after crossing the tracks at Keystone, is Billy Fields' old barn. The surrounding corral

---

* Flooding behind the Tulloch Dam in 1957 destroyed this landmark. A fine covered bridge is preserved at the Wawona Pioneer Village in Yosemite National Park.

sometimes extends hospitality to six or eight of the most tremend-ous Hereford bulls imaginable. Apparently they remain out of sheer courtesy as no ordinary fence would prove very effective as a barrier. The substantial house now pertaining to the barn is the residence of Edward Jasper. It was built on the ranch of a descend-ant of Daniel Boone and was first called "the Boone House." Mr. Jasper purchased and moved it to Keystone where he has lived in it for over fifty years but, so strong is custom in the mountains, that it is sometimes still spoken of by its first owner's name.

Less than half a mile beyond Keystone stands Dunow's Camp, the site of the Green Springs Schoolhouse where, in the '70s, Maggie Fahey, started teaching at the age of sixteen with more than seventy ungraded pupils. Here gathered the children of the Walkers, the Curtins, Boones, Trumpers, Ballards, Aldridges, Stevens, Rosascos, Brunsons, Adams, Bolters and even the DeBer-nardis from over near O'Byrne's Ferry—names that live in the history of the county. It took only a few families to form a large school.

Now, for over a mile Mound Springs Road runs southerly co-incidentally with the new La Grange Highway. The present house of George Bolter, on this stretch, was formerly the H. N. Brunson homestead, a teamsters' stop, and bore the sign "Travelers' Home." Still earlier it was known as Stevens' Place and was operated by L. A. Stevens as a hotel in 1856. It has been enlarged but is built around the nucleus of the 100-year-old chimney and still contains much of the original furniture. The Brunsons ran the freighters' stopping place at Keystone after Field's death.

Two miles from Keystone the Mound Springs Road, in exist-ence years before the highway from La Grange was thought of, twists to the left and starts up a canyon. This corner is one of the most interesting in Tuolumne County. The large meadow west of the highway was the site of the unbelievable Tong War on which the whole countryside so gaily embarked and where a couple of Chinese were killed and several wounded. The story is told in the next chapter as an inseparable part of the history of Chinese Camp, but the imaginative may possibly envision some 2000 Chinese shrilly, happily and above all noisily sparring away at each other with crude hand-made weapons until blood was shed and satisfied the honor of both sides.

In the northeast corner of the intersection, near the fig trees, Ezekiel Brown built a stopping place in 1850 and lived there at least ten years. Then John Stockel took over the property and founded the station that afterward bore the name Crimea House. It was burned in the '70s; a fate that seemed almost inevitable sooner or later in the mountains. A new frame house was put up which did not succumb to flames until 1949. It had a combined kitchen and dining room, both to save steps and because the teamsters liked the homey atmosphere. The rest of the lower floor, outside of the family quarters, was a big clubroom for the men. The upstairs was a dormitory.

While his eight children were still small, John Stockel was bitten by an animal with rabies and died shockingly and speedily. Cyntha Stockel carried on. She put all the resources of a healthy body and an indomitable will into running Crimea House and raising her children and, even in her first days of adversity, she turned no one away but gave food and shelter to any penniless passerby.

Across the road the barn and corral still stand. The corral is circular and was laid out accurately using an oak as the center. It is in good condition, with walls five feet high and two feet thick made of dry-laid rock, and shows the excellence of its patient construction by Chinese labor.

The name "Crimea House," although known to all old residents, seemed to be difficult for them to explain. Finally the authors, with inspired lack of the faintest qualms, sent out questionnaires to anyone who might be expected to know and supplemented this source of information by personally asking everyone in sight for miles. Answers were vague. Everyone was surprised that he or she had not questioned the name before but all said that it had to do with the Chinese; the majority tied the name to the Tong War. We have come to believe that the people of the vicinity, many of them Europeans, were greatly interested in the Crimean War which was raging in 1856—the year of the Tong battle; they spoke of the latter as the local Crimean War and the name stuck to the property as nicknames sometimes do. The late Mrs. Frank Dolling of La Grange, granddaughter of John and Cyntha Stockel, agreed readily that this was the most likely explanation.

We were somewhat confirmed in this supposition by later finding a statement in the Memoirs of Lemuel McKeeby telling of another locality named in just such haphazard fashion by reason of the Crimean conflict: "The little town of Sebastapol," he wrote, "was close by the diggings. It was composed of three houses at that time. ... The Crimean War was then in progress and as two Englishmen —brothers—who had put up a saw mill in that settlement, were eternally talking of Sebastapol, we miners gave that name to the place."

In such casual manner the pioneers bestowed many of our California place names.

The mountains close in beyond Crimea House. Somewhere near Stockel's roadhouse the trail veered to the right and around a hill called in succession Red Mountain, Mount Pleasant or Taylor Mountain. The Taylor Mountain route was not successful because a little creek, soon to be known as Six Bit Gulch, was turbulent in the wet season and had a difficult crossing. It seems probable that the Indians, who traveled mainly in the summer, chose well-watered trails with little regard for their condition in winter. By 1850 the miners had abandoned their course around Taylor Mountain and were traveling the Mound Springs route as it is today. Evidently, in looking for a better crossing of the creek the present road was evolved. So we find that, after 1850, the Mound Springs Road passed what was later Crimea House corner, between the house and the corral; climbed Crimea Hill and proceeded along a brush-filled wash.

The springs for which the road is named flow from a series of spongy tussocks or mounds of sod covered with swamp grass. They are found in a meadow to the right and are the source of a swift gurgling stream. The lavishly watered meadow was, in the days of the cattle kings, a welcome stopover for the herds on the way to and from summer pasturage in the high mountains.

The first proprietor of the Mound Springs Ranch was John Flax who lived and died there and is buried in the flat area just beyond the present dwelling. At that time most of the property was a large vineyard, and his grave was under the vines.

Beyond the springs is abrasive country—full of sharp rocks, stickery weeds and digger pines. It is also full of turkeys who do well in the 1000 to 2000 foot level. Turkey raising seemed at first to be a sublimation of the tendency of the region to propagate grasshoppers. Not since the Indians counted them a dietary luxury had these excitable insects been so popular. Now the industry is so standardized that the pampered birds, raised within fences, never see a hopper. The road, winding north of Mount Pleasant, comes to Six Bit Gulch about where the smaller Picayune Gulch empties into it. Both names were given in derision because of the poor diggings in their neighborhood. On these gulches lived, in peculiar mud huts, a few Chinese of different habits and appearance from

those of Chinese Camp. They were generally known by the townspeople as "Tartars" and never mixed with the other Orientals.
One hut survived until recently and may still be there.

Six Bit Gulch was a welcome sight in early autumn as the cattlemen drove the herds back from the high mountains. It was the first
convenient watering place west of Jacksonville. It was not so welcome in the spring when they made the upward journey, being in
those days a deep and turbulent stream in which, at various times,
riders were drowned. Remembering this, its present inocuous condition requires explanation. Adjoining ranchers tell us that the
creek changed completely after the section around Montezuma was
dredged. It is possible that the drainage slope was altered in some
way or the water supply tapped. The long dry cycle just ending,
no doubt, had something to do with it also.

Beyond the gulch, which now is not even dignified with a bridge,
stood the establishment of John Taylor and his wife, Margaret.
The house was on the left immediately beyond the ford, between
the gulch and the road as it turns and leads north toward Montezuma. Directly across the road was the large barn. The corrals were
between and were so arranged that the road passed through them,
necessitating the opening and closing of two gates. This was primarily for the convenience of the cattlemen who broke their drive
at this point. Taylor's stage and freighter stop was founded after
he had failed in the diggings. He did not maintain a regular dining
room but, of course, any hungry man was welcome to come in and
eat. Taylor was Justice of the Peace and, although hospitable, he
was also practical. This story of early-day court practices came our
way: A jury case was slated to be held at Taylor's Ranch. The court
was assembled at the old house in Six Bit Gulch. The attorney for
the prosecution, a Sonora lawyer who liked his liquor, discovered
upon investigation that there was no great amount of that com-

modity on hand. He rose and requested the judge for a change of venue to Jamestown. Judge Taylor, deciding that if one of the two must be discommoded it might as well be the lawyer and not he, slapped his hand resoundingly on the table and announced firmly, "I've just bought a two dollar roast to feed the jury. Change denied."

At Taylor's the traffic for Big Oak Flat and Yosemite Valley left the Mound Springs Road which continued northward with Six Bit Gulch. Possibly a mile along the course of the latter is the ranch of Robert Sims, in the same family since pioneer days. Farther is the historical marker telling of the settlement of Montezuma which, in 1849, possesesd rich placer mines. A trading post was established there in that year by R. K. Aurand and Sol Miller and was shortly followed by a teamsters' stop and stage station, under the same ownership, known as Montezuma House.

And so, having used the Mound Springs Road from Keystone to Six Bit Gulch, the wagons bound for the Big Oak Flat Road and Yosemite said goodbye to it at Taylor's and turned uphill to the northeast.

The one-mile-long stretch connecting Taylor's with the next town goes through scrub-grown, broken country, beautiful only in spring. It surmounts the hill at an open level filled with yellow tar weed across which is a vista of but medium allure—the outskirts of Chinese Camp.

When the first white men saw this mountain flat it was filled with a stupendous growth of glorious oak trees. In a few months it was a waste of dismal stumps which took much longer to disappear. Now it is a mixture of gravel and red earth, baked in summer but capable of bottomless mud, to which of late years has been added some regrettable landscaping in the form of dumps.

Before the day of black-top surfacing this last half-mile was anathema to the impatient and hungry driver. He might spend hours extricating his wagon and trailer from one sink hole after another while the friendly buildings of what was then a large town stood tantalizingly close and in plain sight across the adhesive waste.

CHAPTER IV

CHINESE CAMP

The town of Chinese Camp appears bigger when approached by way of Six Bit Gulch than when, bowling along Highway 120, one simply skims its upper edge. Even so it has decreased sharply in population and importance since the day, at the height of the Gold Rush, when it is said to have sheltered sketchily some 5000 persons, principally Oriental.

William Heath Davis wrote that two Chinese men and a woman who arrived on the Brig *Eagle*, February 2, 1848, were the first to appear in the port of San Francisco and were looked upon as curiosities. During the ensuing winter the number increased rapidly.

The effort and initiative displayed in arriving at the port of San Francisco by these Chinese, mainly untraveled and speaking no language but their own, is tremendous. To get passage up the river to Stockton and trudge from there to the mines was another chore not lightly to be discounted. There were few if any helping hands. It was not that they were uniquely unwelcome; they were entirely unknown to any but seafaring men and world travelers. Thomas O. Larkin received a letter, dated San Francisco, March 6. 1848, showing that the Chinese immigrants had at least one advocate: ". . . One of my favorite projects is to introduce Chinese emigrants into this country, and desire some encouragement. Any number of Mechanics, Agriculturists, and Servants can be obtained,—they would be willing to sell their services for a certain period to pay their passage across the Pacific,—they would be valuable Miners.

"The Chinese are a sober and industrious people and if a large number could be introduced into California, landed property would increase in value fourfold. . . ."[1]

67

Early in the Gold Rush it occurred to a ship's captain to persuade some Chinese from the crew of a stranded ship to wash gold for him. He brought them to a hilltop encampment called Campo Salvador because it was founded by a group of San Salvadorians.[2] Its site is traversed by Highway 120 just before starting down Shawmut Grade. Here on the timber-grown height above Woods Creek the Chinese built a queer dwelling after their own fashion. It soon formed a nucleus for Chinese who drifted in from other diggings or came straight from the harbor of San Francisco.

Naturally the Caucasians at once pushed in to Campo Salvador to see if the Chinese had uncovered anything worth while; saw the gleam of gold and stayed. Whereupon, in 1850, the Orientals moved out.

This was the procedure all through the gold region. Sometimes, as in this case, they seem to have chosen to leave. Sometimes they were more or less peacefully elbowed out. All too often they were robbed or driven out by violence without regard for common justice or humanity. This was deplored by the majority of decent miners but, before the coming of organized government to the camps, either prevention of crime or its retribution depended upon the busy miners themselves. It took murder or horse stealing to stir them to the concerted action necessary for definite results.

When the Chinese moved they found a group of Americans mining on the west side of Rocky Hill who called their sketchy settlement Camp Washington. It grew; absorbed the incoming Orientals and was soon known as Chinese Camp or Chinee. Washington Street in Chinese Camp is a holdover from those earliest days. Several of the first buildings, including the adobe store belonging to the Morris family, were on Washington rather than on Main Street.

Proof of the use of the name Camp Washington seemed difficult

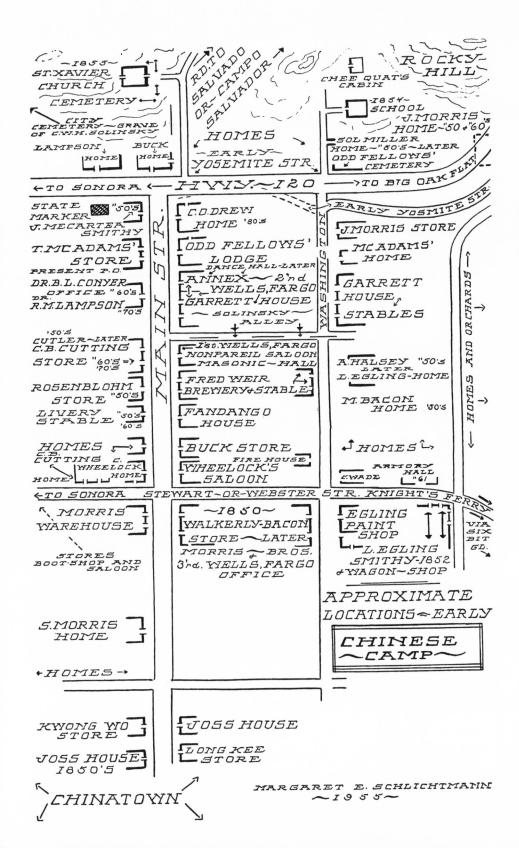

~1855~
ST. XAVIER
CHURCH
CEMETERY

CITY
CEMETERY~GRAVE
OF C.W.H. SOLINSKY
LAMPSON
HOME   BUCK
HOME

RD. TO
SALVADO
OR~CAMPO
SALVADOR

HOMES

~EARLY
YOSEMITE STR.

CHEE QUATS
CABIN

ROCKY-
HILL

~1854~
SCHOOL
J. MORRIS
HOME ~'50 & '60'S
SOL MILLER
HOME~'60'S~LATER
ODD FELLOWS'
CEMETERY

←TO SONORA ←   HWY.~120   → TO BIG OAK FLAT→

STATE
MARKER   "50'S
J. MECARTEA
SMITHY

T. MCADAMS'
STORE
PRESENT P.O.
DR. B.L. CONYER
OFFICE "60'S
DR.
R.M. LAMPSON   "70'S

'50'S
CUTLER~LATER
C.B. CUTTING
STORE "60'S =>
'70'S

ROSENBLOHM
STORE "50'S

LIVERY
STABLE "50'S
'60'S

HOMES
C.B.
CUTTING   C.
HOME   WHEELOCK
HOME

MAIN STR.

C.D. DREW
HOME '80'S

ODD FELLOWS'
LODGE
DANCE HALL~LATER
ANNEX ~ 2nd
WELLS, FARGO
GARRETT HOUSE
~SOLINSKY~
ALLEY

1st WELLS, FARGO
NONPAREIL SALOON
MASONIC~HALL

FRED WEIR
BREWERY & STABLE

FANDANGO
HOUSE

BUCK STORE
FIRE HOUSE
WHEELOCK'S
SALOON

WASHINGTON

EARLY YOSEMITE STR.

J. MORRIS STORE

MCADAMS'
HOME

GARRETT
HOUSE

STABLES

A. HALSEY "50'S
LATER
L. EGLING~HOME

M. BACON
HOME '50'S

↲ HOMES ↳

ARMORY
C. WADE   HALL
"61'

HOMES AND ORCHARDS →

←TO SONORA   STEWART~OR~WEBSTER STR. KNIGHT'S FERRY

MORRIS
WAREHOUSE

STORES
BOOT·SHOP AND
SALOON

S. MORRIS
HOME

←HOMES→

~1850~
WALKERLY-BACON
STORE ~ LATER
MORRIS ~ BROS.
3rd WELLS, FARGO
OFFICE

EGLING
PAINT
SHOP
L. EGLING
SMITHY~1852
& WAGON~SHOP

VIA
SIX
BIT
GL.

APPROXIMATE
LOCATIONS~EARLY

CHINESE
~CAMP~

KWONG WO
STORE

JOSS HOUSE
1850'S

JOSS HOUSE

LONG KEE
STORE

↙ CHINATOWN ↘

MARGARET E. SCHLICHTMANN
~1955~

to find; in fact has only recently materialized. William Solinsky, son of C. W. H. Solinsky of Chinese Camp, wrote a statement which has just been made available to us. He was born in Chinese Camp and lived there most of his mature life. He knew the town perfectly. He wrote: ". . . After a short stay in Carson Hill and other parts of the Southern Mines papa went to Camp Washington, Tuolumne Co. . . . and engaged in mining after which he joined with S. M. Miller & Co. and became agents of Adams Express Co."

Campo Salvador was sometimes called East Chinee. The displaced Chinese miners had not gone far—less than a mile. They had simply put Rocky Hill between them and their ertswhile Caucasian competitors.

Campo Salvador was now composed mainly of Americans, Germans and Chileans. In 1850 E. W. Emory ran a general store. By 1856 there was a blacksmith shop owned and operated by C. W. Ollrich and John Reitz ran a saloon. The camp was rough and tough. It acquired a bad name even in this tolerant section of the mines. The Chinese had established a nucleus of profitable gambling and fandango houses; the Caucasians brought liquor. It had the traditional lynching when the sheriff of Amador County came to arrest a man in John Reitz' saloon. The man killed the sheriff and, so we are told by Robert Curtin, was hanged on a large oak about where the present highway starts down the grade to Jacksonville. It was all quite according to pattern. For a few years the camp was a center of excitement and dissipation for the surrounding mountains, then the diggings dwindled. The gold here had always been of fine quality, but scarce. The miners, one at a time or in small groups, went doggedly off to find a better place.

After it was deserted the Chinese returned in small numbers and frugally sluiced out the tailings. So much for Campo Salvador, destined for complete obliteration.

The new location selected by the Chinese was an entirely different matter. It sat smugly behind little Rocky Hill and began to do very well for itself.

As the Chinese were driven from other camps—notably from Sonora—they congregated here. Chinese Camp was the magnet that drew most of them. It was their "Little Pekin." The diggings were rich but dry, with no water available for sluicing out the gold which may be one reason why the industrious and patient Chinese were able to make a success of their project at this location with, at first, but little interference from the Caucasians. Their colony grew until it is generally accepted that the Mongolian population was several thousand and that four out of the famous Chinese "Six Companies" had their agents on the spot.

At first the gold-bearing dirt was hauled to a creek on the Sims Ranch or, still farther, to Six Bit Gulch and there sluiced out. When it was evident that this process was paying, the white miners edged in but the Chinese were too numerous and too well established to be displaced with impunity, so they worked together amicably enough. The American miners brought more efficient methods. After paying $15.00 a cartload to have dirt hauled to the creeks, they decided to dig ditches and promptly did so, bringing the water from Woods Creek. The miners' meeting in Chinese Camp on September 17, 1850, which decided on the size of claims and laid down the rules, was one of the first in the Southern Mines. They then worked the diggings—lightly once over—with precision and dispatch and, after a few years, moved out.

The Chinese, who had calmly waited for this to happen, panned out the tailings and reaped a fair harvest from the gold which the rough and hasty methods of the Americans had wasted. They continued many years in the town as merchants, cooks and laundrymen after the main bulk of the miners had taken their departure, until

finally but one Chinese remained, Chee Quat, a character affectionately regarded in the settlement, whose tiny cabin stood to the right
of the school house at the foot of Rocky Hill.

During the lusty, swashbuckling first years of gold the town of
Chinese Camp (never, at its best, monotonous) was greatly enlivened by a Tong War—a battle somewhat like a wholesale feud
that took place between opposing clans or families of Chinese.

There were other Tong battles in the California mines, notably
the famous encounter at Weaverville. Old-timers admit that these
conflicts were fomented by drunken white miners who enjoyed the
excitement of the foray. But, although the death rate was by no
means in proportion to the mighty cacophony of yells, tinny clash-
ings of hand-made swords, and scattering revolver shots, enough
deaths resulted to make the admission embarrassing.

The Tong battle proudly claimed by Chinese Camp took place
on September 26, 1856, in the meadow opposite Crimea House
at the junction of the Mound Springs Road with the modern road
to La Grange. It was caused by a dispute between two companies
of Chinese who were mining at Two Mile Bar on the Stanislaus
River; one company having rolled a boulder onto the claim of the
other company and refused to move it. Very few men were involved at the outset but it ended with over a thousand. One account
says 1200 on one side and 900 on the other. History tells us that
the Chinese invented gunpowder, but the Orientals who came to
the gold mines neither owned nor knew how to use fire arms. Their
weapon was the knife. While light-heartedly planning their battle
they beseiged the blacksmiths with orders for swords and spears
which the smith (apparently just as happily) forged for them out
of wagon tires or what not. When all was ready the embattled
Celestials went tearing off in hysterical exultation and had a fine,
impersonal, clattering fight.

Captain Ayres, a resident of Tuolumne County, told of the spectacle when the thousand or so Chinese, accompanied by most of the miners of the vicinity, left Chinese Camp on the four-mile journey to Crimea House. "There was no discipline nor order," he wrote. "Everybody marched as he pleased or ran about hooting and shouting. Chinamen on horseback hovered around the flock and it looked like a band of cattle being driven. One man was killed, one wounded who was bayonetted. He was carried from the field as they carry a hog. His (pig) tail and heels tied to a pole."[3]

After it was over and the accidentally deceased had had an elaborate Chinese funeral, the blacksmith with his helpers went out to the battlefield and collected the debris. George Egling stated that the swords and other weapons stayed in their scrap heap at the smithy until he sold them for old iron at the time of the first World War.

At one time Chinese Camp had three Joss houses in town, large structures filled with carvings and images covered with gold leaf—rich and surprisingly luxurious; but, by a strange contrast, provided with no floor but the hard-packed earth. Chee Quat faithfully frequented the last of these.

The Chinese made industrious residents of the settlement, kept to themselves and took care of their own indigent—if any. The white merchants appreciated them as customers, for, although frugal, they were scrupulously honest. The only drawback seemed to be that dozens of them had the same name. There were so many called Lim, Chew, Hoy or Hong that it became simpler to describe them; so the records in the accounting books show: Blind Chinaman, Squint Eye, Lame One, Flat Nose and many more.

However, freely granting the fundamental honesty and industry of the man from China, a large Oriental quarter in a mining town did not add to its moral tone. They were quick to establish gambling shacks; to bring prostitutes into the settlement and to house them comfortably in accessible spots; to bring opium along as a matter of course and to sell it openly. In short, they had a good many of the less presentable proclivities of a modern Chicago gangster tucked away behind their fat bland faces. And, when approached with opprobrium by reform-minded citizens, did not under any condition worth mentioning speak English.

One good thing, the Chinese did not particularly care for their American neighbor's whiskey nor for their morphine which was equally easy to purchase; but fortunately neither did the Anglo-Saxon care for their sickly and outlandish-smelling opium.

By 1852 or '53 two small hotels had appeared in Chinese Camp, the Eagle under the proprietorship of Mr. O. Waltze and the Garrett Hotel and livery stable run by Hiram and Peter Garrett, the latter answering amiably to the local title of "Stovepipe Pete." Other hotels, the Belvidere—H. Mattison, proprietor, and the El Dorado, owned by Ramon and Peacock, appeared in 1856. About the same year the Garrett Hotel was purchased by one of the most colorful characters to enter the Southern Mines, C. W. H. Solinsky; or, to give him his lawful title, Count Christian William Hugo Solinsky[4] forced to leave Poland for fear of exile to Siberia.

He arrived in the United States in the middle 1830s; served as a lieutenant in the Mexican War and then came around the Horn, arriving in San Francisco about January of 1849 where he struck out immediately for the mines. By 1852 he was located in Chinese Camp where he and "Sol" M. Miller became agents for the Adam's Express Co. When their employers failed they continued with the Pacific Express Co. and later, in 1857, Wells, Fargo & Company. They managed also a branch agency of Fretz & Ralston, San Francisco bankers, and shipped gold dust and nuggets. The partners remained in business together until 1870. According to a written statement by a son, William Solinsky, they had five offices located at Montezuma, Big Oak Flat, Camp Washington (Chinese Camp), Coulterville and Don Pedro Bar.

The same year, 1856, that Solinsky bought the Garrett Hotel, he married Mary Amelia Sprague and settled down to run a truly first class hostelry. As it became necessary he enlarged and improved his property. Next to the hotel was a building used as a dance hall. Eventually, to house the embarrassingly large number of guests, this property was purchased and divided into rooms by seven-foot partitions. By standing on a bed the occupant had a view at once comprehensive and uninterrupted. It was necessary to go into the hotel proper to wash. No provision was made for heating and the building was usually referred to as "the Morgue." Garrett House became famous throughout the Mother Lode country and, its scrupulously upright host was favorably known over a wide area. Many persons of distinction were guests here before Solinsky's death in 1896. Their names, including that of Sir Thomas Lipton, are recorded in the old register recently presented to the Sonora Museum.[5]

C. W. H. Solinsky's daughter Margaret married Thomas Jackson, one of the drivers of the stage line passing through the town. In those early days the bachelor stage drivers were the catch of the community.

From the beginning the town maintained excellent stores. Mr. Buck (forerunner of Hedges and Buck of Stockton) managed a business there, as did also at various times, Thomas McAdams; the Gamble family; Brock and Blake; Wass, Veader and Cutler; C. O. Drew; Charles B. Cutting, and Mr. Rosenblohm. At least as early as 1850 the Walkerley Brothers, William and Martin, owned and operated a general store housed in a substantial brick building. A nephew and namesake, Martin Bacon, came from England at the

Keystone House, about 1890. Billy Fields in center.

Brunson's Stage and Freighter at Keystone House, 1898. Mr. and Mrs. Horatio
Brunson at right foreground.

Perkins

O'Byrnes Ferry Bridge. The construction of the Tulloch Dam and flooding of reservoir destroyed this landmark in 1958.

Courtesy of Grace Morris

Burning of the Morris Store, Chinese Camp, 1918.

age of seventeen; served in the Civil War and then came to Chinese Camp to help out in the business which he later took over. He married Mary Elizabeth Shepley, daughter of Robert Shepley who arrived in '52 and took up land east of the town. Martin Bacon became a very active citizen, serving as a banker and also as treasurer for the Yosemite Turnpike Road Company when that organization was founded, but left the mountains about 1876 to go into the stock and bond business in San Francisco.

The store, founded by James and Pauline Morris, which developed into an institution in the town, began in a large adobe structure on Washington Street, but as the business section shifted and, probably, as Martin Bacon moved away they purchased Walkerley Brothers' interests. James Morris founded a family greatly beloved throughout the Southern Mines. He was succeeded by his sons, Paul, Henry, George and Saul and by a daughter, Grace. To the last surviving son, Saul, now recently deceased, we are indebted for much of our detailed local information. "Our store was typical of the times," he wrote, "with not much order and with mining supplies scattered all about. We carried everything from a needle to an anchor, even including fine imported china and glass from England, France and Bavaria. We prided ourselves on well-stocked shelves, often buying in carload lots which then had to be freighted from the railroad or from the Stockton boat levee. The books showed more than $250,000 in business. As a very young man I was deeply opposed to the railroad coming any closer because we all liked the teamsters and were afraid that they would lose their jobs. It was a misconception. The closer the railroads came, the more work they had."

Blacksmith and wheelwright shops were vital to the life of the times. Louis Egling, a strapping young fellow of twenty-two just over from Germany began to shoe horses for the miners early in the history of the camp and is said to have founded his famous wheelwright shop in 1852. He specialized in the building of wagons, stages and freighters. The shop remained in active service until about 1920 and, after a century, occasional wagons made by Egling still may be found standing in the blackened and weather-beaten barns of the nearby towns and ranches. Louis married Emilie Krautter who had likewise come from Germany with the laudable intention of keeping house for her father in Big Oak Flat. Such good intentions seldom lasted in the early mountain towns where women were at a premium, but Emilie had plenty to do, as, after the hospitable custom of the times, out-of-town customers with blacksmith work to occupy a day or so moved into town with their families and stayed in the blacksmith's home.

Egling kept several helpers busy. Six forges held heaps of red hot coals, blown to fury by bellows when extra heat was needed. Every object used in the shop was made by hand—horseshoes, nails, hammers, many of the implements in common use by the miners and farmers, wheelbarrows, picks, shovels, and the scythes which were used for harvesting to the exclusion of any other method. Even the truss rods of the Knight's Ferry Bridge were turned out by this shop.

Recently the authors received a letter from Howard Egling, grandson of Louis, in which he states that the young John Studebaker, founder of the famous manufacturing company, makers of wagons and later of automobiles, worked in the Egling shop as a helper of such juvenile obscurity that his name apparently has not been remembered as a part of the history of Chinese Camp. From there John went north to the mining camp of Placerville where he became a partner in a firm "that could shoe a mustang or make a wagon." He furnished the mechanical skill while his partners did the blacksmithing. In 1858 he returned to South Bend Indiana, where he helped to establish the beginnings of the Studebaker Company.[6]

In all of the data that came to him through his own father, Mr. Egling is corroborated by his uncle, George Egling of San Jose, only surviving son of Louis. It was his job on Saturdays, at the responsible age of eight, to wash the chimneys, trim the wicks and fill with kerosene all the lamps at the Garrett House. For this he received fifty cents.

Louis Egling had another helper, James Mecartea, who later branched out with a shop of his own in Chinese Camp which he ran until 1872 and then moved to Big Oak Flat. All but two of his thirteen children were born in Chinese Camp; his son James being probably the first white baby to appear on the scene.

As the placer mines were worked out the town gradually grew into an ordinary American trading center with a large Chinese quarter. It had a head start on the towns higher in the mountains and drew the trade of a large area. In the early '60s many persons moved to California on account of the Civil War. The East suffered and the West prospered. Luxuries came in from China and the Orient. The families who had arrived early and were, by this time, well established built fine homes and often furnished them elegantly.

The town was sharply divided into two elements: Chinatown, peaceful and law-abiding in the main but with a fringe of rough hangers-on, and the families of merchants, doctors, lawyers and other professional men. In 1854 a school was built close to the site of the present one and here the small, pig-tailed sons of the Chinese residents played with the other boys, were taught to read by the teacher, Benjamin Butler, and hung around the blacksmith shop after school with the rest to watch the sparks fly and to see which of them could best stomach the nauseating smell of burned hair and hooves.

Two years after the Chinese Camp School appeared there were eight scattered schools in the county.

By the late '50s there were several lodges in town, supported by the more far-seeing among the citizens. They were a steadying influence, furnishing focal points for gatherings among miners of the higher type and among those men who intended to remain and grow with the country.

There was also a Vigilance Committee.

At first the religious life of the people was cared for by traveling ministers and priests. Beginning in 1851 priests were allotted territory by Bishop Alemany from his headquarters in San Francisco. The one assigned to this section, Father Henry Aleric, lived in Sonora and visited the camps between Knight's Ferry and Second Garrote, riding mule-back. These men of religion traveled untold dangerous miles on mule-back to hold services wherever they could find men gathered together. Reverend James Woods, a Presbyterian minister, wrote: "I have preached in churches, school houses, theaters, halls, gambling saloons, drinking saloons, and twice have preached funeral sermons in houses of ill fame . . ."[7]

Father Chan, a Chinese priest, is mentioned by Henry L. Walsh in his book, *Hallowed Were the Gold Dust Trails*. The Oriental was ordained in Rome and assigned to Chinese Camp for work among his fellow countrymen but did not meet with outstanding success and remained but a few years.

The Caucasian population in Chinese Camp was predominantly Catholic. The potato famine in 1848-49 caused thousands to emigrate from Ireland;[8] the discovery of gold in California gave them an objective. Vessels carrying food and succor from the United States took the news of gold to Ireland and brought back many of the destitute who seem to have been more or less officially deported to the States, Australia and elsewhere. These newcomers provided a strong motivating force for the establishment of churches by bringing to the gold towns respectable family women in sufficient numbers to insist upon places of worship. By 1855 beautiful little St. Xavier Church was built on a knoll beside the present highway. It has been restored and is still in use. Most of the early wooden markers in the adjoining cemetery have long since fallen and rotted or have burned.

Later, during the Civil War, the Chinese Camp Military Company was formed under Captain W. H. Utter and named the "Tuolumne Volunteers." On its roster were some of the leading citizens. Armory Hall was built in 1861.

As Chinese Camp grew and gathered the trade of outlying mining communities and ranches, roads became of paramount importance—wagon roads to replace pack trails. An act of the Legislature, approved May 12, 1853, made it possible to form a joint stock company for the purpose of constructing "plank and turnpike roads" in the counties of Tuolumne and Mariposa.

It was possible, yes. But for some years little was done about it. Still the roads continued to improve without any legal procedure. Miners widened Indian trails to permit passage of laden pack mules; merchants encouraged road-work enabling the much needed freight wagons to pass thus allowing them to buy in larger quantities and to reduce the exorbitant prices; private individuals constructed sections of road useful to themselves, personally.[9]

By 1853 conditions had improved to the extent that stages now passed between Chinese Camp and Sonora every two or three hours.

The town, naturally, had grown and prospered but growth did not always mean improvement in the mines. Along with the sterling citizens came the riffraff of the world. They seldom worked. It was easier to hold up a miner and take his gold than to obtain it lawfully. Chinese Camp, being the first large settlement above the foothills, acquired a wagon road early and had her fair share of bandits and road-agents of all kinds.

In December of 1852 the Sonora *Union Democrat* told the story of two of these unwelcome "bad-men" who viciously attacked a livery stable proprietor. They were apprehended quickly and put in jail. That same night a bell rang once to collect the citizens who took them from their cell and hanged them without much formality from a nearby tree.[10] This was considered only fair to the town's respectable element. Other settlements along the Big Oak Flat Road won notoriety by hangings of this nature, but the lynching in Chinese Camp is seldom mentioned.

For the most part, the bandits of the vicinity were unglamorous, cold-hearted killers, stopping solitary travelers and often leaving the bodies where they fell without so much as dragging them off the road. If they could put a day's ride between themselves and retribution they felt quite safe. Especially they picked on Chinese victims as offering even less chance for an unpleasant aftermath. References to such sordid characters will appear now and then as this history of the Big Oak Flat Road unfolds but, right now while probing into the past of Chinese Camp, we may as well touch on the two rather "different" bad men of whom old-timers of the vicinity speak almost with affection: Joaquín Murieta and Black Bart.

This is not the life story of either one. If such a chronicle interests you, you can't do better than to read *Bad Company*, by Joseph Henry Jackson. But their lives did touch the community and, by the contact, managed to add color, spice and gossip interest to its history.

Joaquín Murieta was a Mexican of pleasant manners and superior bearing. His adventures in the Southern Mines took place between 1850 and 1853 and, by some strange alchemy, time and the legends of the gold camps have altered their base metal to something rather precious in the memories of the old-timers. No one living now remembers him but some have heard of him from their parents; from their fathers of his occasional appearances in town; from their mothers of his courtly manners and old-world fashion of bowing from the waist.

Those who have done extensive research on the life of this man, tell us that the name served as a peg on which to hang the exploits of several different bandits, all claiming the name Joaquín. No doubt they are right. We give only the simple statements that have come down from father to son, and, of those, only the ones they will put in writing and sign.

From George Egling, son of Louis Egling, blacksmith of Chinese Camp, and from Eugene and Austin, sons of his helper, James Mecartea, we get the statement that a man who said he was Murieta and for that reason demanded, and got, instant service, came more than once to the smithy with several mounted men and had emergency horse-shoeing done. He came quite openly but was in a hurry to be gone. He always paid lavishly.

From Robert Curtin, son of John Curtin, we get the account of Murieta riding out of the shrubbery to stop a Cloudman freighting outfit; selecting the best horse with a shrewd eye and causing it to be taken from the team and put under the saddle from his spent animal. For this he paid far above its value and rode on.

This man who rode openly but hurriedly and was always attended by other mounted men, gave his name unhesitatingly and was known by sight to many in Tuolumne County especially around Sonora, Sawmill Flat, Chinese Camp and Moccasin Creek which he habitually passed on his way to a hangout at Marsh's Flat. We have never met anyone who claimed to know anything about his family, nor have we met anyone with an especially detrimental incident to recount. It was too bad, everyone felt, that he was on the wrong side of the law but even so his entertainment value was enormous.

When his outlawry finally came to its logical conclusion and a posse caught up with him near modern Coalinga a battle took place. His head was severed from his body for identification purposes, as was the hand of his companion Three Fingered Jack. Among the men of the posse who knew Murieta by sight were William Byrnes of Columbia, George S. Evans of Sonora and T. T. Howard who lived on a ranch in Mariposa County. The head, not too sightly after several hot days in a saddle bag, was then positively identified by Caleb Dorsey, a lawyer and prominent citizen of Sonora.[11] To the end of a long life Mr. Howard told the incident and insisted that the head belonged to the leader of the outlaw riders who had haunted the Sonora-Chinese Camp portion of the Southern Mines. The prevalent and persistent story that the wrong man had been killed and decapitated sprang (so these men maintained) from the fact that the original posse had split and over half had followed an objector who insisted that Joaquín Murieta had gone north. Captain Love, in command of the posse, had held fast to the idea that Murieta would head for Mexico. He and his men tracked down and killed their familiar Tuolumne County outlaw; collected the reward and were gratified to note later that he had indeed vanished from their midst.[12]

Probably there *was* another Joaquín. The chances are excellent that he *had* gone north. One faction said that the objectionable head (by this time preserved in alcohol) should have had brown hair instead of black. The large Mexican population which had founded and named Sonora followed their spokesman and agreed. Mr. Howard and Mr. Dorsey always insisted that this was partly because they had no love for the Americans—nor had, indeed, any reason to love them—and would not admit that their fellow countryman had been brought low; but it is quite possible that they had only known the brown-haired Joaquín.

Whether or not the original owner of the head was the true Joaquín Murieta, he had publicly accepted the title and with it the blame that was inseparable from it; he died the death that was appropriate to the name and Murieta he will always be to the folks along the Big Oak Flat Road.

Of much later date was the second bad man in whom Tuolumne County claims an interest. His twenty-eight holdups extended from 1875 to 1883.

Black Bart, sometimes known in private life as Charles Bolton, was a natty-looking gentleman, preceded by a mustache and wearing a bowler hat and three-quarter length coat with a velvet collar. So slick was Mr. Bolton that he probably kept his Prince Albert on his person with glue. He represented perfectly a respectable business man or even a clergyman. Apparently he used no horse, but always paid his way into the mountains on the stage, cheered by the thought that he would get it all back on the morrow. He did not carry a loaded gun, and trusted for security to the fact that no one saw his face during hold-ups and to his utter respectability at other times. His mask was a sort of pillow case with eye-holes, inside of which he continued to wear the bowler hat presumably to add to his height and to tempt a possible recalcitrant holdup-ee to aim too high.

There was another reason for the long continued immunity from the normal results of his transgressions. Black Bart's ability to travel fast on foot and his habit of turning up within twenty-four hours at an unconscionable distance from the scene of the robbery prevented the suspicions of any one from turning in his direction. Meanwhile, to all but his victims he offered no end of pleasurable excitement. Where would he strike next? How much gold would he make away with? Would he ever hurt any one? But this latter he never did.

In his guise of respectability he was a somewhat familiar figure at the stage stops between Stockton and Sonora. Robert Curtin remembers him leisurely pacing up and down on the porch of their home at Cloudman, stretching his legs as he waited for the stage to go on. Never drinking as did most of the men; never smoking; just cheerfully passing the time of day and then effacing himself. Saul Morris remembers him as sauntering into his father's store at Chinese Camp while the horses were being changed; remembers that he always bought candy.

After he was apprehended and his picture was in all the papers they knew whom they had seen.

Robert Curtin adds a couple of interesting anecdotes to the story of Black Bart's last, or 28th, hold-up: "In early staging days," wrote Mr. Curtin, "the express was carried loose in the stage except for a wooden box with a heavy padlock for jewelry and papers and an iron box in which was gold dust, bullion or money for the payroll for some mine. A road agent simply had the boxes thrown out and ordered the stage to drive on. But the stage company soon devised a plan whereby the iron box was bolted to the floor of the stage. After that the highwayman ordered the driver to unhitch the horses and drive them up the road leaving the stage behind so that he might be free to knock the box apart. When Bart robbed the stage on Funk Hill he ordered the driver, whom I knew, to unhitch the horses and to go up the road with them. In no time he had hammered the box open and disappeared but not before a young lad who was hunting had taken a shot at him and wounded him in the hand, causing him to lose a handkerchief.

"This was his last robbery and, in the days before his capture, it was the talk of everyone in these parts that the famous Black Bart must be a stage driver or hostler familiar with stages, for he had cut a length of scantling that exactly fitted between the ground and the bottom of the stage. This he wedged under the spot where the iron box was bolted and thus had a firm foundation on which to hammer it apart. Otherwise it would have crashed through the floor boards before it would have opened."

Eventually he turned up, smug and respectable, at his San Francisco lodging—a middle-aged unpretentious man who had been away on business. The story of his apprehension by means of a laundry mark on the lost handkerchief is well known.

We quote again from Mr. Curtin: "He served but a short term in San Quentin, helped by the fact that he had never fired a shot or bodily harmed any person. I saw him in the streets of San Francisco several times after his release in 1888 but, as I was in the uniform of a police officer, he never gave me recognition. As far as I know he was never seen after the great fire and earthquake of '06."

By the late seventies the settlement of Chinese Camp had completely evolved from a riotous mining camp into a reasonably staid family town with all of the comforts and many of the luxuries obtainable at the time. It, in common with most of the mountain towns, had been practically demolished by fire more than once but, for the most part, was rebuilt of more durable materials, the native schist rock slabs held together by lime mortar being more popular than expensive brick. Population was decreasing steadily. Mining, except in a few large quartz mines, was a thing of the past and men had left for the lumber camps.

Prior to 1856 a "female seminary" or, in other words, a private school for girls was conducted in his home by Allen T. Bartlett, a

Presbyterian minister. It was located near the Shepley Ranch of those days and not far from the W. E. Menke residence southeast of town. A book of the verses of Thomas Moore still exists which was given as a prize by this institution to Mary Elizabeth Shepley at the age of eleven. Prosperous families preferred to have their daughters educated away from the rough elements in the camp.

The town, or at least that portion of it which held meetings and formed policies, was now almost belligerently right-minded. A maiden could flutter a flounce along Main Street without seeing (more than maybe two or three times a week) anything to bring the blush of shame to the cheek of youth.

* * *

Coming in from Six Bit Gulch one enters the town of Chinese Camp by way of Webster Street. An orchard spreads to the right. On the left is the site of Egling's wheelwright and paint shops. On Washington Street the house on the southeast side behind a picket fence was built by Judge Abraham Halsey and later was the home of Louis and Emilie Egling and is the oldest dwelling in town. The original portion is in the rear and the timber used was brought around the Horn. Lumber had become so scarce in the early '50s that the partitions were tailored economically from a white cotton material called "drill." Afterward came the luxury of wallpaper—simply pasted to either side of the drill where it added a certain stiffening but very little else.

With the years have come major improvements but Mrs. N. R. Turner who now occupies the house says that the enormous fig trees date back to the Egling occupancy.

"The Garrett House stables were up Washington Street a little ways, on the right side," she explained, "but the Garrett House itself faced on Main Street—that's the next one over, so the stables were right in back of it. There's a little alley all covered with trees that led from the stables to where the hotel stood. You see, almost everything in this town has burned down at one time or another, so many of the famous old buildings are gone. China-town was at the west end of town, below Webster."

Main Street, from Webster to the highway provides the most fascinating block in Chinese Camp. Unfortunately, the Morris store, purchased from Walkerley Brothers, vanished long since. In the '90s it held the Wells, Fargo & Company's office. Here young George Morris, resisting a bandit, baptized the records with his blood and brains so that one of their old account books was burned for that reason and is lost to history. The Wells, Fargo & Company Museum in San Francisco shows an old-fashioned iron shutter punctured by a bullet fired in this encounter.

Fandango Frank's still stands. Fandango House was full of "cribs" and "fancy women" and boasted both a saloon and a dance hall.

The Rosenblohm store, built in 1851, still boasts its strong iron doors. It is constructed of rock with a wooden top. The brick front was added later. Its genteel coat of whitewash is peeling off into the tall weeds.

Next to Fandango House is a ruined wall—all that remains of the three-storied Fred Weir brewery that ran clear through the block to Washington Street. On the wall is a painted sign, "Levi Strauss." It is barely decipherable, almost covered with the feathery branches of tree of heaven. The sign was intended merely as an announcement that Levi Strauss overalls were a staple in the mountains but it served to remind us of a story prevalent in the Southern Mines: A miner, disgusted with his inability to keep work pants from ripping, finally took those unmentionables to a shoemaker in the town of Coulterville and asked him if there was no way to keep seams from tearing out at the end. Levi Strauss, then a young man, was much interested when the cobbler experimented by putting in a rivet. The result of this small incident is known to all wearers of workmen's clothes and even to our children who wear the blue riveted overalls. Several variations of this basic story may be heard.

An adobe store originally owned by a Mr. Cutler and later purchased by C. B. Cutting was across Main Street, roughly opposite the brewery; then, still on the north side comes the attractive home of Mrs. Fox which was originally built in Montezuma and moved to its present location. After the death of Count Solinsky the Fox family took over the management of the Garrett House and it was during their regime that it burned.

The town's physician, Dr. R. M. Lampson, who arrived in 1870 to succeed Dr. Benj. L. Conyers, had served previously at Montezuma. Like most mountain physicians he was respected, loved and overworked. There was no doctor between Chinese Camp and Yosemite and, in case of serious illness, Dr. Lampson's little buggy traveled to the most remote portions along the Big Oak Flat Road.

The present post office is in good repair, made of stone with a brick front. Its narrow flat porch is also the sidewalk. The ubiquitous, modern corrugated iron forms its roof, but the heavy iron shutters are old and are the authentic insignia of the early mining town where the threat and the fear of fire was always oppressive during the dry season. It was at one time the Thomas McAdam's store. The building is dark and cool and is presided over, as postmistress, by the granddaughter of Charles B. Cutting.

Nearly opposite the post office is a lonely stone wall which marks the property of the early Wells, Fargo & Company's office run by Solinsky and Sol Miller. We know that it was in operation as early as 1857. Almost every large mining town had such an office and, in the days when honesty was no longer an expected quality, when "Sidney Ducks" from Australia and slick confidence men from all over the world infested the towns and road-agents terrorized the thoroughfares, Wells, Fargo & Company with its promise of armed guards and at least an attempt at security for the gold dust en route to San Francisco banks or to the family at home, was a name by which to conjure.

In later years this was the site of the Nonpareil Saloon Building operated by J. A. Cogswell and M. K. Graham. On the second floor was the Masonic Hall.

East of the remaining wall of the Wells, Fargo & Company's Building is the tiny passageway known as Solinsky Alley, connecting Main Street with Washington. At first it is almost hidden by tree of heaven but breaks through to sunlight and glistening wild oats as it nears the end of its course. The alley separated Solinsky's express office from his especial pride, the Garrett House. Nothing remains of the latter but the cellar and foundations, smothered in feathery branches. It is impossible to form any idea of this gold-town hostelry—the acme of elegance for its time and place. Saul Morris told that the bricks of which it was constructed chanced to be made from gold-flecked clay and were often defaced by exploring pen knives.[13]

The Odd Fellows' Building has long been used as a home by Dr. and Mrs. D. E. Stratton. He was, in the early 1900s, physician and surgeon for the Eagle-Shawmut Mine. In what is now their garden stood the home of C. O. Drew, pioneer cattleman and his wife, Maria, daughter of Albert Snow, well-known hotel man of Yosemite. Mrs. Stratton is a daughter of Charles B. Cutting, and Helen Anthony Cutting of Farmington. He was active in his day in the construction of the Big Oak Flat Road. She readily gave her memories of the town which were, of course, of its later period. She told of the feeble remainder of the once prosperous Chinese quarter and of its final disappearance; of the beautiful Chinese girl, Yung Ida, born in the Camp, who was sold for $3000 and taken across the Pacific by her purchaser to China which she had never seen; of "Duck Mary" who came as a slave girl aged eleven and who spent her old age raising the fowl for which she was named and was usually followed about her tiny place by a waddling procession of fat ducks. She was 85 when the last of the Chinese went back to China; cried bitterly and begged to stay but there was no one who could keep her and she went with the rest. Ah Chee was still able-bodied and remained in his little cabin on the hill near the Odd Fellows' Cemetery. There was no way, after the exodus, that the old Chinese could get his customary opium and Dr. Stratton, out of humanity undertook to break him gradually from the habit. Often, on returning from a hard day's round of visits Ah Chee would be found waiting with his customary plea, "Please give me some wind in my head," whereupon the good doctor doled out a slight breeze.

"Mecartea's blacksmith shop used to be on the opposite corner," Mrs. Stratton said, "right next to the historical marker. And I think that Sol Miller had what was probably the most pretentious house in town. It was on a knoll at the corner of Washington Street and Highway 120, where the Odd Fellows' Cemetery is now. It burned in one of the big fires. We had four cemeteries here," she continued. "The Catholics buried their dead in the churchyard at Saint Xavier's. The Protestant, or City Cemetery, was just north of it on the east side of the highway. Count Solinsky was buried in the City Cemetery. His grave is boxed up and easy to find but most of the headstones were wooden slabs carved with the name and date and the fires destroyed almost all. Quite a few had small shallow niches gouged out into which were fitted tintypes of the deceased. A piece of shaped zinc, flush with the surface of the picture, pivoted on a nail so that it could be swung up, exposing the tintype, and then allowed to fall back over it to protect it from the weather. As children we used to wander from one headstone to another looking at the faces, making up stories about them and covering them up again. It was a strange art gallery."

We have since found this appropriate sentiment in "Ballou's Pictorial," dated August 25, 1855, and published in Boston: "Gravestones are now being prepared with daguerreotypes of the deceased set in marble. The idea, says a New Hampshire paper, is poetic, and if generally adopted, would make living galleries, through which the eye would delight to wander."

Mrs. Stratton finished a running commentary on the landmarks of her neighborhood. "There was a last and terrible fire in the '90s," she said. "The town was so depleted in population that it was never properly rebuilt and is only a fraction of what it once was, but we who live here love it."

Before leaving the town, a continuation of Main Street across Highway 120 will lead to the knoll where Saint Xavier's white steeple points upward and the cross-topped gravestones of old and revered residents remind one that the most exciting portion of Chinese Camp's Century of Progress was its beginning.

CHAPTER V

THE TOWN ON THE TUOLUMNE

The Big Oak Flat Road, proper, began in Chinese Camp and carefully picked its way between digger pines and scrub oak to the brink of the hill above Woods Creek. The present highway would have nothing to do with this route and keeps well to the north of it. To see a couple of the landmarks on the abandoned section turn right about half a mile out of Chinese Camp and follow the Menke-Hess Road.

Those who turn aside here with permission from its owners, will find themselves crossing Shepley's Flat, originally known as Red Flat, but which is passion-fruit yellow a good part of the year and redolent of tarweed. Less than a mile sights the buildings owned in the '60s by William and Levi Null and known simply as "Null's." Beside the Wells, Fargo & Company's Express agency, a change station was kept for the stage lines. In pack-mule days this was an important stop and scores of animals were stalled in barns of which one large specimen remains. A tiny building next to the road, built of wide boards and battens of an outdated fashion, is said to have been the express office. There is a gate to pass through at this point.

Usually one may drive unquestioned as far as a second gate but, at that point, the old road becomes almost indistinguishable in a grassy field to the left and the fire hazard in mid-summer is so great that the gate is chained and strung with a bangle bracelet of padlocks.

This was the West property but was purchased many years ago by William H. Menke, father of the present owner, W. E. Menke, who personally conducted us along the old road on his ranch. He

93

lives over the next knoll in a handsome house constructed in 1908 out of brick salvaged from the Garrett House after it burned.

West preëmpted the land by squatter's right and, for three years, his property marked the end of wagon travel. At this point everything had to be unpacked and loaded on mules. There were not always mules enough to carry the freight from a large wagon so it filled a real need when a shelter was built to hold the overflow. It was called West's Warehouse. Almost obliterated adobe foundations protrude through the weeds, guarded by a few ancient and untidy fig trees; a trash pile crowds a feeble little creek. This is all that remains of the nine or ten buildings that formed the first terminus of the road and were its connecting link with the Big Oak Flat Trail until the year 1852. At that time the trail was improved sufficiently to permit wagons as far as Jacksonville.

The spacious home of the Shepley family stood conveniently near and was the favored gathering place for the young teamsters from the ranches up and down the road. Every excuse was made to break the journey at West's in order to enjoy a musical evening. The Shepley organ played by the women-folk provided accompaniment for the voices and fiddles of the young "knights of the ribbons."

A small village of Indians lived nearby in West's era; lazying away the summer days in the shelter of the oaks, waiting until the acorns should be ripe enough to gather. The burial place of this primitive people is of indeterminate extent and new activities on the Menke Ranch, such as road building or excavating, are apt to be accompanied by the disconcerting appearance of dead Indians.

Returning to the junction of the highway and the Menke-Hess Road, the traveler follows the highway about .4 miles to the site of the inelegant Campo Salvador. The Big Oak Flat Road kept well to the right of the highway, now called the Shawmut Grade and built after the turn of the century.

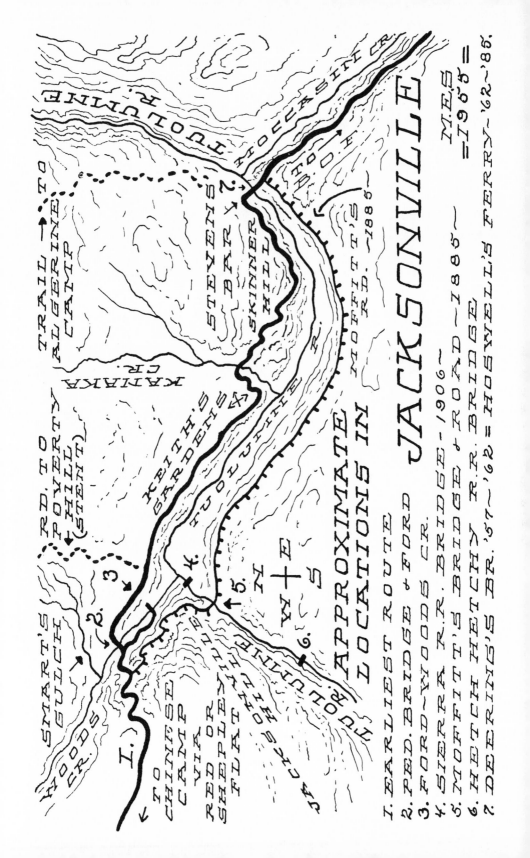

APPROXIMATE
LOCATIONS IN JACKSONVILLE

1. EARLIEST ROUTE
2. PED. BRIDGE & FORD
3. FORD-WOODS CR.
4. SIERRA R.R. BRIDGE - 1906 ~
5. MOFFITT'S BRIDGE & ROAD - 1885 ~
6. HETCH HETCHY R.R. BRIDGE
7. DEERING'S BR. '57 ~ '62 = HOSWELL'S FERRY ~ '62 - '85.

M.E.S.
= 1965 =

At the crest of the present Shawmut Grade, a trail led northward down a gully. One branch went to Algerine Camp, forming a short cut to the diggings along Rough and Ready Creek. Another led off to the Eagle-Shawmut Mine on Woods Creek, richest in Tuolumne County. The latter path connected with a heavy suspension bridge over Woods Creek nearly in front of the dumps of the Tarantula Mine which are still visible upstream and higher on the hill than the Eagle-Shawmut. This swinging bridge would carry a mule and the trail was intended for people who lived in Chinese Camp and worked at the mine but was frequently traveled furiously by Dr. Stratton in his light buggy; for almost any summons from the mine was bound to be an emergency and the wagon road, which detoured clear to Jacksonville and back the other side of the canyon, took too long. About one-quarter mile downstream from the mule-bridge was a lighter foot-bridge connecting the tunnel with the chlorination works on the west side of the stream. It was near the present Miners' Club.

The Eagle-Shawmut Mine, situated on Blue Gulch and feeding 100 stamps, was by long odds the most important project of Jacksonville and its payroll did everything from keeping the town a going concern to lining the purses of the shoddy bandits of the area. All freight for the mine went down the Big Oak Flat Road—its first grade (paralleling the present Shawmut Grade but just above it) being known as the Jacksonville Hill. Jacksonville lay at the foot of the grade, between the mountain and the main Tuolumne River, on the far side of Woods Creek. The wagons headed for the mine forded Woods Creek at the edge of town and went back up its canyon on the far bank to where the big stamp mill stood, opposite the midsection of the Shawmut Grade.

Originally the project was the "Eagle Mine," owned by Mr. Musser who ran it with an overshot mill, meaning one powered by flume water striking the top of a water wheel. Later the mine merged with the Shawmut.

The mine buildings were torn down in 1951. Previously they had been a seemingly indissoluble part of the landscape.

The Jacksonville Hill was a one-way road with infrequent turn-outs. It lies in the digger pine country. Many of its curves are densely wooded and, in the days when stages often carried fortunes in gold dust, the drivers dreaded it with good reason. Road agents were a part of the regular scheme of things. A story is told for truth that, on a suitable stretch of the hill, a lone bandit once held up seven stages filled with visitors for Yosemite. They had left Chinese Camp at timed intervals. The bandit, having thoroughly informed himself as to the spacing, had just sufficient time to line up the passangers of each in turn, get their valuables and guns, bundle them back in the stage and have them drive down the road. Then he was ready for the next. The seventh coach, filled with baggage, he didn't touch; feeling, with some justice, that it was time to go.

The bandit (name not supplied) could not have done such a job with impunity if there had been, for instance, a shipment of gold dust in the express box. In that case there should have been a "messenger" with a sawed-off shotgun loaded with whatever his individual taste dictated. Failing that, the driver would have done his best. It is a good bet that someone would at least have pulled a trigger. But it was far safer for the passengers to permit the melodrama to be played as scheduled even though, as in this case, the chief actor bowed out and was never seen again. Their valuables were nothing to the driver but he had engaged to see that they, themselves, arrived at the end of their journey—and preferably arrived intact.

Woods Creek was named for one of the first four men to sample the mines of Tuolumne County. He, Rev. James Woods, arrived in the summer of 1848 with three companions, J. H. Rider, Charles Bassett and James Savage of whom we will hear more later. Their encampment, up the stream and just south of Sonora, is credited with being the first white settlement in the county. It was called Woods. Nearby a Mexican headquarters, Sonorian Camp, came into notice. It was dubbed Stewart from one of the early non-Latin arrivals. When the state was divided into counties, February 18, 1850, Stewart was selected as the "Seat of Justice" for Tuolumne County. The name Sonora came into common use later but it is still the county seat.[1]

At the foot of either the old road or the newer Shawmut Grade, Woods Creek had to be crossed before the traveler could enter Jacksonville. Miners and freight must get across somehow. For many years pack mules and wagons forded. "A six horse team," wrote the unperturbed Saul Morris, "had no difficulty although the water sometimes ran over the horses backs." The earliest fording place, according to the same authority was almost at the mouth of the creek but it proved disadvantageous during high water and it was later customary to ford farther up stream, above the pedestrian bridge.

Miners afoot fared much better. The early business men of Jacksonville combined to build a pedestrian suspension bridge. The motive was frankly that of bringing as much gold dust as possible into town to be passed over counters and bars.

Jacksonville was founded by Col. Alden M. Jackson in June of 1849, although he was not the first settler. An individual named Smart had located there earlier in the spring but was too busy planting his famous "Spring Garden" to worry about starting a town. Instead of looking for nuggets he raised potatoes. Within a few months he asked, and got, $1.00 a pound for his carrots, turnips and beets. And at that he was a public benefactor. There were many cases of scurvy among the miners and a dollar expended for vegetables was well spent. In a remarkably few months he had fruit, which, from its rarity brought even higher profits. Possibly the owner of the garden was "Julian" Smart. Most persons whom we interviewed seemed to lean to that opinion but *The Miners' and Business Mens' Directory* for 1856 gives W. S. Smart from Louisiana as the proprietor of Spring Garden and Nursery and "Julius Smart" as attorney at law. In the cemetery a marble slab marks the grave of Ann Elizabeth Frederick, wife of W. S. Smart. Died Feb. 1862. At first Colonel Jackson mined along the creek but, by the summer of 1851, he was operating the first trading post. The town owes its name to him as does also Jackson, Amador County.

James Marshall, famed as the discoverer of California's gold, mined here quietly and not too successfully for a time but left no mark on the future of the place.[2]

Chinese Camp was always hampered by too little water. Jacksonville had too much, but river gold is said to have been worth $6.00 an ounce more than "grass-roots gold" which was porous and full of dross, so the men persisted. Mining along the river could only be accomplished when the current was low. This led to the building of dams and the digging of large diversion ditches by amazing cooperative effort.[3] One, of which we have record, was 2380 feet long by 20 feet wide and 18 inches deep. At least two of these attempts were washed out by the uncaring winter floods of the Tuolumne. They form, however, good examples of the seemingly spontaneous organization and self government so characteristic of the California miners.

For many of the miners homesickness was the greatest drawback to life in the diggings. David S. Smith and party were typical. They happened to work a waterless claim in the mountains east of

Stockton and spent months piling up dirt to pan out when the rains should come. When the better part of a year had passed without one line from their families David and another man couldn't endure the separation and the anxiety and agreed suddenly to leave for home. To get funds for the trip they carried some of the dirt to the nearest water supply and found it quite rich, including a nine dollar nugget. But the pull was too strong. They left the next day, although David wrote, "It was a little hard to leave that pile of dirt even for home and babies."[4]

Mail delivery—any kind of mail delivery was a Godsend to these lonely men. In The Adventures of William T. Ballou we read that he, operating alone, started the first express in California. He worked in and through the Southern Mines charging $4.00 apiece for letters and newspapers. Later he sold his line to Adam's Express Company. However, old-timers have stated that, in 1849, young Johnny Metson, equipped only with horse and gun, started a short-lived mail delivery between Jacksonville and the neighboring camps which was the forerunner of the numerous express companies that flourished throughout Tuolumne and Mariposa Counties. In some manner Johnny faded from the picture and Alexander H. Todd brought a shrewd mind to bear on the subject. His own health was not up to the heavy work demanded by mining but he *could* bring in the mail. Each man expecting to hear from home paid Todd a dollar to have his name placed on the list. Then Todd journeyed to San Francisco and collected mail for the men listed. The fortunate recipients paid one ounce of fine gold per letter on delivery. The plan was a great success. Those who received mail paid gladly. It also sheds light on certain passages in letters, written by men in the diggings to their wives or families, telling of the improbable sums it cost them to get the mail from home, but always adding "write again at once. It was worth it." One can understand, after learning of Mr. Todd, that an accumulation of letters such as might arrive by boat during several months, would prove expensive. Certain side lines were also profitable. For instance, a New York Herald sold readily in the mines for eight dollars a copy. Todd himself stated, "I had at one time over two thousand names on my express list. . . . For months and months these over net earnings were a thousand dollars a day."[5]

As the business grew the name became Todd & Company's Express, taking in every camp between Stockton, Jacksonville, and all parts of the Southern Mines south of the Stanislaus River, until, in 1851, it merged with its competitor, Reynolds and Co. of Stockton. It was for this firm that the well known rider, Pillsbury "Chips" Hodgkins, rode from camp to camp. Reynolds and Co. served both Tuolumne and Mariposa Counties since late in 1850— but it was by no means unique. One paper stated rather resignedly, "There are so many express companies daily starting that we can scarcely keep the run of them."[6]

By this time Jacksonville was second largest town in the county, exceeded only by Sonora. It assumed the aspects of any mining settlement. George B. Keyes, who had reaped a harvest as an early comer to the Southern Mines, erected a hotel, the Tuolumne House, in 1852 and was postmaster as well. At that time he was but 31 years of age. By June, 1855, Snow's Express advertised four regular trips a week, running a double wagon and accommodating half a dozen passengers. In '56 S. B. Kingsley was also running a hotel. An early newspaper tells us that, in July of the same year, Miss Sophia A. Thomas was married to Mr. Isaac Dessler, blacksmith and livery stable owner—a gala and extremely social occasion which took place in the Tuolumne House Hotel. In the '60s and '70s Dave Ackermann ran still another hotel on the south side of the road about where Woods Creek empties into the Tuolumne River.

Kanaka Gardens, owned by John Keith, were in full production in the '60s. They were just out of town upstream and above the river, on a slope known as Skinner Hill and near the road which followed up Kanaka Creek. It provided a spot of beauty in the days when the abandoned diggings were both ugly and depressing. Helen Hunt Jackson passed Keith's low, cabin-like house in the '70s. It was bowered in honeysuckle and oleanders while a low table was piled with pears, figs, apricots, plums and apples. A spring gurgled beside the house. Later in the season S. B. Kingsley's vineyard, also near Kanaka Creek, produced wagon-loads of grapes. Passing on Mrs. Hunt saw deserted cabins, wheels, sluice boxes, rusty mining tins and great piles of crushed quartz presided over by ragged Chinamen looking "like galvanized mummies," panning for a few pennies worth of gold.[7]

The main Tuolumne at this point is rough and dangerous; it is visibly narrowing down for entrance into the canyon just below. Consequently Jacksonville had no river crossing at first, but went about two miles upstream to ford at a wide, shallow riffle called Stevens' Bar. A miner on foot could jump dry shod from rock to rock during the season of low water and wagons crossed easily. The only trouble with this simple solution was that everything for use in the camps above had to be thought of and provided before the river rose again.

Stevens' Bar, named for Simon Stevens who ran a trading post and miners' hotel, was a tiny community but was a voting precinct in its own right casting some thirty votes. It seems better, however, to consider it as an adjunct of Jacksonville, at least while discussing bridges. It was an enterprising little place. James H. Deering, a '49er, ran a miners' supply store and loaned his own small home on the river's north bank as a school for whatever children happened to be available. In the '60s Tyler Bither ran a "comfortable hotel" near the crossing and prided himself on a large supply of assorted liquors.

Immediately above the low water crossing was a suitable place for a toll bridge—narrow with good anchorage. In 1857 James Deering, his brother, Ed, and a partner named Davis constructed one. The firm was known as Deering & Bros. Because it preceded the ferry there has been much controversy as to whether it ever existed but it had some five years of active use.

Came, however, the deluge—the incomparable, never-to-be-forgotten flood of 1862. According to W. H. Brewer, who traveled with Whitney on the Geological Survey of 1863, seventy-two inches (six feet) of rain fell at Sonora between November 11, 1861 and January 14, 1862. Even in the level lands of the Sacramento Valley roads were impassable, mails cut off and the telegraph rendered inoperative by reason of the flood waters submerging the tops of the poles.[8] At Stevens' Bar the tossing current tore the bridge from its foundations. According to Samuel E. McGlynn of Moccasin who was an eye witness, the bridge ". . . looked like a ship floating down the river and when it reached the turn near Jacksonville it went to pieces." The public-spirited owner, James Deering, was drowned; his brother, Ed, en route to Jacksonville, was drowned crossing Sullivan's Creek. The San Joaquin *Republican* of January 11, 1862, and the *Alta California* of the 17th, told the story and added that during this overwhelming flood the mining camps were scenes of despair and illness and that a great many unfortunate Chinese were washed down the canyons and never seen again. In Jacksonville the river backed up into Woods Creek and inundated the community from two sides with ten to twelve feet of turbulent water. The Daniel Munn family was rescued precariously from the second story window of their home.

Mr. Deering's property was acquired by one, Charles Hoswell, who decided in his own mind that, as an institution, bridges were too transitory for the Tuolumne and made arrangements to start a ferry. Joseph G. Skinner, a local mechanic, built a suitable scow to be operated by pulling on a rope. Hoswell then personally shuttled it back and forth on a patch of clear water below the bridge site but above the white-water riffle where they still forded at low water. Indians with canoes of which we have never had an adequate description ferried occasionally at their own pleasure but Hoswell's was an all day, every day service during suitable river conditions. He also allowed the school to continue in his house as it had when the building belonged to James Deering.

"Charlie," as Hoswell was called by everyone, became part of the life of the vicinity. Catherine Munn Phelan, of Moccasin, spoke about him: "When we lived at the base of Moccasin Hill," she said, "we children walked to school to Stevens' Bar—a good three miles—and there good-hearted Charlie took us over the river and never charged us a cent. He did that twice a day, back and forth, and even donated a part of his house as a school. There were about twenty of us. Mr. Gamble was our teacher and he handled all the grades, coming horseback from Big Oak Flat each day."

The late Charles Schmidt, of Second Garrote, remembered Charlie Hoswell: "When I was sixteen," he said, "I used to haul freight into Yosemite with a six-horse team. I'd often start from Oakdale and go along the old route to Charlie's ferry. I had to pay two and a half to get my team across the river. Coming back, if the water was low and my wagon empty, I'd cross the riffles and save the toll. The miners had some row boats they used when the river was just too high to ford, but the Indians had much less trouble with their canoes than the miners with their boats."

Old-timers report that Charlie Hoswell did a thriving business, an optimistic estimate in which he did not share; but, until 1885, he continued to run the ferry. And then Moffitt's bridge was built opposite the town of Jacksonville.

Charlie had all his eggs in one basket. He had counted on a bridgeless river. He went down to Chinese Camp; took room 13 at the Garrett House and ended his life with a bullet. He was forty-six years old. His ferry lay in the river near his home until it disintegrated and gradually floated down with the current.

J. H. Moffitt was a man of parts, a doctor, engineer and inventor. Rumor has it that he built his famous bridge at Jacksonville as the result of a quarrel with Hoswell when the latter lost from his ferry some crates of chickens belonging to Moffitt. There is little doubt as to the quarrel but the bridge had probably been planned to the last spike long before. Its total length was 300 feet with one span of 160 feet which hung high above low water in the Tuolumne. It was but twelve feet wide and was supposed to be capable of supporting one hundred tons.

As the bridge neared completion in 1885 a road was run on the south side of Woods Creek from the bottom of Jacksonville Hill to the bridge approach. "I remember," Robert Curtin told us, "it was always a relief to have the bridge in back of me while driving our cattle up to the high mountains in the spring when the Tuolumne was high. The bridge would rattle and shake in every direction. This caused the cattle to run and made my hair stand on end. I thought at any moment the bridge, cattle and I would all go down together."

One of Moffitt's main projects was to recover from the river bed, about three-quarters of a mile below Woods Creek, a great mass of rich dirt which had been accumulated by the men of Jacksonville to await winter panning and had then been swept resistlessly into the river by the first freshet of the season. To this end, about the

Freighter on Moffitt's Bridge, Big Oak Flat Road, descending hill on left.
Jacksonville in distance, center.

26 Mule Team and Wagon, Tuolumne County.

Courtesy of Edwin Harper

Big Oak Flat after the fire of 1863. Trunk of Big Oak stands at right.

Perkins

The Big Oak Flat Road in 1885. The Big Oak now has fallen.

year 1885, he had the main current of the river deflected. The entire population of the town (by this time very small) was on hand to see the first shovelful tested. John V. Ferretti, now of Alameda but born and raised in Tuolumne County, was in the group and says that the result was richer than had been seen on the Mother Lode since early days. Excitement mounted high, but during the night the jealous river rose and produced a surprise freshet out of season. All their laborious and expensive work was erased in a few hours. The project was not repeated.

Moffitt married Eugenia, daughter of Joseph Ferretti of Moccasin, and they maintained a health resort on the northwest bank of the river. His bridge made a great change in the habits of the nearby townspeople. It was no longer necessary to go through Jacksonville or Stevens' Bar. The new route came from the foot of Jacksonville Hill straight across the river. After crossing, traffic now had to go upstream a couple of miles along the south bank of the Tuolumne to a spot opposite Stevens' Bar before being able to turn away from the river up the canyon of Moccasin Creek. Moffitt constructed this new road at his own expense.

About 1890 Paul and Saul Morris of Chinese Camp took over the management of the bridge and had the toll collected until the turn of the century when, through the efforts of Supervisor John D. Phelan, a new toll bridge was put up at Stevens' Bar. It, too, served its day and has been replaced by a steel structure.

Moffiitt's Bridge went the way of the others, only this time the destroying force was dynamite, and travel came back through Jacksonville and along the north bank to Stevens' Bar.

* * *

On entering Jacksonville, Smart's property spread on both sides of the road. The "Spring Garden" lay between road and creek while just back of it was one of the two early pedestrian bridges.

Glimpses still can be seen through the trees of the Big Oak Flat Road coming down Jacksonville Hill. On the knoll to the left, and above what is still known as Smart's Gulch, is the early citizens' cemetery, while below it, completely obliterated, lies the inevitable Chinese burial place. Col. Alden Jackson's property reputedly extended from the gulch to the present Stent Road, once known as the trail to Poverty Hill.

In the near angle of the highway and the Stent Road was the Orcutt Hotel, afterward L. B. Sheafe's of the town's later decades. Part of its concrete watering trough may be seen close to the intersection. Dave Ackermann's Hotel stood on the right and Isaac Dessler's livery stable, erected in 1851, to the left just east of modern Penrose Service Station. Just beyond the site of Ackermann's Hotel was the other suspension bridge over Woods Creek.

From this point there is a good view, down river and partly around the bend, of the two small black pitons that remained after the demolition of Moffitt's bridge. They should not be confused with the two much larger pitons that are nearer to the town. These are the remnants of a bridge begun in 1904 to carry the tracks of Yosemite Short Line, a 30-inch gauge railroad then being built down the west bank of Woods Creek, and intended to connect the Sierra Railroad Company at Jamestown with Yosemite. About twenty miles of track had been laid; the bridge was well under way and the piling had been driven in '06 when the financial recession of 1907 made it impossible to resume operations in the spring.

The two flood years of 1907 and 1909 then not only washed the bridge away but tore out the tracks all along Woods Creek Canyon.

The project died right there.

Then, because the city of San Francisco needed water, the O'Shaughnessy Dam was begun on the Tuolumne River at the mouth of Hetch Hetchy, the beautiful companion valley to Yosemite and, at that time, almost as deep and unbelievable. Supplies and men must be transported so another railroad was planned to cross the river near Jacksonville and to use the low-level shelf along the south bank of the river graded first for Moffitt's Road to Stevens' Bar. This time the project was completed and functioned. The bridge over which the Hetch Hetchy Railroad trundled with supplies for the dam may, at this date, still be seen in the mouth of the canyon below the town.

The history of Jacksonville is tied up with that of its bridges.

* * *

The early freight road leaving Jacksonville didn't go as the highway now does, entirely along the river. It took to the north bank hills after leaving the last houses, followed Kanaka Creek a short distance and then went over what they then called Skinner Hill. It was along this section that Mrs. Hunt regaled her eyes, and probably her appetite, with the products of Kanaka Gardens. Some of Keith's fruit trees are still there.

At the place where Kanaka Creek crosses the highway, a glance upward to the left will disclose the rock work of the terraces of Kanaka Gardens. Palm and figs are still green and healthy.

In another half mile, near the Cleo-Harriman Mine, the Skinner Hill Road came back into the highway from the left. The riffles where the wagons forded the river are unmistakable. Then, at the near end of the steel bridge and north of the highway, was the site of Deering's home and trading post, one room of which was used for the school, and which later came into the possession of Charlie Hoswell. A foot trail led from here over the mountain to Algerine Camp and Jamestown.

At the far end of the bridge on the upstream side, some of the ferry cables still are at the water's edge; while, looking back across the bridge and also on the upstream side, the rock work that anchored the previous bridges stands firm and solid.

The towering dark rock that crowds the highway at the southern bridge-end is called, with unfortunate lack of originality, Robbers' Roost. Just up river from the steel bridge Moccasin Creek flows in from the southeast. A smaller span immediately crosses the creek and takes Highway 120 up Priest's Grade, used since 1912. It is a winding course—curve after excruciating curve but has recently been subjected to a "permanent straight" and has had some kinks removed. The grade is not over 5 per cent. The early Big Oak Flat Road may be followed by taking Highway 49 to the town of Moccasin and from there up "Old Priest's Grade" which is about a quarter as long as the new one with the resultant effect on the steepness of the pitch. A connecting road will take you from Moccasin to a point about midway of the new grade if conditions make it unwise to take the shorter and steeper one. They both end at Priest's Resort at the top of the mountain.

We could not get names or dates for specific holdups at Robbers' Roost. It simply bore a bad name and the stage drivers were glad to be safely past its shadow. But in days when a private individual was known to transport (Brewer tells us) as much as $28,000 in his carriage, banditry was to be expected. One gentleman of the road with a predilection for other folks' jewelry is said to have frustrated several posses of riders and hounds by the inexpensive expedient of tying open sardine cans to the soles of his shoes.

Certainly all such nefarious practices at Robbers' Roost must have occurred in the lonely days after the placer mining boom was over; for, during the height of the mania the entire canyon of Moccasin Creek was teeming with miners and there was little of the privacy necessary for the best regulated banditry. The side hills were lined with tents and the whole sphere of activity was open to view in the shallow creek bottom. The banks were measled with red shirts.

The men who first populated Moccasin Creek shoveled dirt into sluice boxes or squatted at the current's edge slopping water from shallow-beveled mining pans. Every daytime hour was marked by beehive action. If a miner stopped to eat, the watchful but hitherto inert Indians moved in on his claim and the squaws panned industriously until he returned to drive them off. Every foot of the bottom was turned over and for years the long low mounds—tailings from the long toms—remained above highwater mark, having evidently been operated from a supplementary ditch. Broken picks, rusted pans, disintegrating gold cradles, old tin cans and whisky bottles lay under the bushes. Now it is all a forgotten thing, buried under tons of rock from recent dredging.

When the miners gradually moved out, the mountain lions just as gradually moved in. Evidently the canyon had been a favorite haunt for them and now the coming of ranches with cattle formed an attraction to call back the hungry beasts.

The first settlers seem to have been a miner named Powell, a '49er, and a man named Cassassa who ran a trading post possibly a mile from Robbers' Roost and established squatters' rights in his land. In 1871 Daniel Munn purchased a holding from Cassassa and moved his family down the creek from the foot of Old Priest's Grade (or Moccasin Hill) where they had lived since being flooded out at Jacksonville. Meeting a large mountain lion between the house and the barn was fairly nerve shattering; and Mr. Munn recalled one occasion when he shot four within twenty-four hours.

Catherine Munn married John M. Phelan, of a prominent family in the county living at Noisy Flat, between Big Oak Flat and Groveland. For many terms he was a county supervisor and was responsible for the immediate predecessor of the present steel bridge at Stevens' Bar.

The Munn Ranch of the '70s is represented by a small structure on the right of the road with a stone base and wooden top. It is built over an unfailing spring and sheltered by an oak tree. Across the road and a few yards upstream was the first school house of this section. It replaced the classes held in Mr. Deering's home.

The road up Moccasin Creek is an easy trek in the very footsteps of the '49ers. It is almost level and shaded in the afternoon by a low bluff from whose top black-trunked digger pines lean out precariously. Two miles from the bridge is another landmark which has been looked at with interest, and usually misinterpreted, for decades. It was the hospitable home of Guiseppi or Joseph Ferretti. His daughter, Maria Ferretti Sandner wrote: "In 1869 father, whom every one knew as 'Happy Joe' Ferretti, bought squatters rights from Mr. Cassassa and took over his small store or trading post. At that time 1500 people of all nationalities lived and mined along the creek. Fourteen years before at the peak of the gold diggings about 2000 were in the canyon. You know, of course, that after awhile the government made a regulation that the early squatters' rights must be homesteaded to be legal, so father and many others got government patents, or homesteads. Father got his in 1884 and, about the same time, decided to build a little roadside shrine such as he had seen in his native Italy. He intended to put a figure of St. Joseph in it but somehow never got to it. Many present day travelers think it is a drinking fountain."

The Ferretti house, built by Charles L. Harper of Big Oak Flat, with its accompanying winery and vineyards, have vanished; just some foundations are left, and walls breaking up into piles of loose rock. A few straggling apple and pear trees remain with the seemingly indestructible figs. But across Highway 49, landscaped with dry weeds and the silver filagree of wild oats, the shrine stands high. It was meant to be seen and heeded. "Happy Joe" did what he could. Rocks were plenty and so the body of the shrine took form. Very likely it was difficult to get the statue of his patron Saint Joseph and, from one year to the next, it was delayed. His dream never was completed but it was a better dream than most.

Mr. Ferretti was a powerful, stocky man who wore earrings, loved his accordion and told stories inimitably. He gained his nickname from a trivial incident and bore it the rest of his life.

Mrs. Sandner's letter continued: "One day a very aloof woman traveler with her husband stopped at our place for refreshment, as father made and served delicious wine. These travelers were on their way by stage to Chinese Camp. Father, who was always jolly and very informal apparently didn't impress the woman favorably, for, when she arrived at the Garrett House she asked Mr. Solinsky who 'that character' up the road might be. Mr. Solinsky, who was a good friend, laughed heartily and said, 'Oh, that's Ferretti—Happy Joe Ferretti.' Some other friends overhead this and from that day he was always called 'Happy Joe'."

Mr. Ferretti was known as the leader of the Italians in the vicinity and it is said that his preference ruled on election day. There were Italians along the canyon of Moccasin Creek, just as they were to be found scattered all through the Southern Mines. Good solid family men who had come to live as well as to mine; who brought their skills and their wives from the mother country; planted their orchards and vineyards; made their wines and raised their families to be a stalwart bulwark of society and a force for good in their counties and in the state.

The road passes the hillside where the Raggio winery stood and the vineyard ripened its grapes in the warm autumn sunshine. It dated back into mining days, as Joseph Raggio came into the canyon about 1852, just after his arrival from Genoa, Italy.

The Hughes Ranch of the '60s is marked, at the present time, by a fish hatchery. The old covered bridge over Moccasin Creek was built by Charles Harper who did much of the heavy construction work of the surrounding settlements. It stood possibly 200 yards upstream from the present dam. Hung at either end were the signs, once so familiar, "Ten dollars fine for riding or driving over this bridge faster than a walk." The low stone abutments may still be seen.

A statement from Thomas Hughes was obtained nearly twenty years ago: "The first white settler at Moccasin," he said, "was a miner named Powell in 1849, and in '55 the gold fever really hit the place. Of course all these paths that the miners used in getting into the mountains were actually Indian trails. The one that comes in from Coulterville to Moccasin was always used by Indians and also the road up Moccasin Hill, or the Old Priest's Grade as some call it. Pack trains began to come over the trail from Coulterville and before many years the packers got the miners to widen it. When this vicinity became thick with new arrivals the widened trail was made into a road so that ox-drawn freighters could get through to the upper mines. In fact, from 1852 on, most of the merchandise that the old Sun Sun Wo store in Coulterville carried was sold and freighted up Moccasin Hill. The Marsh's Flat Road and the Coulterville Road through to Penon Blanca started right here at the covered bridge over Moccasin Creek.

"My father knew all the owners and drivers of the stage line. In the '60s my folks served supper to the drivers and passengers as the stages arrived at the next station on the crest of the hill [Priest's Station] too late for that meal. We served breakfast too. The down stage left above too early for that.

"Some mighty good friends used to live along this creek in early days. Joseph Cavagnaro and Luigi Segale were successful miners. There were Paddy Welsh, Mr. Powell, Mike Donahue, Daniel

Newhall and George Culbertson. Everybody mined to begin with. It was exciting but it didn't last. Joseph Raggio was a good neighbor; his daughter, Caroline, married Mr. Cavagnaro. When the mining gave out they became ranchers or vineyardists. They were all fine people." The trail down Moccasin Creek from Coulterville, mentioned by Mr. Hughes, passed by the small, unruly settlement of Italians and Chinese miners known as Sebastopol. It was about one and a half miles upstream from the Hughes Ranch.

A small portion of the old road, as it made an exit from the covered bridge, may still be seen approaching Moccasin.

To get into the village of Moccasin the present road crosses the creek on a dam. The power house through which flows the water supply for San Francisco stands in handsome dignity just upstream. It is apparent that lots of water has always rolled down the canyon during the wet season but, for all that, it was never bridged until 1880.

At the end of the dam, immediately at the foot of the mountain, is a snuggle of small, contented houses. They are vine-covered, lawn-surrounded, tree-shaded—really beautiful, and are occupied by the employees of the Moccasin Creek Power House.

We are greatly indebted to Mrs. Catherine Munn Phelan and to Mr. and Mrs. Lynn Owen Brabazon of Moccasin for assistance. Mrs. Brabazon collected historical information of the region for the Native Daughters of the Golden West using Mrs. Munn as a prime source and was able to confirm the names of the old-timers and the proprietors of the Moccasin stage stop. Mr. Brabazon gave us valuable data on the sequence of bridges at Jacksonville.

From a modern point of view this foot-of-the-mountain village is one of the most attractive spots on the road to Yosemite.

When the first miners arrived they found here (and extending north along the right bank of the creek) a few Miwoks. They led a placid, torpescent existence. In summer they were very comfortable. In winter it wasn't to be expected so they didn't worry about it. Meat and acorns were plentiful. The canyon seemed to be a favored hunting ground for deer and, almost every year, a visiting tribe of 50 to 100 people would come from higher in the mountains to replenish their food supply, taking the meat back with them.

Among the things that add spice to the study of the town's history is the good-humored controversy over the reason for the name, Moccasin. One theory exploits the abundance at the old ford of tiny slithering watersnakes, causing the wading stage horses to shy and frightening the lady passengers. The first comers, it is thought, might have mistaken them for water moccasins. Another (and probably more likely) theory was told by Ellen Harper May, daughter of Cornelius McLaughlin, a '49er, and whose first husband was Charles Harper, the builder. She was told that, when the first prospectors were making their way along the Indian trail leading up the mountain, they saw an Indian moccasin hanging from a branch beside the footway. In speaking afterward of their route they said "the hill where we saw the moccasin," and it soon became shortened to Moccasin Hill. The trail was widened to a road and, after Priest's Hotel was established in the '70s, it received the name Priest's Grade; but everyone with the exception of a very few who said either "Rattlesnake Grade" or "Big Oak Flat Hill" spoke of it as Moccasin Hill. The creek and later the town fell heir to the name from proximity.

George F. Culbertson was the first, we are told, to homestead in the community. He was a '49er. In '56 he settled down and planted a vineyard. He and his partner, Daniel B. Newhall, had a winery and also made brandy of such excellence and potency that its memory is cherished with suitable regret. In 1871 it took first prize in the state. Their vineyards spread over the space where the power house and town now stand.[9] For twenty years Culbertson was county treasurer and, being an excellent manager, was called "the Watchdog of the Treasury." Sometime in his career a man who owed him $100 settled that onerous debt by building him a two-story house of native rock south of the road and at the base of the hill. Culbertson and Newhall lived there for an indefinite time and then rented it to the Munns. It was one of the most pretentious houses on the road and was so gratifyingly permanent that it had to be torn down at last to make way for the improvements around the power house. How much, one wonders, could you get for $100 in those days if you really put your mind to it.

Daniel Newhall was equally well known and well thought of in the county, being a director of the Yosemite Turnpike Road Company. The stone house stood on a site within the gates of the private road to the power house and at the rear of the first dwelling.

Close to Culbertson's was the home of Augustine Gardella, a friend of Mark Twain.

It was in the stone house that the Munn family lived from '62 for almost a decade before moving down Moccasin Canyon to contend with mountain lions just south of Robbers' Roost. While still renting from Culbertson, Daniel and Mrs. Munn kept a small general store. They had six children. To one of them, Catherine Munn Phelan, we are indebted for valuable information generously given. She was born here in 1867. She wrote: "Moccasin had no church and my father, being a devout Catholic, arranged to have mass said in our parlor whenever a traveling priest from Sonora came our way. Often it was Father Slattery who came. Baptisms and confirmations took place in our house also.

"Mother worked hard, living as she did at the foot of the grade. It was the stopping place for teamsters to rest themselves and their animals. The freighters came from all directions, Stockton, Oakdale, and Sonora, filled with miners' supplies and goods for their families. Mother served the drivers a meal, but fortunately only one or two arrived at a time."

It was '71 when the Munns moved down to Robbers' Roost and we know from Nelson's Pictorial Guide Book that in 1878 the stopping place at the foot of Moccasin Hill was again known as Culbertson's.

Mr. Newhall died in 1879 and Culbertson then sold his stone house to Fred Cavagnaro who ran the mountain store and stopping place in much the same manner.

As ridiculous as it sounds, the California Associated Cycling Club's Touring Guide and Road Book of 1898 strongly recommends Cavagnaro's, at the foot of Moccasin Hill (then a 20 per cent grade), as a stopping place for cyclists. Granting that they had arrived thus far, one would certainly recommend that they stop before going one hundred yards farther.

In the last five years the grade has been widened, straightened and the worst parts eliminated. Its two miles of continuous climbing may not be pleasant in the middle of the day for there is no shade but it has the advantage of getting one to the top without fooling around. There is no particular object in going that way, though, as there is a connecting road from the foot of the old grade to the middle of the new one and each may be seen plainly from the vantage point of the other.

The route taken will depend on each driver's idea of what constitutes a pleasant ride.

CHAPTER VI

THE BIG OAK ON THE FLAT

The grade that leads up from the town of Moccasin to Priest's is a dilly, whether called by its earliest name, Moccasin Hill, Rattle-snake Hill, Big Oak Flat Hill or the more familiar "Old Priest's Grade." Somehow or another any vehicle traveling its stark contours must hoist itself 1575 feet in a matter of two miles.

The new Priest's Grade on Highway 120 which, so transitory is fame, even now is old and is subjected to reconstruction every year or so, takes about eight miles to reach the same point.

The ascending travelers of yesteryear all walked the full distance of Moccasin Hill as it was difficult for the teams to pull even an empty stage. Fortunately, a spring issued from the mountain about half way up the old grade. Miners, weary under heavy packs, found odd companions as they rested here. Sometimes the welcome patch of shade held strange Miwoks from the mountains returning from a hunt; their women, burdened with deer meat covered with dust and flies, were unable to rise with their loads unless pulled to their feet by the men who carried simply bows and arrows. The hunters never objected to assisting their help-mates to that extent. Again the resting miners might find themselves in company with a circuit riding clergyman, a traveling priest, or even an occasional masked bandit with a predatory eye on the buckskin bags of gold dust so universally carried. One rather impulsive highwayman killed a perfectly run-of-the-mill traveler under the impression that he was the tax collector. In staging days a small building containing tools and ropes was installed near the spring. No person nor vehicle going uphill passed without pausing. As automobiles gradually replaced other modes of transportation the cars all stopped here to pant and both car and driver took on all the water they were capable of containing.

It is no longer necessary to stop at the spring. Any well-driven modern car in good condition can, in the cool of the day, go straight up. Many automobilists (including ourselves) prefer it to the numerous curves on New Priest's Grade which are all too often traveled in discomfort and from which one is apt to emerge with one's inwards out of alignment.

The canyon lying between the old and new grade is called Grizzly Gulch and is filled with heavy brush, notably toyon. On the north slope about opposite the spring is a subsidiary gully humorously named Cub Gulch. The small mines visible on the north slope were well known as the Eureka and the Grizzly belonging to Charles and Edwin Harper of Big Oak Flat. From them some of the most beautiful exhibition specimens of leaf gold in the Mother Lode have been taken.

Immediately at the top of the grade was Priest's Hotel or Station founded in 1855, of which the mainspring and motive force seemed to be its handsome Scotch hostess. She was, in the first and hardest period, Mrs. Alexander Kirkwood and with her husband managed to place "Kirkwood's" in an enviable position among the hotels of the country. After Mr. Kirkwood died in 1870 his wife eventually married a fine-looking Kentuckian, William Priest, and the attractive couple carried on the old tradition. Many of their guests were journeying by wagon to Yosemite. They came at all hours for it was considered worth traveling long after dark to arrive at Priest's Hotel.

At that period there seems to have been no employment thought suitable for a young girl except some type of domestic work where she might be constantly under the supervision of an older woman. A job in a superior hotel was at the head of the list.

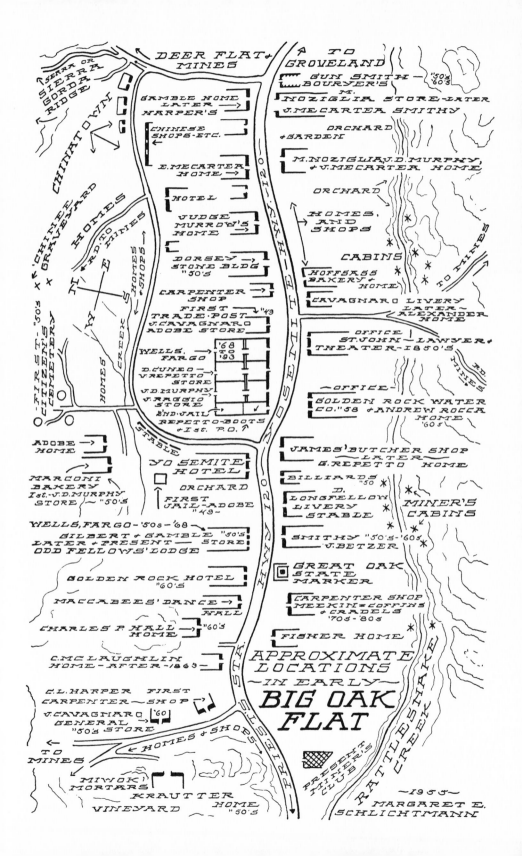

DEER FLAT & MINES

SIERRA OR SIERRA GORDA RIDGE

CHINATOWN

TO GROVELAND

GUN SMITH — BOURYER'S "50's '60's"

M. NOZIGLIA STORE-LATER

J. McCARTEA SMITHY

GAMBLE HOME LATER HARPER'S →

CHINESE SHOPS-ETC.

ORCHARD & GARDEN

E. McCARTER HOME →

M. NOZIGLIA, J. D. MURPHY, & V. McCARTER HOME

HOTEL

ORCHARD

HOMES, AND SHOPS

JUDGE MURROW'S HOME

CABINS

CHINEE GRAVEYARD

HOMES

R. D. TO E. MINES →

SHOPS

CREEK HOMES + SHOPS

DORSEY → STONE BLDG "50's"

CARPENTER SHOP →

FIRST TRADE-POST "49" J. CAVAGNARO ADOBE STORE

WELLS → FARGO "68 TO '93"

D. CUNEO — V. REPETTO STORE

J. D. MURPHY J. RAGGIO STORE

2ND JAIL

REPETTO-BOOTS & 1st P.O.

HOFFSASS BAKERY + HOME

TO MINES

CAVAGNARO LIVERY LATER — ALEXANDER HOME

OFFICE | ST. JOHN — LAWYER + THEATER-1850's

R. D. MINES

~OFFICE~ GOLDEN ROCK WATER CO. "58 & ANDREW ROCCA HOME "60's"

STABLE

ADOBE → HOME

MARCONI BAKERY 1st-J.D. MURPHY STORE ~ "50's"

YO SEMITE HOTEL

ORCHARD

FIRST JAIL-ADOBE "49"

JAMES' BUTCHER SHOP LATER G. REPETTO HOME

BILLIARDS "50"

D. LONGFELLOW LIVERY STABLE

MINER'S CABINS

WELLS, FARGO - '50s-'68 →

GILBERT & GAMBLE "50's" — STORE LATER + PRESENT — ODD FELLOWS' LODGE

SMITHY "50's-'60's" J. BETZER

GOLDEN ROCK HOTEL "60's"

GREAT OAK STATE MARKER

MACCABEES' DANCE → HALL

CARPENTER SHOP MEEKIN = COFFINS & CRADELS '70's-'80s

CHARLES P. HALL → HOME "60's"

FISHER HOME

C. McLAUGHLIN HOME - AFTER ~ 1863

APPROXIMATE LOCATIONS ~IN EARLY~ BIG OAK FLAT

C. L. HARPER FIRST CARPENTER — SHOP

J. CAVAGNARO "60" GENERAL → "50's STORE"

HOMES & SHOPS

TO MINES

MIWOK MORTARS

KRAUTTER HOME "50's"

VINEYARD

PRESENT MINER'S CLUB'S

~1955~ MARGARET E. SCHLICHTMANN

·FIRST "50's CITIZEN'S CEMETERY

HWY 120 — YOSEMITE — HWY 120 STA.

PRIEST STA.

RATTLESNAKE CREEK

Eunice Watson Fisher of Big Oak Flat, was kind enough to give us a word picture of life at the top of the grade. In part it reads: "Mother worked for the Priests three months out of the year and we all stayed there during that time. I was what you would call a 'bull cook' when I was only thirteen years old for which I received five dollars a month with room and board. Later I was a real cook for which I was given twenty-five dollars. We used to get up at all hours of the night—just whenever the travelers arrived. Mrs. Priest would call us herself. Often we'd hear, 'Whoo hoo, girls! A party of eight.' Then we'd get out of bed, dress, and cook up anything the people ordered and it wasn't easy, especially if we had had a busy day. But that didn't matter. There were no set hours of work in those days."

Eunice Fisher was most loyal to the establishment. "I was very fond of my employers," she went on, "and when Mr. Kirkwood died I helped to lay him away. We didn't have funeral parlors to take care of such things. Young though I was the responsibilities and sorrows of life were never kept from me. We children of the pioneers helped with everything to the best of our ability."

John Ferretti, who lived near by in Spring Gulch, was completely familiar with Priest's Hotel. As a boy of fifteen he was general handyman, errand boy, and the nearest substitute for a modern bell hop considered necessary in the '90s. "It was a high-class establishment," he assured us, "and well known from one end of the state to the other. The cuisine was excellent and Mr. and Mrs. Priest were fine people. It was a privilege to know them."

William C. Priest was a man of affairs in the county also and became a director of the Great Sierra Stage Company's Yosemite Run when it was re-incorporated in 1886 and was superintendent of construction of the Tioga Road. The couple were general favorites. The new Priest's Grade was not opened until about

1915 and, although Mrs. Priest had died ten years before, it was formally named in her honor.

The establishment is maintained by Mr. and Mrs. Joseph L. Anker. Mrs. Anker is a grandniece of Mrs. Priest so it may be said to be "in the family." It is still Priest's Station and the old and the new grades meet directly in front of the office so that many cars stop with a sense of achievement on the part of the driver as it is certain that every horse-drawn stage and freighter has done since the roads opened.

Eunice Watson Fisher watched the coming of the automobiles. She wasn't too favorably impressed. "Give a horse time and he'll get to the top," she remarked. "Some of the old cars never did get there."

Priest's is on the height between Grizzly Gulch and the canyon of Rattlesnake Creek. Originally the latter was allowed the privilege of going down its own canyon but Rattlesnake, what with mines and miners, was admitted to be a dirty little stream and a detriment to the relatively pure flow of Moccasin Creek. No objection was made to the project of having it detoured for the use of several mines. So its waters were conveyed into Grizzly Gulch by means of a tunnel beneath the highway in front of Priest's, utilizing one partially dug by miners in search of pay dirt many years ago. After passage through the mountain Rattlesnake Creek comes out to sunshine in the toyon-covered box canyon, finding its way into the Tuolumne River even more directly than before.

At Priest's Hotel a road swings in from the south. It leads to Coulterville about ten miles away. In freighting days a tiny, scattered settlement known as Boneyard strung along the road about half way between the two places. Its name was bestowed because of a large number of Indian bones which, the story has it, came to light when any excavating was done. On this same road about three miles from Priest's, at Spring Gulch, lived Frank Ferretti, brother of "Happy Joe," with his family. The rock wall still standing farther along beside the road was built by Frank. The James Lumsdens, another prominent family of Tuolumne County, lived at Boneyard. So also did the German roadhouse keeper, Ike Meyers, with his 300 pound wife. These families and several others divided their shopping and social activities between Coulterville and Big Oak Flat, so their small cluster of houses should not be omitted from the roster of settlements along the Big Oak Flat Road.

East of the summit the highway is slightly farther from Rattlesnake Creek than was the original road which kept faithfully to the edge of the water. A miners' settlement called "Rattlesnake" existed briefly in the 1850s. Three-tenths of a mile from Priest's, Slate Gulch comes in from the left. A high flume used to carry the waters of the Golden Rock Water Company across the road at this point, releasing them into a ditch on the opposite side of the creek. where they flowed down into Mariposa County.

The road wound through the open canyon, bordered with a hodgepodge of miners' tents and temporary shelters, until it emerged to the awe-inspiring vision of the big oak on the flat. In the first few years of the white man's invasion of the "California Mountains" the trees were apt to be large but widely spaced with no underbrush. Each year the Indians burned the grass to facilitate hunting and also because they had found it prevented fires hot enough to ignite the acorn oaks. The custom was an effective deterrent to the growth of small bushes and to the propagation of young saplings. The scattered grove shading the gravelly flat was composed of magnificent trees but the "Big Oak" was king of them all, a giant both in height and girth.

Here, in the fall of '48, came James D. Savage. He was a

strange young man and beyond all doubt a brave and competent one—best remembered as the commander of the Mariposa Battalion which entered Yosemite Valley and conquered its belligerent Indians in the spring of 1851[1].

Savage had been much associated with the Indians in his home state, Illinois, and on his arrival in California affiliated himself with the natives of the Sierra Foothills. He spoke five Indian tongues, some of them as well (we are assured by an old comrade) as the Indians themselves. He secured safety and trading privileges with the most important tribes by taking a wife from each. He never became part of an Indian village as the fur trappers sometimes did, but remained with his own projects keeping his Indian intimates with him; trying to guide their actions and to stand between them and trouble. It was not particularly altruistic as he fully intended to profit by their services, but he *was* concerned with their welfare and had probably more influence with them than any other white man.

There seems to have been but little exact personal information about Savage available. His age was any man's guess; because of his effortless strength and tirelessness his stature was usually presumed to be above average; his hair was called blonde. Dr. Carl P. Russell questioned an old Indian woman (the only person then living who had ever seen him) and gained the information that he always wore red shirts, but little more as to his appearance. So it was with great interest that we read the diary of Robert Eccleston, who served under him in the Mariposa Battalion, which gives at the end a short description of this almost fabulous character: "He is a man of about 28 years of age, rather small but very muscular & extremely active, his features are regular & his hair light brown which hangs in a neglege manner over his shoulders, he however generally wears it tied up. His skin is dark tanned by the exposure to the sun. He has I believe 33 wives among the mountain females of California, 5 or 6 only however of which are now living with him   They are from the ages of 10 to 22 & are generally sprightly young squaws, they are dressed neatly, their white chemise with low neck & short sleeves, to which is appended either a red or blue skirt, they are mostly low in stature & not unhandsome   they always look clean and sew neatly." This complimentary picture is partly corroborated by an unknown "Robert" who, in 1850, wrote to his wife from Sonora: "Generally the Mexican women have bad figures, but the Indian girls are slender and strait as arrows . . ."² Eccleston continues: "The major has a little house built for their accomodation. Major Savage is now connected with Col Freemont & Capt Haler³ in the contract for supplying the Indians with provisions."

In another paragraph Eccleston gives this additional information: James D. Savage emigrated to the west with Col. John C. Fremont "on his Expedition of Survey of this Country." He saw action as an officer during the California revolution. He ingratiated himself with the Indians and became a trader. He took a contract for collecting "the Freemont stock of cattle" and afterward for digging the race for Capt. Sutter in which James Marshall discovered gold. He continued trading until late spring when it was possible to ascend the mountains. He then "worked his Indians" until uprisings among the nearby tribes led to the formation of the Mariposa Battalion.

When it became known that gold was all around him for the taking James Savage had been as well equipped as any man in the mountains to make a fortune. His Indians were amazed that a little work (done for the most part by their women) in gathering the heavy golden dust should be so delightfully productive of food and tin cups and dirty shirts and blankets. He accumulated in barrels gold dust and nuggets that assumed in the telling legendary proportions.

But his dusky in-laws were not emotionally organized to live peaceably with the miners who were not themselves noticeably self-controlled. A miner knifed an Indian who retaliated much more efficiently. And Savage took his protegees away—higher in the mountains.

He was only in the flat of the big oak a short time but because of him it received its first name "Savage's Diggings."

Rufus Keys, a young prospector, is supposed to have spear-headed the invasion of some six thousand miners who succeeded Savage on the flat. They found a gold-bearing gravel bed two to twenty feet thick—far too much to work out in a few months and leave. The place was so rich that according to Eugene Mecartea, claims were limited to ten feet square so, unless the owner lived in a tent, his shelter was rarely where he worked. Later the miners' convention of 1851 allowed more generous holdings. A rather childlike condition of perfect trust prevailed during the first year at the diggings. Stealing was unknown. In spite of the fact that it is a hackneyed statement and appears in most publications dealing with the mining camps, we need not learn this fact at second hand. John R. Maben wrote to his wife November 15th, 1849: ". . . There is no such thing as stealing here   men leave everything no matter what it may be where he was using it even their Gold dirt they will leave it on a rock or in their boxes where they work it and be gone half the day."[4]

As cold weather came on houses were needed and there was but little in the way of small timber with which to build. The following description is completely typical although it happened to be written a few miles away. It is given because Jason Chamberlain, from whose diary it comes, was one of the best-known residents of the Big Oak Flat Road. His story will be told later. A few words are illegible but the statement is plain enough.

"Commenced building a place to sleep or in other words a house most of the houses here are cloth but we have no cloth nor means to get any fifty cents is all that remains of our scanty supply between Cutes, [illegible], Chaffee and self so must do as they used to before cloth was invented We select the mountainside to build digging down some six feet to make it level we have nearly three sides inclosed we put [illegible] in front and run rafters back into the bank to support the roof We throw pine boughs on the rafters and cover the boughs with dirt build a chimney in one end and fix a place to sleep by laying logs on the ground and covering them with boughs one bed answering for five of us our house is now comfortable and if we have no rain will be very comfortable much more than tents in warm weather

April 16, 1851

"Commences raining which prevents our work. A (sic) rains hard all day and our house stands it finely until about 9 oclock evening then it comes down through by bucketsfull pretty well thickened with mud Now we have a fine time we stand it awhile till we are completely drenched we then repair to a tent that is deserted which leaks about as bad as the one we left but the water that comes through is clean and that makes it the more endurable four of the party find places to lie down and I find a bucket to sit on and with my blanket over my shoulders soon fall asleep but do not sleep near as sound as I have in days of yore in the land of feather beds "

By the approach of winter in '49 the diggings were thick with such uninhabitable shelters. The miners had, of course, everything to do for themselves—no matter how foreign to their former habits—cooking, washing, nursing, even sewing.

Wilton R. Hayes wrote from the California mines to a friend in New Jersey: "I have just completed the astonishing feat of making a pair of pants. And I defy all the tailors in Nottingham to make a pair that will come as near like the negro's shirt, touching nowhere. I was led to this desperate undertaking by seeing others do it."

Among other unusual but necessary accomplishments every miner was obliged to be his own lawyer. That he took it seriously the following copy of an original document will bear witness:

"This is to certify that I have Sold to Luigi Noziglia my interst in the lot that have Sold to Mr Manuel Flores on account that Mr, Manuel Flores hase not appier withing Six Months from that time that Sel was made I sel to L. Noziglia the above Said mention person for Sum Ten Dollers to me paide and

Tigh nechuer My Mema   M. Noziglia "   [Undated]

There were a few skirmishes between the miners and the Indians who either lived on the spot or came in season to gather acorns, evidenced by a large stationary mortar rock with many grinding holes north of the road at the entrance to the town. The affairs, in which a few arrows and pistol shots were let loose happily and at random, resulted in little but a pleasurable relief from monotony as far as the white men were concerned. There is, however, a story that some Indians were killed in a fight and buried across the trail from the big oak and that, peace being made a day or two later, their friends were permitted to exhume the bodies and take them elsewhere for burial according to tribal rites. If so the Indians seemed to bear no grudge and this, as far as we knew, ended real hostilities between red man and white along the Big Oak Flat Road.

More deadly than Indians was the "fever and ague" that attended the damp and steamy mining camps during the summer.

The ailing men would pay "an ounce of gold for the visit of a medical man." Often they paid three times that much for a single dose of medicine.[5]

Even so the mining camp grew and prospered and became a settlement.

A trading post appeared at once. Rufus Keys inaugurated the first mail delivery, bringing it from Chinese Camp by pack animal.[6] Gio Batta Repetto came soon after and settled down as a maker of fine boots. In 1852 one of the finest and largest stone store buildings in the whole Mother Lode country was erected by the roadside. Lodges and a fire department appeared. The Yo Semite House took care of travelers. Various types of business were established by persons whose names are almost as well known today as then.

In 1856 the wagon road was extended to Big Oak Flat. And, in the following year, Tom McGee, who operated a liquor store and ran a pack train at irregular intervals, decided to blaze and open the Mono Indian Trail to saddle traffic. He cleared out the hindering growth and blazed trees to identify the route many of which may still be found—notably at Tamarack Flat.

On February 26, 1859, the first real stage came into town from Chinese Camp, solving the problem of transportation[7] and about the same time the town decided that it must have more water. All through the diggings the "more water" fever was only slightly less virulent than the gold fever. As the placer mines waned quartz mines were discovered and went into production. The people of the flat were in good fettle *if*, they told themselves and each other, they could just get water enough; it was essential to any type of mining and Rattlesnake Creek was small, seldom lasting through the summer.

Influential men formed the Golden Rock Water Company[8] and issued stock to the amount of $200,000.00 which, in its day, was a large sum but was less than one-third of the cost of other ditches in the mining area. Heedless of the fact that placer mining was literally "all washed up" they rushed the project. The company built a dam on the South Fork of the Tuolumne at Hardin's Mill and brought the water down from there by ditch and by flume, one section of which stood aloft on giant wooden piers the height of a twenty-story building. The story of the dam and flume will be given in its proper place.[9] The water came 38 miles, serving First and Second Garrote on the way, and reached the flat of the big oak on March 29, 1860. Miners and merchants were wildly excited and it was then, in the full pride of achievement, that the town was incorporated and named. Those were peak days. The Golden Rock Ditch was under the management of Otis Perrin, a '49er.

In order to concentrate the inappropriately dry data on Tuolumne County's great water project we will give most of it here: The ditch divided on the height just west of First Garrote (Groveland), one branch passing around the south side of Big Oak Flat and proceeding by ditch down Spring Gulch. It crossed Cobb's Creek and the Coulterville Road by means of flumes and served mines in Mariposa County, the excess water finally finding its way into Moccasin Creek. The other branch passed north of Big Oak Flat and served the quartz mines on the divide between that settlement and Deer Flat, from whence the surplus water was allowed to run into Slate Gulch and from there by flume across Rattlesnake Creek just above Priest's Station and on toward the south.

The ditch was nine feet across the top, six at the bottom and thirty inches deep. The water was sold by the sluice-head (or fifty miner's inches) which cost $5.00 a day. A miner's inch, they tell us, is the amount of water that flows through an orifice one inch square with the water a given depth over the top of the hole, usually four or six inches depending on the rules of the locality.[10]

Although most of the promoters of the ditch cannot be proved to have made money and some lost a great deal, they were benefactors to the country in general. They prolonged placer mining and made possible the firm establishment of several quartz mines which produced for years, maintaining large payrolls and stimulating business. But, by the '70s there was a decline in mine production and the owners could no longer afford high prices for water. Costs for upkeep on the ditch and flume were prohibitive and, by the turn of the century, the ditch was as dry as the details of its actually colorful existence.

From '59 to '63 the town boomed. The California Division of Mines states that the immediate vicinity produced in excess of $25,000,000 from its placer mines. It had four hotels and a large brick theater seating 800 people for which the actors came from San Francisco. It was the accepted shopping center for its section of the county. Its many saloons were crowded. Stages ran two or even more wagons to accommodate the passengers. In 1860 Wells, Fargo & Co. served Big Oak Flat and the Garrotes daily; mail, however, came but once a week.[11] The men were avid for entertainment. A feeble and dessicated circus appeared but the never-failing source of noisy enjoyment was the "hurdy-gurdy." Mrs. Whipple-Haslam describes this group as consisting of four girls with a man to manage them and to play the violin. "The girls," she wrote, "were mostly German and more decent than the dance-hall girls. Instead of drinking strong liquor, they drank something light. This was necessary because every dance brought to the house fifty cents for drinks and fifty cents to the girl. Each and every dance cost the miner one dollar. But dollars were plentiful in those days." Apparently the "hurdy-gurdy" never stayed long in one place.

Except from pure habit the flood of '62 could be passed over without mention in the history of Big Oak Flat, but the drought of the following year caused a fire that all but wiped out the settlement. Ellen Harper May of that town recalled the catastrophe: "It was early October and everything was terribly dry. Suddenly the fire started. Water was low and the sparks flew in all directions and started new blazes. About the only buildings that didn't burn were those built of stone and there were hardly any trees left. All of Chinatown burned. It was on the north side of the road. The entire business section was wiped out with the exception of the big stone building and the fireproof store of Gilbert and Gamble in which Wells, Fargo had its office. The Odd Fellows' Lodge burned; the Yo Semite House, owned by Mr. James Kenny, was destroyed at a loss of $5000. The loss of Mr. Longfellow's livery stable and hay amounted to $800. Jacob Betzer realized a loss of $5000 when his saloon, house and blacksmith shop were destroyed. The total loss to the community was $48,900, a terrific amount in those days. Columbia, Chinese Camp and Coulterville each had a fire in the year we had ours. '63 was one of the driest years in the history of the state. Fires were a terrible hazard before we learned to build of stone and adobe. How our hearts did beat whenever we smelled smoke! We were living in First Garrote at that time. Every wagon was filled with men and boys to help fight the fire. Many of my father's friends were burned out. Shortly after he built a home for us in Big Oak Flat and planted young cedar trees all around. It still stands close to the road at the edge of the town."

This volume is indebted beyond measure to the patience and goodwill of the older citizens of the Road who have answered questions without number, dozens more than could be entered here for lack of space but which have found their way to historical libraries and will never be lost. Of these friends Ellen Harper May, interviewed almost twenty years ago, was the oldest.

The Yo Semite House had been the best stopping place but its owner immediately built another which he called the Kenny Hotel. In 1872 another Yosemite Hotel was in existence in the town— Proprietor Thomas R. Barnes. Ellen Harper May had memories of James Kenny's second hotel also and of her girlhood in the Flat. "When I was very young," she said, "I was employed as a maid in the Kenny Hotel. It was a two-story affair and John Wootton owned a saloon in the same building. I had to work hard but they were good to me. While I was there I met Charles Harper. He was well educated and could quote Shakespeare lengthily. He was shocked when he first came to the diggings with its swearing and drunkeness. He arrived on Sunday and the town was celebrating the day with cock fighting and horse racing. Those painted women he didn't like at all. He was also shocked at the gambling but he soon got on to some of the ways of the other miners although he always remained a gentleman. He bought a horse before long and raced him on Mr. Robert Simmons' ranch in Deer Flat. But he never raced on Sunday. It wasn't long, though, before his jockey was killed in a race and, after that, he wasn't so interested in the sport.

"Well, we were married. Charles was a fine carpenter and specialized in big barns. He put up many of them here and in Deer Flat. He built the covered bridge at Moccasin. But, more than anything else, he loved the theater. He named one son, Edwin, for Edwin Forrest the great tragedian. When any of the towns showed advertising pictures of the plays in San Francisco he would ride a horse to Stockton and from there he'd take a boat just to see a play. Especially if Lotta Crabtree or Mr. Booth were there."

When one thinks of what that journey by horse and boat entailed it is doubtful if Lotta Crabtree and Mr. Booth ever received a more sincere compliment.

John Wootton, earlyday citizen, was born in England but was in

Australia at the time of the California gold strike. He, with his wife and small son took a sailing vessel for San Francisco some time in May, 1848. There were other young people aboard similarly bound and they were aghast when much of their household goods was thrown overboard to lighten the ship during a storm. Then the little boy contracted measles and was buried at sea. After they reached port a daughter, Louisa, was born but the young mother died. It is almost frightening when one thinks how much stark living is contained in three or four sentences.

John Wootton took his baby girl and started for the diggings. By some chance he settled at the top of Moccasin Hill, building a small shack there in 1855, the same year that the Kirkwoods arrived. Later he settled in Big Oak Flat and eventually bought Kenny's Hotel.

The Cavagnaro family were well known throughout the Southern Mines and in Yosemite. Their first store in Big Oak Flat was at the west end of town close to Harper's first carpenter shop. In the '70s John Cavagnaro kept a general merchandise store in what had been the original adobe trading post. He maintained a livery stable across the road.

James Mecartea moved his family from Chinese Camp to Big Oak Flat in 1872 buying a pretty frame house, already old, which had belonged to the merchant Michael Noziglia. Next to the house but separated by an ancient grape arbor was a stone building which the latter had used as a general store and which Mecartea converted into a smithy by adding a layer of earth on the roof as a precaution against fire. In spite of this forethought the building was gutted many years later, laying bare a neat hole under the cellar steps which had been the hiding place of Mr. Noziglia's gold dust.

In considering the two men last named it seems a good time to say that we disclaim all responsibility for the spelling of the proper names so well known in the Southern Mines. Members of the same family often had varying ideas and even individuals refused to be coerced and, from time to time, used a bewildering assortment of spellings. Where we have found a signature on a legal document we have adopted it as probably correct and, to save confusion, have used it to designate all members of that family.

To the eleven Mecartea children who had arrived in Chinese Camp were added two more, born in the new home. The last child before they moved was Austin. The first after coming to Big Oak Flat was Eugene. These two brothers became landmarks in the town and never left it. At some time Mecartea ran a smithy farther west down the main street on a lot just east of what is called "the big stone building," but the exact date is not known.

Blacksmith shops were lively places. James Mecartea was far too busy making picks at one dollar apiece and ox shoes, six for seventy-five cents, to think of gold dust except as a means of exchange. So it happened that the ground under his smithy was never panned. When his numerous children asked for spending money it was his custom to suggest that they take a pan and shovel and repair to the cellar which, on several notable occasions, they actually did. During this decade it was usual to be paid for blacksmith work in produce as money was scarce. The Golden Rock Water Company paid in cash and was considered a very special customer.

In January, 1864, this exciting item appeared in a Sonora paper: "Greenbacks—Greenbacks. Bendix Danielson and Oliver Moore, his partner, have this day paid me their store bill of $140 in Greenbacks at par. (Signed) Alex Kirkwood, Big Oak Flat, Dec. 29, 1864."[12]

Indian women were hired to help Elvira Smith Mecartea with

the enormous washings and heavy cleaning, but just to bake bread for so many was a chore almost inconceivable today. A housewife of that generation earned her passage through the world. All clothes for women and some for boys were generally made at home; but, in respect to the sewing problem, Mrs. Mecartea was lucky. Only one of her thirteen children was a girl—Alice, a blonde and notably pretty.

At the age of seventy-five James Mecartea contracted pneumonia and quit work and this life at the same time. His son Austin took over and kept up the business until automobiles replaced the horse-drawn vehicles, when he locked the heavy iron doors of his shop with the five-inch key and retired into the old family home. Like many another mountain bachelor he used only the kitchen, a bedroom and side porch. Most of the cupboards had not been opened for so many years that they had lost the knack and Austin had long since forgotten what was in them. In the garden the figs still bore, the roses bloomed spicily and the grape arbor increased to tremendous size. Eugene lived just across the street. On the edge of his front porch stood a rain barrel where dozens of song birds drank while a neighbor's cat with sleepy eyes but switching tail sat nearby and schemed. The brothers spent hours together on one porch or the other and, on many unhurried occasions, told us of their happy childhood, of how the thirteen young Mecarteas worked, played, studied, got sick and got well again. "We didn't have many doctors and they lived a long way off," said Austin reminiscently. "There was a Dr. Williamson in early days when the mines were good but in my time Dr. Lampson of Chinese Camp would have to ride up here in a great emergency. But the women folks could handle most kinds of sickness. Our mother could anyway."

Across from the smithy lives another pair of brothers, Edwin and Charles Harper, sons of Ellen Harper May and her first husband, Charles L. Harper. To them, also, we were indebted for much of the information contained in this exposition of life as it used to be along the Big Oak Flat Road.

They have told us of the big oak—early symbol of the community. Accounts of its size vary. Those who paced around the spreading roots gave sixteen feet as its diameter. Elbridge Locke of Knight's Ferry, who was given to understatement, tallied eleven feet, one inch in his diary.

Accounts also vary as to the reason for its untimely demise. It was protected by a town ordinance but the fire of '63 stripped it to its great charred trunk. Through many interviews we have learned that, previous to that event, greedy miners had worked all one dark night removing the earth from around the roots and taking it away to be panned in private and that it died as a result. If the angry men of the settlement could have found out who did it blood might have been shed, so the secret was well guarded. William Brewer visited the town on June 10, 1863, some four months before the conflagration. He wrote in his personal journal: "The 'Big Oak' that gave name to the place [is] nearly undermined, a grand old tree, over 28 ft circum, but now dilapidated although once protected, Town ordinance." In '69 the top fell off and left just the lower trunk. Finally that fell and lay on the ground for over thirty years, so bulky that a tall man on horseback could not see over it. Then in 1900 a camper on a cold night accidentally set fire to it. The fire got away from him and he decided that he had better leave. The townspeople were angry all over again, for even as a fallen monarch the big oak was impressive and it was peculiarly their mascot.

The highway, crooked as it is, was the original Big Oak Flat Road and has always been the main street of the town. The miners dug under it too, in their frantic search for dust and nuggets, and the heavy freight wagons sometimes broke through the crust into holes.

In the '50s the settlement had a schoolhouse about half a mile east of the small group of stores but it was soon abandoned and the children walked to First Garrote (Groveland) for their schooling. In 1860 Mount Carmel Church was erected on a knoll immediately beyond the town.

Robert Curtin assures us that a telegraph line was installed from Big Oak Flat to Yosemite as early as 1866 and that it used a special type of insulator some of which are still in existence. Within his memory there was an old sign on the east end of the Oddfellows' Building which read "American District Telegraph Company" and he believes that this indicated the company in question. There is also evidence that, in June, 1871, a telegraph office was established in the Savory Hotel at Groveland. Apparently there was not enough business transacted on this short line to insure its success and, in 1875, Harlow Street of Sonora installed a telegraph from that town to Yosemite, via Big Oak Flat, which functioned well.

Wells, Fargo & Co., rated, of course, as one of the town's important institutions, and we know that, in 1868, William Urich, Wells, Fargo & Company's agent, used one of the largest pair of gold scales in the Mother Lode country. In the earliest mining days when gold scales had not yet arrived, the amount of gold particles, or "dust," that could be held between the thumb and forefinger was generally considered a dollar's worth. The buyer held up his poke of gold dust and the seller took the pinch. Whatever spilled on the counter was supposed also to belong to the seller and at first blankets were often spread and, after a period of time, burned to recover the gold. Various ingenious expedients were utilized. A '49er wrote: "There was at that time no means of weighing the gold dust; there were no scales to be had; until finally we got a thimble. It w - - - - [would] just hold $ 4. worth of gold dust."[13]

A block north of Main Street was the ordinary goldcamp Chinatown. It was not especially large nor outstanding but it maintained its own cemetery and the odd funeral ceremony is remembered by some of the older citizens. Food, especially a fine roasted pig, was taken to the grave and after the service the porker was carried back to the home where everyone had a feast. The other food was usually left at the cemetery.

We asked Mr. Saul Morris of Chinese Camp for a description of a typical Chinese funeral and received his reply: "I attended the funeral of Kwong Wo, Sr. He was probably the first Chinese child born in Tuolumne County and possibly in the state. He was born in 1851 in Chinese Camp where his father conducted a store. Kwong succeeded to his father's business. Thirty years later he purchased a store in Sonora's Chinatown. He was a prominent officer in the local Chinese Masonic Order and was held in high esteem by people of all races. Every American attending the funeral was given a ten cent piece and some incense for good luck. Boys old enough to know better would line up in the procession, get their ten cents, then crawl through the fence and get at the end of the procession again and receive another dime. Some of them got thirty cents before they were caught. Bodies did not rest many years in this country. Periodically the remains were exhumed and sent back to China to remain forever among their ancestors."

Mr. Edwin Harper, born in Big Oak Flat in the late '70s, told us more about this custom: "I remember," he said, "when a boy, that a group of us used to watch a certain Chinaman when he came here from San Francisco. He was a priest or some important official. We would hide in the bushes to watch the priest with several others as they walked slowly, in single file, to the graveyard. They wore fine Chinese clothing and hung bright-colored banners on the shrubs around the grave they had come to open. Then they chanted and gestured for a time. The officials brought Chinese laborers to do the actual digging but they were most particular to see that every tiny bone was gathered. A piece of silk was spread at one side of the grave and the bones placed on that. When every single one was found and accounted for they were placed in a small wooden box which was given to the Chinese priest with a good deal of ceremony and they all went back to Chinatown." Mrs. Stratton of Chinese Camp added the information that the box was always the length of the human thigh-bone; that the contents were scraped clean and that the cue was carefully placed on top just before the box was sealed. Mr. Harper continued, "I was too young to have seen Chinese funerals. They took place during early mining days. But I well remember that at Chinese New Year they all gathered at the cemetery with bowls of cooked rice and little roasted pigs which they put on the graves. On some of the graves where they thought it would be appreciated they added a container of Chinese gin. Then they had a ceremony and went home. They left the rice and the gin but they always took the roast pork along and had a grand feast in their cabins. Then they gambled for the rest of the holiday." Only the bones of the men were disinterred. Where the women were buried was immaterial.

Big Oak Flat depended on mines and miners. Its prosperity and lack of prosperity ran the usual gamut. Placer mining lasted longer than in other places because the level land was many feet thick with gold bearing gravel, but in the '60s the rockers, cradles and sluice boxes disappeared and the quartz mines took over. The Mack Mine, owned at one time by the storekeeper of '49, Albert Mack, and later by James Kenny and Otis Perrin, the Tip Top Mine owned by Jules McCauley, the Lumsden, the Butler (later the

Longfellow), the Nonpareil, the Rattlesnake Mill, the Jackson Mill, the Burns, the Cross, the Mohrman, the Mississippi and others kept the town going. They operated intermittently, their pounding stamp mills only noticed when they ceased to thunder. Possibly one would stop production because of the increasing depth of its gold bearing vein, only to be placed again on a profitable basis by more modern machinery and wiped out, after an interval, by advanced costs of operation. Gold discoveries in Alaska and elsewhere rendered Tuolumne's gold mines of less importance. About 1909 there was a revival due to greatly improved deep shaft methods, but in the 1920's inflation reduced the condition of the mining towns to a long and dismal slump. This was broken during the depression of the 1930s by a busy scattering of lone operators along the creeks, glad to have the dollar or two that they might accidentally pan out. Then, quite suddenly, the price of gold (which had been as low as $14.00 per ounce in 1849) was raised from $20.67 to $35.00 per fine ounce. This put many districts back into production. In 1940 mines were active and the town was prosperous until 1942 when war mandates practically ended the saga of gold in the Southern Mines.

Now, as far as Big Oak Flat is concerned, but few profitable veins are being worked.

The decline of the quartz mines had a corresponding effect on the towns. As the payrolls fell off the smaller business men left the vicinity; fewer hotels and livery stables were needed; there was less travel on the stage lines and many went out of operation. There was little outlook for the future and the young people left taking with them the life of the settlements, the dances, theatrical performances and band concerts. The Chinese, who are canny business people, left too. Only those remained whose roots had sunk too deeply for removal.

The last half century has been drab along the Mother Lode in comparison with its golden beginnings; but with the coming of year-around play lands in the Sierra Nevada, the building of wide and safe mountain highways and the almost universal possession of a family automobile everything is changed. Give an old-time mining community an interesting history, some authentic ruins and a clean restaurant and the American public will be sure to come sooner or later and to leave good money behind.

* * *

To the left as one enters Big Oak Flat is the site of the early Indian village which the miners under Rufus Keys rudely displaced. A few yards to the north a large mortar rock with several holes for the grinding of acorns may still be seen. Some years later Mr. Krautter, fresh from Germany, built a beautiful one-story home close to the mortars and sent for his daughter Emilie to keep house for him. Immediately to the rear of the home, Krautter constructed rock retaining walls that separated his large vineyard on the knoll from his lower gardens and found time between his sausage and wine making to assist his countryman Ferdinand Stachler in the building of a brewery a few miles east of Big Oak Flat.

It is hard to remember that this was once a lovely flat; the sharp declivity toward Rattlesnake Creek came as a result of surface gold mining operations.

On the north side of the highway, and atop a scenic elevation, is the home of Charles P. Hall, once manager of the Tip Top Mine and son of Capt. Perry W. Hall, one of the founders of the Odd Fellows' Lodge and a prominent pioneer. Charles Hall married Alice Mecartea. Farther along on the south side and almost hidden in trees is the home of Eunice Watson Fisher, at this time the oldest resident. The large Maccabees' Dance Hall at one time stood opposite. Near her house, and also on the south side, is the marker commemorating the Big Oak. The lower part of the monument is recessed and grated heavily with iron bars behind which large chunks of the great white oak were placed by the older citizens who had watched with regret the various accidents and acts of vandalism; saving at last a few pieces for memory's sake.

The Golden Rock Hotel stood, in 1860, opposite the oak and probably was burned along with it in '63.

The Odd Fellows' Hall stands alone. Its two neat stories are a study in contrast. The lower floor was built in the early '50s of dressed schist slabs set in lime mortar. Schist was plentiful but lime was scarce and expensive, having to be freighted in from a quarry near Sonora. It has, however, proved its worth, for many of the buildings which have weathered the years in the Southern Mines are of that construction. The five iron doors that space the front wall are set in perfectly squared frames by the use of bricks which were far too costly to be used for the complete building if suitable rock could be obtained. At first it had but one story and the pitched roof was of cedar shakes. The second story, reached by a covered outdoor stairway, is of sheet metal and was added much later.

The building was used as a grocery by Gilbert and Gamble[14] before it survived the fire of 1863. It was then purchased by the Oddfellows who had lost their meeting place and were assisted by other lodges. Yosemite Lodge, No. 97, was instituted in 1860 and is still in active service in the same building.

Nearly opposite the Oddfellows' Building was the smithy operated by G. Betzer in the '50s and '60s.

The "big stone building," the town's most impressive landmark, was one of the largest stone structures in the Mother Lode country. According to Mr. H. A. Cobden, its erection was commenced in 1850 or '51, but he states that some of the rear masonry shows crude Indian labor and that he has evidence that this earlier portion was used as a summer trading post by the Hudson's Bay Company long before the Gold Rush.

Within the building a stone partition divides it in the middle lengthwise while two other crosswise partitions divide the space in thirds, so that three stores face the street and a corresponding number of rear rooms or offices face the back. An iron door led from each front room to its companion in the rear, helping immensely in fire protection. At first it was known as "the Company's store" and one could walk from one third to the next and then the next through arches. These were closed later, causing it to be treated as if it were three separate buildings. It was completed in 1852 and had a wooden roof over the front porch which did not survive the fires of its first 75 years. A replacement of corrugated iron blew off in a windstorm and now the narrow porch gets along without a roof. Back of the ponderous iron doors are more conventional inner doors with glass panels. Tree of heaven shades them delicately.

We have been informed by two long-time residents, Clotilda Repetto De Paoli and Edwin Harper, that the suite on the left was first occupied by J. D. Murphy and Luigi Marconi who ran a general merchandise store. Later it came into the hands of Joseph Raggio who did a wide-spread business in surprisingly choice foodstuffs and liquors. The Raggio family were prominent pioneers who also had mining interests.

On the west (or left) end of the building and toward the rear, built as a separate compartment out of rock and adobe, was the room utilized as a jail after the first one was abandoned. It has been a storeroom for many years but the tiny barred windows may still be noted. The Repetto family quote their father as saying that the first jail was of adobe and was across the small side road, west of the big building and somewhat north of the highway.

The small inclosure covered with corrugated metal and just in front of the second jail is an adobe building fully as old as the big stone building, say the old-timers, and possibly older. It was the place of business of Repetto and Chase—makers of boots and shoes that they sold at a uniform price of $20.00 with a guarantee of a year. We have also been told that this little building housed the first post office and that, in 1852, Joseph W. Britton was the postmaster.

The center suite of two rooms seems to have been first occupied by Dominic Cuneo. Afterward it became the Noziglia store for a period and, at different times, was rented to a Mr. Cody and to a Colonel Roote who ran a drug store. When Mr. Cuneo died the three children of Gio Batta Repetto inherited the suite under his will. It was then listed under the name Victor J. Repetto and the Post Office of the 1900s was maintained in the Repetto store.

The right hand suite contained the offices of Wells, Fargo & Co. Sometimes the post office turned up even here and, in 1868, toward the end of a period of prosperity, William Urich was both agent for the express company and postmaster. Court was held in this office. We have some inconclusive evidence that Judge McGehee (or Magee) presided about 1870, with Judge John Gamble and Judge Fred Murrow (known as the marrying judge) following in less than ten years. Wells, Fargo & Co. closed its office and left the town in 1893.

This information takes a little fine dovetailing but, if all the data could be found and compared, is probably quite correct.

The Raggio store was the last to do business in the big stone building. Joseph Raggio had married Emanuella, sometimes called Amelia, the widow of Mr. Marconi who was the baker of the settlement. He produced hot and fragrant bread in an adobe building with iron doors and large ovens of rock and adobe. It stood between the back of the stone building and the town's first cemetery. The bakery and a nearby small adobe dwelling faced the back road which led to Deer Flat and the rear section of the Yo Semite House. In that period of prosperity between the coming of the ditch water and the devastating fire, families drove many miles to buy Marconi's tempting pasteries. After the death of Joseph, Amelia Marconi Raggio lived alone in the big building for a time but it was eventually closed by the grandchildren.

Across the highway from the big stone building was the office of the Golden Rock Water Company and the home of its one-time owner, Andrew Rocca, who sold out in 1875 and left Big Oak Flat still a wealthy man. Across the side road from the stone building was the well-known Kenny Hotel. Both the office structure and the Kenny Hotel are completely effaced. But south of the highway still stands the home of Gio Batta Repetto.

It is a neat residence with a picket fence to ward traffic away from the low porch. A hill drops away sharply so that the house is an extra story high in the back. This was not the case in early days when the town was on a true flat. A heavy stone wall under the front of the house prevents the foundations from slipping in wet weather. It was built before 1852 and was there to greet Mr. Repetto (fresh from Italy, speaking five languages and greatly disturbed by Vigilante rule in San Francisco) when he retreated into the simpler living conditions of the mountains. At that time the house had iron hooks in the fireplace for cooking purposes and was occupied by the butcher shop of the James Brothers. Mr. Repetto later bought it and it has been the family home ever since the early '70s. It is now occupied by his two daughters, Sylvia Vail and Clotilda De Paoli.

Mrs. De Paoli remembers "the Citizens' Cemetery," when it had many wooden markers, especially over the graves of children, but fire has gradually wiped them out. It is the oldest burial place of the town. The marble monument marks the resting place of Johannah, wife of August Voight, who was placed here in 1856 when her little daughter Josephine was but two years old—a tragedy all too common in the gold camps. Josephine, later Mrs. Von Offen, may have been the first white child born in the Flat. She never forgot her mother's grave which originally was outlined according to custom with large chunks of white quartz and had a wooden marker. She had it inclosed with an iron fence, placed the stone headpiece and now lies there herself in the town where she was born.

Above the Citizens' Cemetery was the burial place of the Chinese. The removal of their bodies to China was a definite obligation on the survivors and there used to be shallow depressions where the soil of the graves had settled after the bodies were taken away. Mining operations in the 1930s effaced these evidences.

The modern post office was built on the site of the original two-roomed stone and adobe trading post which was later occupied by John Cavagnaro's store.

Beyond the early trading post stood the stone building of Caleb Dorsey and it was there that Charles Harper maintained his second carpenter shop. In later years, so Mrs. De Paoli told us, it was acquired by Judge Redmond and held the Justice Court. After the town was surveyed, about 1879, property deeds were given out signed by J. D. Redmond, County Judge.

Fig and pear trees and a tremendous grapevine mark the site of the Mecartea home. Next to it the blacksmith shop still stands flush with the road. In the '60s and '70s there was a tiny building on the east side of the smithy with only a three-foot alley separating the two. In it William Bouryer ran a gun-smithy. When he died it was added to the Mecartea property. Just across the highway is the Harper house, residence of Charles and Edwin Harper and once the home of John Gamble and family.

Mount Carmel, atop a knoll of gleaming white quartz and surrounded by its pioneer graves, is the last point of interest.

CHAPTER VII

THE RANCHES AND THE RANCHERIA

The expanse of rolling, oak-studded farming country known as Deer Flat cannot be omitted from any study of the Big Oak Flat Road; neither can the community of Miwoks who lived peacefully within its environs. It lies north and over the Serra or Sierra Gorda Ridge from the neighboring town of Big Oak Flat and west of Groveland. A road which began its career as a pack trail comes southeast from Sonora, splits in Deer Flat and sends one branch to Big Oak Flat and one to Groveland. Between Sonora and Deer Flat it crosses the main Tuolumne River at what used to be Ward's Ferry and is now Ward's Ferry bridge.

The canyon of the Tuolumne lies among the mountains just here, high, rocky and covered with chemise. The bridge, dwarfed by its surroundings, seems spidery and slender and from it one may look down on blue slate boulders far below which wear in their buttonholes fragile purple flowers. On the north side of the bridge and possibly 100 yards up the road a ruined stone and log cabin crouches on the steep long mountainside. It may have been a toll house connected with the bridge.

The overhanging northside cliffs are formed of rock in which small birds have built nests and during the spring freshets the thunder of the tumultuous waters so echoes and re-echoes that one wonders how the tiny creatures endure it. The spot is indescribably lonely. Few cars and no pedestrians come here.

From a vantage point on the bridge one can see the old pack-mule trail coming down the brush covered mountain—just one switch-back after another. Before the shelflike, one-way road was cut across it, the trail dropped precipitously to the edge of the

147

snarling river without a break. It is completely impassable now, of course, and only glimpses are visible here and there. To have ridden it in pack-mule days (which is a daring assumption as any sane person would rather have walked) would have rendered the side-saddle equestrienne grateful for the stiff shrubbery which interposed its not inconsiderable barrier between her and a non-stop trip.

Below the log cabin the mule trail struck the inhospitable narrow footing of the river's edge at a stretch of pansy-dark smooth water; and it was here that, in 1850, Joseph Ward built a ferry of hand hewn logs and ran it himself.

His fares were reasonable: footmen—twenty-five cents, horsemen—fifty cents. In fact, he sold his life cheaply as he was soon murdered for his profits in gold dust.

By 1854 James Berger and Sam White were operating both the ferry and a store carrying miners' supplies and kept their gold dust profits unpretentiously in a baking powder can.

This cutoff from the Sonora country, when made possible by a ferry, was very tempting. Why go clear down to Chinese Camp and climb up again by way of Moccasin Hill when, by means of even a rough and unattractive trail, one could travel more directly? Countless miners, afoot and mounted, came by Ward's Ferry. As in the case of Knight's Ferry and others, the name stuck even though Knight never finished his ferry and Ward ran the one that bore his name less than four years.

On the south side of the Tuolumne, soaring up from a landing beach apparently the size of a soda cracker, runs Murderers' Gulch. It grooves deeply a mountain darkly smudged as the miners' cheeks. The trail can be seen ascending in three or four large switchbacks before it disappears to the left around a jutting, brushy shoulder. Each zigzag is built up on the lower side with rock work to keep the whole thing from washing out during wet weather and has lasted a full century. Tall, many-branched diggers thrusting up from the bottom of the canyon obscure the view but, by looking for the smooth place in the river where it was alone possible to cross, the trail can be located easily.

Murderers' Gulch was dangerous and bandit infested. Early travelers, if possible, made this portion of their journey in groups, being careful that they knew of whom the group consisted; but many a lone man left his bones to be scattered by coyotes in the thick growth beside the trail. Death always knew his way along the Mother Lode.

In the '60s Berger and White were murdered and the baking powder can preëmpted. Then a Mr. Tuttle, who ran the ferry and collected the fare in dust, was eliminated by the same system. Posses searched unsuccessfully in the heavily timbered country. In the 1870s a bridge was built and years later, the tolltaker, Charles Pease, was killed as was also a visiting friend, Joseph Lowe. The bridge and toll house were burned. This time the bandits had their trouble for nothing as the can of gold dust was found melted in the ashes.

None of the criminals were apprehended and the route bore a bad reputation but, with all its disadvantages, it was shorter and people would chance it.

In the fall of '54 Ellen Harper May, then a baby of three or four months, rode over the Murderers' Gulch Trail. Her father, Cornelius McLaughlin, had come from Australia to Sullivan's Creek near Sonora. She was the fifth child of her twenty-two year old mother. There were no white women. There were no supplies to speak of. The little mother made her own soap and candles from cooking grease but there came a time when she had no bread. It was flood season and they were isolated from their supply base in

Sonora but their need was so acute that Cornelius managed to swim the raging creek both ways, arriving home in some miraculous manner with a sack of damp flour. When they opened it a mass of weevils greeted them. She, who had not wept from cold, hunger nor fright, cried bitterly at the thought of disappointing her children; she was so worn and so in need of food. So they dumped the flour on a large clean piece of cloth and picked out the weevils, one by one.

Shortly two of their children died and they became desperate enough for desperate measures. When Ellen was barely old enough to travel they sold their claim to James G. Fair and started on the journey. They had heard of Garrote and would settle there. Mr. Fair was later to make money from the claim but they were mercifully ignorant of that.

All the household goods and mining equipment were packed on mule back. The little mother wore a long alpaca dress and sunbonnet and rode a sidesaddle, holding her baby on one arm while she guided her riding animal with the other. The combination of a sidesaddle, a baby and the descent to the ferry was cause for prayer and, one has no doubt, occasioned it. Now and then the anxious mother looked back to see how Johnny and Adeline were faring on the horse with their father which brought up the rear of the little procession. But their bad luck was over and the children remained safely atop the animal until their new home was reached.

As settlements along the Big Oak Flat Road grew and prospered and fertile Deer Flat filled with ranches, such sticky progress as the pack trains were able to make up Murderers' Gulch was no longer to be tolerated. The merchants and farmers conceived of a bridge instead of a ferry and a better road lying to the east of the Gulch. It was then, in 1870, that the first bridge was built. The trail up the Gulch was abandoned gradually and the new road finished.

The present road from Ward's Ferry bridge to Deer Flat is not for anyone unaccustomed to mountain driving but is full of interest. In May the flowers are lovely, vivid red Indian paint brush, tangerine-colored daisies on long stems, duller gold "monkey flowers," long lavender spears of mountain balm, the white stars of wild syringa, and red bud, fifteen feet high. The crossing of Deer Creek south of Ward's Ferry bridge is negotiated on a tiny iron bridge, bright red with rust and draped at both ends with wild grape. Quail bob across the road which is often marked with coon tracks. Cattle, invisible in the brush of the steep hillside, low continually and, frightened by the unusual advent of a car, crash heavily away from the noise.

Still farther south and immediately at the road's edge stands the old schoolhouse. At noon its weather-fringed roof-shakes cast long shadows down the walls, across the many-paned windows and almost to the ground. All the children of the Deer Flat ranchers attended here. For a long time this ungraded school was taught by various members of the Ortega family from Sonora. Later D. M. Ortega went as teacher to the school in Groveland, succeeding John Gamble.

The farmers might have had trouble keeping the opulent pasturage of Deer Flat if the miners had coveted the land; but it was composed of a peculiar sticky clay and was troublesome. James E. Hunt wrote, "it was what we called gold stealer for it would roll in little balls in the pan while washing and collect all the fine gold."[1]

So the ranches of Deer Flat were prosperous. The fields, orchards and homes well cared for; but the outstanding landmarks were the big barns, some of them built by Charles Harper whose handiwork has outlasted him by over half a century.

About five miles north of Groveland is the present Gookin Ranch which used to be the home of Giovanni Batiste Boitano, a '49er, and still boasts the old stone and adobe dwelling. It is long and narrow with a heavy shake roof and seems originally to have been divided into two large rooms but is rapidly crumbling and partially overgrown with grapevines.

At the well-known Carlon Ranch, Nora Carlon Mogan, now deceased, was happy to talk about her parents, John and Kate Carlon. "They were born in Ireland," she said, "and came to Tuolumne County in 1849. They had to reload all their belongings onto mules at West's Warehouse. They were true "pack saddle pioneers" and had eight children all born in this county. Father didn't stay long with mining and soon transferred his interest to cattle. His brand was known all over this part of the state."

Some of the ranchers were also mine owners. Dearborn Longfellow, known always as "Derb," was one of these. A pertinent letter from Mrs. Frank Cassaretto of Piedmont, California, who was Lula Longfellow, gave us first-hand information: The Longfellow family came from Maine where their son Dearborn was born. They were reserved and competent and Mr. Longfellow was proud to tell that he was the nephew of Henry Wadsworth Longfellow. Primarily he was a rancher and soon moved over the divide from Big Oak Flat into Deer Flat where a number of households were already living comfortably in the midst of their fields and herds.

When Dearborn Longfellow was twenty-nine and Louisa Wootton was fourteen they were married and took up housekeeping on the Longfellow Ranch where they raised cattle and race horses. Louisa had five children; but Civil War days, no matter how comfortably upholstered with money, were not easy for children in the Mother Lode. There were never enough doctors and often it was not possible to get any trained help in time of sickness. Two of the five died in the terrible diphtheria epidemic of 1879 while another succumbed to an accidental gunshot wound. But the ranch and the rich Longfellow Mine came down to those who remained. The name will be remembered.

Another well-known family who mined in the ridge west of Groveland was Augustine and Maria De Ferrari with their off-spring. They came directly from Italy in 1862, making the long dangerous journey around the Horn and settling in the Mother Lode country, which their descendants have never left.

The Meyer brothers, Diedrich and Heinrich—called Dick and Henry—with a brother, John, left Germany, as they said, so "hell-bent for the diggings" that they couldn't be bothered with a large city lot on Montgomery Street, San Francisco, offered them in 1850 for $20.00. They had no time for small deals. They soon lost interest in mining but did well in cattle; their holdings in the rolling hills east of the James Ranch were supplemented by the customary summer grazing land in the high mountains. They acquired it in an interesting way. Some of their horses were stolen by Indians and John started out with a posse to recover their property. While riding they came upon a lovely alpine meadow on what was later the old Tioga Road. An Indian encampment was poised there temporarily and they named the place White Wolf for the chief. When it became possible they patented the land. It is still a place of beauty where bear wander harmlessly and deer frequent the salt lick in the clearing at dusk. It is still called White Wolf and is in the Yosemite National Park.

Other ranchers of the vicinity whose names were known throughout the county were James Ballentine, John Gray who purchased the Samuel Ayres ranch, Patrick Murphy, Thomas Clark, Lurain Hunt, Robert Simmons, the O'Neils, the Woodruffs, the Lumsdens, the Corcorans, and others.

Scenic Deer Flat is watered by Deer Creek; while Big Creek and Big Humbug flow to the east of Deer Flat and Ward's Ferry. All three empty into the Tuolumne River and their small tributaries, winding through the ranches, provide water for the livestock.

* * *

The well-known Miwok tribe living in this vicinity was a branch of the Mokelumnes, a larger division of western Indians, and its individuals were too comfortable to be warlike. They were competent and well adapted to their existence in the low mountains which abounded in food throughout the year. They made watertight baskets in which to cook. They sewed skins together to make exceedingly sketchy clothing but soon found that it was easier to beg for cast-off breeches which the neighboring whites were only too glad to donate.

The first known location of the Miwok rancheria was on the old Reid Ranch, somewhat north of Groveland, whose crumbling and vine-covered adobe now stands empty. Nearby is Garrote Creek where many mortars have been found. A century-old apple and cherry orchard still bears heavily and the Indian village was on a sunny hillside just south of it. About sixteen slightly flattened sites are all that mark the locations of the little houses made of cedar bark. The Miwoks scrupulously kept their hillside bare of brush, but now timber and other growth is fast encroaching. In 1857, when the Reid family built their house, the Miwoks had just transferred their belongings from this first site down to Big Creek. Later Edmund James preëmpted the land surrounding their new village but apparently the Indians didn't mind having a neighbor and continued to occupy their hillside near the creek without disturbing him. Their village site (now deserted) is visible from the present county road, just within the fence and north of the gate to "Big Creek Ranch," but in early days the road from Groveland turned east before getting that far and went past the ranch house, crossing Big Creek on an ungainly long wooden bridge still in existence, so that the Indian village was off the beaten track. About once a month the residents of nearby ranches could count on a sleepless night as the men of the tribe really settled down to a good powwow in their "round house" or gathering place which was on a bare knoll north of the village.

In 1898 the James Ranch was sold to S. A. Ferretti of Groveland and later to Dunn and McLellan.

The funeral rites of these Miwoks were interesting. Fred De Ferrari of Groveland told of the last two to be buried on the rancheria sometime in the '90s, an Indian named Jimmie Bill and his wife called simply "Sullivan." The body of the deceased was placed in a hut and a constant marathon was maintained about the place where it lay. Sometimes the participants walked and sometimes danced but were always supervised by a person of authority. The ceremony was to prevent an invasion of evil spirits. The dancers took turns resting but the movement around the body never stopped. Four slabs of native rock mark the two graves which are about four hundred yards from the ranch house. There is no other indication of a cemetery.

Before the coming of the white man the Miwoks cremated their dead according to the old-timers.

All Indians were fond of visiting and sometimes a whole village would arrive and practically take up residence in a tribe with whose members they were friendly.

One year the snow came early and without warning even to the keen weather-sense of the Indians. It caught a large party of acorn gatherers at Big Creek village, marooning them west of the passes. Although the braves never did anything about the acorn gathering they were possessed of cavernous appetites and had to be fed.

The food gave out; any remaining acorns were under the snow; the deer had sought lower levels and there were exceedingly dim prospects for a comfortable winter. When there was nothing else left to do the braves staged a ceremonial dance, chanting and stamping in the melting, snowy mud around their camp fires. It was reported in the settlements and the citizens of the Garrotes were legitimately worried. They hoped that the dance had a religious significance but weren't quite sure. The Indians might be working themselves up to a raid. The common humanity of the pioneers, who only existed because they helped each other, also asserted itself; they couldn't let a group of fellow creatures starve. James Tannahill, Jacob Boitano, the Meyer brothers and others visited the camp.

The braves regarded them through sullen slit eyes and went right on curveting and vaulting in the dance, tensely curved as leaping trout one moment, then bent almost double as they tramped in a circle chanting, "We are hungry. We are hungry."

The men decided to feed them. Tannahill gave an adequate supply of flour and staples from his store and the others gave what they had.

Whether prayerful or threatening, the dance had been effective. The affair simmered down into a feast and the citizens were given affectionate names by their grateful red friends. One (which we can only hope was Mr. Tannahill) was called "Moss Covered Rock," denoting dependability.

Partly because of this incident the Indians from the Mono country seem to have been always friendly to the travelers they encountered on their age-old trails over the Sierra.

When the Indians from Cherry Creek and the Jawbone country foisted themselves on the Miwoks of Big Creek they crossed the main Tuolumne River by an ingenious grapevine bridge. A vine clinging to a tree on the north side was strengthened and lengthened by braiding other runners into a strong rope. Then the best swimmer of the band threw himself into the river's chilly race and took the rope across to be fastened to the vines in a tree on the south bank. When it was swinging above the current the Indians went across hand over hand, getting a foothold now and then on the rocks that bared themselves like white expectant teeth.

The valley of Big Creek was a nice location with fertile soil and good pasturage but, of course, that was not its main appeal for the Miwoks. Excellent hunting, fishing and abundance of acorns were the reasons that they had elected to live on the spot.

The men were a lazy lot and seldom exerted themselves although they occasionally panned out dust and nuggets on the fringe of the diggings. They were very good at it, preferring to use the Mexican wooden batea rather than the miners' pan. Even though they enjoyed it, however, it was much easier to let the women do it. Mr. Edwin Harper contributed a colorful item to our knowledge of the Indian in the days of gold. Every year, he said, after the beginning of the rainy season, the Indian women came with their wooden bateas and panned the gold dust out of the wagon ruts in Big Oak Flat, squatting imperturbably in the midst of the hoofed and wheeled traffic of the day. It seemed to pay fairly well.

Accepted outdoor attire for an Indian woman apparently included a burden on her back—more often than not her baby. But during acorn season the papoose carrier made way for the heavy cone-shaped basket whose weight was supported by a band around the forehead and in which she endlessly garnered acorns; snatching them up swiftly with both hands at once; cleverly keeping a continuous barrage over her shoulders and into the flaring receptacle. Meanwhile her baby was not neglected. It was either hung from a convenient branch or propped against a tree as the mother worked and chattered with other women similarly encumbered. Seldom did a woman go out to work alone but always as a sort of village project.

Each year the acorn crop was carefully stored for the winter as acorn meal was a staple in the Miwok diet but they did not lack for variety. Fish and game were abundant; also grasshoppers which they collected by building a large circular fire in a suitable flat, grassy spot and letting it burn slowly toward the middle where a hole had been dug. This took care of everything except ladling the hoppers out after they had been roasted. Sometimes, if toasted extra dry, they ground them into meal in their stone mortars and made cakes from them which were palatable to the ordinary diner if he didn't happen to know whereupon he was dining. General John Bidwell occasionally had them served to unsuspecting guests. Fat earthworms also were collected, dumped on hard ground and trampled by the bare feet of the squaws into an indescribable mass. The long white wood grub was a compact little item and full of calories. Because of the peculiar pungency of their cuisine few whites, except children, went to the rancheria. Of course the latter were not supposed to trespass but, judging from interviews given in their later life when too old to be held to account for childhood transgressions, most of them went to see the Indians whenever they got a chance.

The Miwoks were fond of visiting especially when profitable, so they often roamed abroad to do a little concentrated mingling. Once a year they came into the towns of Big Oak Flat and Groveland and put on a fandango dressed in their native garb, during which they jumped up and down and chanted, not forgetting to pass the hat afterward. At other times a few wandered about singly, begging. "Old Grizzly" was a rancheria character often seen in town. Some remember him as the chief, for a while at least.

He was covered from neck to ankles with bagging shirt and pants but always with naked feet—one of which was a shapeless mass. Eunice Watson Fisher said, "I remember his horrible foot, all twisted and knotted. He was chased by a bear and managed to reach a tree and start to climb, but the bear got him by one foot and held on until he had chewed it all up. I don't know how he got away without being killed because a bear can climb a tree pretty well unless the trunk is too small for him to get a good grip."

"Old Capitan" or Captain Luis, was another well known rancheria Indian probably at one time chief of the tribe. He always wore a loose shirt and very little else, but invariably carried his bow and arrows. "It was rather disconcerting to the women of the community," said Mrs. Fisher, "to encounter him in the stores begging for sugar and tobacco, but they finally got used to him."

The Indians had interesting, sometimes beautiful names but cheerfully went by whatever appellation was applied to them by the whites. Mrs. Fisher continued, "We always called Old Grizzly's wife 'Lucy.' She died of a stone bruise on her heel. It might have been from blood poisoning. They were all dirty but mostly were harmless although they would always steal if they got a chance. They didn't seem to think it was wrong; it was just a convenient way to get things they needed. They spoke to us in garbled Indian, Spanish and English—mostly just names of things and verbs, like 'Give me carne, sugar, pan, salt.' We always knew what they meant. Except when they came into town in all their regalia and paraded around, most of them kept to themselves and it seemed as if we children were the only ones who paid any attention to them.

"They were always curious, though, and would press their noses against our windows to see what we were doing. When Mother got tired of it she would walk up and put her face close to the inside of the pane and drop her false teeth. There was nothing that scared them more."

Ellen Harper May remembered the Miwoks best as door to door visitors. "One day a poor old squaw knocked at our kitchen door," she said, "and mother felt sorry for her. So she cut the crusty end off a fresh loaf of bread, still warm from the oven, and gave her the spongy thick slice. It looked and smelled wonderful to me for I loved the crust. The old Indian woman said 'Gracias' and with her wrinkled dirty hand took a wet mass of pulpy earthworms from her pocket and mashed them into that delicious new bread. My mother ran and tried to stop her, but she backed off and just smiled and said 'Muy bueno, muy bueno.' She was an inveterate beggar and it seemed as if she could always smell fresh bread."

With the exception of certain well known characters who enjoyed the white man's town the members of the Miwok village stayed in their own domain most of the time. Many of the Deer Flat ranches can show portable mortars and pestles of stone used by the Indians for grinding acorn meal and some of them can boast the large stationary mortars consisting of twenty or thirty grinding holes in one boulder. These are always found near a creek or spring. Sometimes the pestles have been found in the holes as if the users intended to return.

Until twenty years ago obsidian arrow and spear heads were frequently picked up on the Flat. The obsidian was brought by the Mono Indians from east of the Sierra Nevada to exchange for the superior baskets of the Miwoks, for acorns which they did not have in their country and also for hunting privileges. The Miwoks made surprisingly perfect arrow heads of this black volcanic glass by a simple treatment which took, nevertheless, a high degree of skill. Suitable fragments were heated in the fire, so we were told by Mr. John De Martini of Groveland, then icy water from the creek was sucked into a straw and retained by closing the upper end with a finger or the thumb. Drop by drop the arrow maker released the water around the edge of the projected arrow head and at each application a chip popped off. Only the jet black obsidian was used.

The native food supply of the Miwoks being plentiful and varied, resulted, through generations, in a better stature than, for instance, that of the Indians of the Mono country. They seemed more intelligent and, consequently, cleaner, although the latter attribute might not have been perceptible to the casual observer. They also had culinary arts in advance of the habits of the Mono Indians.

Mr. W. D. McLean, grandson of the founders of Dudley's Station on the Coulterville Road, often ate acorn mush, or chimuk, with his Indian friends. He said, "It would have been fairly good if they could have been persuaded to add salt, but salt was a scarce commodity in the Sierra tribes—something they had to trade for— and was not to be wasted. Even after it became plentiful they retained their old habit of putting a pinch on the tongue and making that do for a whole meal. They also stayed with the old-time method of leaching the bitterness out of the pulverized acorn meal by placing it in a bowl-like hole scooped in clean coarse sand and pouring hot water through it. Seven washings was usually the rule. The only concession they finally made to modern labor-saving devices was to put the meal in a flour sack or other cloth so that it could be lifted free of the sand. They cooked it," he added upon being questioned, "in a basket with water by dropping in hot rocks as became necessary just like mush. Dulce, an old Indian woman who lived near Cascade Creek, used to invite me to eat chimuk now and then. It was very rich, had no grain at all and always looked to me like pork gravy made with milk. They ate it hot sometimes but more often she floated the basket in which she cooked the meal in cold water until it solidified. Then they just broke it into chunks and ate it when they pleased.

"Black oak acorns made the best meal. When the acorn crop failed the Indians were in real trouble. In very bad years they gathered buckeye balls and leached them until they were just dry pulp. They had little food value but they filled the stomach and prevented starvation."

Observing the more utilitarian qualities of the early miners' cabins the Miwoks gradually abandoned the picturesque but sketchy bark abodes and built ramshackle frame huts. We know that in 1877 there were only sixteen Indian families remaining on the rancheria and that their buildings were in the white man's style.

One at a time the family units left. Some moved to Tuolumne, a small settlement near Sonora; but, in the main, they have been profitably absorbed into the white population.

A bizarre item in the economic system of Deer Flat was an outlander, Ah Chew. He came with the first of the Orientals and was left stranded by the backwash of their tide of retreat. He lived alone in a tiny cabin and was a person of privilege, especially with the children. Mrs. Frank Cassaretto remembered the old Chinese with affection. "He was a part of our childhood," she said. "We went to his cabin every now and then. He used to give us odd-tasting Chinese candy and little pies that were made out of a short dough and filled with mincemeat. He was very clean and we thought they were delicious.

"The old man did a certain amount of prospecting and mining and, every week, went to Garrote for supplies. He would just put his tin box of nuggets and gold dust on the counter and enough would be measured out to pay for what he wanted. He didn't seem to know his own age, but men who came into the country about 1849 estimated it as over ninety years. When he began to get too old to work some of the citizens in Garrote gave him a pension. We always liked to see him bobbing along the street with his cue swinging down his back. He was a real part of the life of the community."

After his death Ah Chew's single weapon of defense was found in his lonely cabin. It is possibly eighteen inches long—too big for a dagger, too small for a sword. Hand made and crude both as to handle and blade, but beyond any doubt effective.

There is necromancy in the homely scenes of the ranching country. Stalwart barns, blackened by time and weather, under giant oaks. Hyacinth sky bracketed between curving branches. Far-off sun-slants on fields where long grasses swing their tasseled tops. In leaving it one can fairly feel the silence rolling back to linger undisturbed.

* * *

The Serra or Sierra Gorda Ridge that separates Deer Flat from its neighboring towns is brush-covered and spiked with scrubby trees along the top. Beneath the unattractive apron of chaparral the innards of the mountain are scarred and depleted from mining operations, for several of the best known of the hardrock mines are located here: the Mack, the Mississippi, the Tip Top, the Nonpareil, the Longfellow and others. Several branches of the Golden Rock Ditch wandered through, maintaining their grade level and serving the mines.

For the person who enjoys nothing more than an hour spent idly in a country graveyard there are two spots between Big Oak Flat and Groveland that are mandatory, Mount Carmel and Oak Grove Cemeteries. The first, just east of Big Oak Flat, is marked by a little white Catholic church on a knoll. It was built in 1861; burned but was rebuilt in duplicate and the vestments saved. It stands guard over sacred ground in use for almost a century. Some of the graves bear familiar names and are bordered by ornate iron fences. Anna Jones Reid, of Groveland, to whom we were indebted for much first-hand information of pioneer days, was the first to be baptised here, in July of 1862, and, at the present reading, the last to be buried in its confines. She was the first child of the first marriage to be performed at Mount Carmel—Margaret McCarty to Martin Jones, September 1, 1861.

Beyond the church and on the north side of the road is a small flat where the Miwoks were in the habit of camping. Nothing outstanding remains to distinguish the place but, in the past, interesting relics have been found.

Indefinitely near the top of the divide (some say 500 feet before reaching the crest) the Big Oak Flat School of the '50s stood on the left. While still atop the hill a road turns south to Oak Grove Cemetery and its older companion, The Oddfellows' Cemetery. The title first used was St. John's Cemetery in honor of Mr. C. A. St. John who was a lawyer living in Big Oak Flat during the '60s and who donated the land. He further recommended himself to history by being in the first party to ascend Mount Dana. The name was eventually changed because, it is said, of its misleading implication—strangers often mistaking it for a Catholic Cemetery.

The untended plots are fascinating. The markers range from small slabs to marble monuments of fair size and elegance. There are tight little wrought iron fences just the shape of the graves they outline, as well as simple wooden rails. Naturally, the older markers are of wood.

Moving from plot to plot one can pay respects to the memory of many a familiar name. Here lies Ellen Harper May. Nearby is the grave of her first husband, Charles Lukens Harper, builder extraordinary for the community, creator of bridges and barns. Markers bear the names of Tannahill, Woodruff, Longfellow, Crocker and James, so tolerant of the complexities of his Indian neighbors. Under a slim stone shaft lie the four children of Colwell Owens Drew, victims of the terrible diphtheria epidemic of 1879. One can imagine the disappointment of the family when the monument proved too slender even for the short inscription they had planned, but the stone mason did his best with the space provided:

"Earth counts 4 mortals l's
Heaven 4 angels more."

The family, crushed beyond bearing, left their high mountain home and moved to Chinese Camp.

The Repetto family is buried here, reminiscent of the days of '49; also many of the Mecarteas. The dates spread over the passing of a century and the names range from unknown miners to Charles and Fred Schmidt of Second Garrote, brother companions who died in 1953 within forty-eight days of one another and on whose graves during our last visit the flowers were fresh.

In spring this is a hushed and peaceful spot sheltered by black-trunked oaks with foliage of a glossy, living green; clustered with fairy lanterns and mariposa lilies. Pine scented breezes from the forested peaks make it a happy and uplifting place of serene memories. These pioneers founded an era; saw it through and some of them outlived it. They have their places in the very foundations of our state.

A reunion of Big Oak Flat Road '49ers. Top row, left to right: George F. Culbertson of Moccasin, Nathan Screech of First Garrote, Barna Fox of Big Oak Flat, Jack Bell, and Caspar Cook. Lower row, left to right: James A. Chaffie of Second Garrote, Jason P. Chamberlain of Second Garrote, James Ballentine, Tom Maxey, who participated in the first Indian trouble in Big Oak Flat during Savage's time (Savage's Diggings), and Winslow Hubbard.

Chamberlain and Chaffie at their mine near
Second Garrote, 1898.

James A. Chaffie and Jason P. Chamberlain at home, Second Garrote, 1892.

CHAPTER VIII

THE GARROTES—FIRST AND SECOND

In considering the history and problems of the Garrotes, one asks, quite naturally, why should there have been a First and a Second and why should the First, in a modest moment, have re-christened itself Groveland?

The last-named settlement had its beginnings in 1849. The earliest permanent building was an adobe trading post established by a Frenchman known as Raboul. In July of the same year a couple of men, said to be Mexican, stole some gold dust said to amount to $200. It is impossible to be positive in this incident—that is, up to the lynching which was both positive and irrevocable. To kill a man, the miners reasoned, might be justifiable; to steal from him was not. So they picked a fine oak tree growing conveniently near the trading post and the hanging took place thereupon. The camp was promptly dubbed "Garrote," the Spanish term for death by choking or hanging, and through the years the word has retained a Spanish cast to its pronunciation.

Shortly afterward it seems probable that history repeated itself on another fine oak tree in another settlement some two miles southeast. The scene of the second un-blessed event was called Second Garrote. This necessitated that the hanging having priority be recognized and, instead of plain "Garrote," the first camp became known as "Garrote I"[1] or "First Garrote."

The hanging at Second Garrote has been questioned and two of our most reliable sources of information differ. Both are entirely thoughtful and honest in their decision; both give the facts as they have been handed down to them. It will be taken up in its place in this narrative.[2]

167

The settlement of First Garrote bore that title, or was called simply Garrote, until the middle '70s when the more conservative of the population began to think that, as an address, the name might be just a bit lacking in gentility. At the suggestion of Benjamin Savory it was changed to Groveland in honor of the town in Massachusetts from which he came. Many of the inhabitants heartily approved. Many did not. The Sonora *Union Democrat*, in an issue of January, 1875, offered this disparaging criticism: "Among the recent orders issued by the Postoffice Department at Washington is one changing the name of the Garrote Postoffice to Groveland. Garrote is not a very pretty name, and has unpleasant associations, yet for all that the pioneers of Tuolumne County will stick to it and call Jim Tannahill's post-office Garrote whether the government likes it or not." A prophecy which some of the old-timers fulfill to this day.

When the Frenchman, Raboul, built his adobe trading post as a nucleus around which the settlement of First Garrote was destined to grow, he started a long-term business; for the building, known for many years as Cassaretto's store and now as the Red and White Grocery, is still busy at the old stand.

A word picture depicting some of the scenes in the family store was given to us by Mr. Frank Cassaretto: During the days when more gold dust than coin of the realm was taken over the counter, Louis Cassaretto was doing a thriving business and had a large Indian custom from the Miwok Rancheria in Deer Flat. "The Indian trade was mainly in staples," said Mr. Cassaretto, "especially sugar. They would come into the store with their gold dust and make a bee line for the sugar barrel. They would even work to get it. That was one sure way that the pioneer women could get much-needed help. My mother could get a heavy washing done for fifty cents worth of sugar.

"The Indians were usually quiet but the miners from the hills would come into town for Sunday and spend the day drinking and gambling. Then they'd get boisterous and come into the store to make trouble. One day father got thoroughly disgusted; picked up a weight from the scales and threw it, hit or miss, at the bunch of them. It 'hit' all right and the man it connected with was out for three hours. After that he didn't have so much trouble."

Mrs. Louis Cassaretto, who was Adelina Bruschi of Coulterville, was typical of other early day wives and mothers. It was imperative that they have help for the multiplicity of daily tasks and by far the most accessible source of unskilled labor was each housewife's own older children. In talking with the men and women who were born in the '60s along the Mother Lode it becomes noticeable that, as lads and girls, they have done practically everything from riding with the sheriff's posse to laying out the dead for burial. The picture of self-reliance is amazing. Mother and father simply couldn't do everything; the Indians were lazy and unwilling; so the children were kept at it until the tasks were done. Every single member of the family had his responsibilities—even the four-year-old.

The family took its pleasures together also. There were no baby sitters. If, by any chance, a neighbor's daughter was helping out as "hired girl," no one questioned her right to go to the dances and picnics and the children who were old enough to take care of the younger ones wanted to go too. So everybody went.

This family solidarity in work and play included father, mother and the younger children. As the boys grew to a man's strength at fifteen or sixteen, their chosen employments, teamster, stage-driver, guide, Wells, Fargo & Co. messenger, miner, etc., threw them out into grave, often terrible situations where they could look to no one for help. Between the ages of fourteen and twenty the girls usually married and, from then on, they faced whatever of danger childbirth had to offer without doctor or hospital care.

Childhood ended early, but the parent pair were a pair until death.

These children of the '60s, now grown old, remember with affection the schoolhouse at the edge of town which was known through decades of its existence as the "Big Oak Flat School." The earlier schoolhouse serving Big Oak Flat stood for just a few years near the top of the divide between the two towns. It was soon discontinued. By an uncommon spirit of reciprocity Groveland, which had no church, attended Mount Carmel in its neighbor town and the children of Big Oak Flat and even of Priest's Hill trudged to Groveland to school. In modern times Big Oak Flat has a school of its own and the Groveland institution is called by its rightful name.

John Gamble was the early day teacher, an unusually tall and powerful man with a black spade beard, who did not hesitate to use his fists if necessary to keep order. He was succeeded by his daughter, Lucy; his son taught the school at Stevens' Bar, so among them the Gamble family trained much of the countryside. There are men and women who can still remember Lucy Gamble sitting atop of a cast iron stool with a horsehair cushion—minus, in the later days, every vestige of horsehair—while the small organ vibrated heroically to the Battle Hymn of the Republic.

Mrs. Thomas Reid, lately deceased, was an accepted source of accurate information on the county's early history. She was born in Groveland and, with the exception of one short visit out of state, lived continuously in this, her chosen town, for over ninety years. She was an exceptionally tall, slender woman, sweet-faced and gracious; had seen the better part of a century of excitement in the Mother Lode and remembered a surprising amount.

One day she was induced to talk to us of old times. "There was a period," she said, "during the fading out of the gold fever when the mining communities were rather rough. I think it partly coincided with the high feeling over the Civil War. As a rule it didn't touch the women, though. They had enough to do without being out very much. A tragic affair happened in the first store. Mr. Raboul still owned it. My father could remember the excitement in town. You know almost every place sold liquor in those days and men were apt to meet and drink together. Several men were standing talking, and after awhile one of them turned around and invited everyone in the store to come up to the bar and drink with him. One of the men waiting at the counter for his groceries happened to be colored and the man who was treating gathered him in with the rest and wouldn't take no for an answer. Then a gambler from the South, named Andy Hunter, made a big scene and shouted that he wouldn't drink with a 'nigger' and pulled a bowie knife. The colored man moved away. He didn't want trouble but Hunter kept right after him. He backed him against the wall and there they were. Hunter had the knife high in the air when the Negro clutched the hand that was gripped around the handle. He was a powerful man and fighting for his life. The hand came down but he had forced it around so that it was away from him. When the other men rushed over Hunter still gripped the knife handle but the blade was buried in his own body. It was he who was dead."

The gentle woman who had taken Garrote for better or for worse since Civil War days thought about the incident for a moment with apparent serenity and then added, "Nobody did anything more about it. There was no need to."

Questioned about her family she said, "My father, Martin Jones, came here in '52. Four years later when, at twenty-seven, he got married he built a frame house about a mile northeast of town and lived and died in it. Mother was Margaret McCarty and was heir to a large estate in Ireland but it made no difference in her life as a pioneer. She was married at sixteen and had eleven children without being attended by a doctor and not one of them weighed less than twelve pounds at birth. Father was a farmer, freighter and cattleman. There was always plenty to do around the place.

"My husband's father was Thomas C. Reid and he came around the Horn in '49. He and several others bought a ship called the *Velasco* on the east coast and, after they got to San Francisco, were fortunate enough to sell it to a party that wished to return. My husband was Thomas R. Reid. He was born in Garrote in '56 and, when he was thirteen, worked as a guide with the mule train that took tourists into Yosemite. After the telegraph line came through in '75 he was the operator here in town with an office in the Savory Hotel.

"Just before we were married my husband bought the Savory Hotel and we ran it three years. It was the first one in Garrote and was built in 1852 by Otis Perrin and Dr. J. L. Cogswell, one of the other owners of the ship that brought Mr. Reid to California. They called it the Washington Hotel. After about ten years they sold it to Albert Snow who re-sold it quickly to a French woman called Elizabeth Bottleier. She married Ben Savory and the name was changed to Savory Hotel sometime in the early '70s.

"It was just an ordinary mountain hotel," she went on. "The boarders were mostly miners. No woman or child ever set foot in the bar. In fact, I was well along in years before I was ever in company where I saw a woman take a drink of liquor. The Savory was torn down years ago. It stood across the road from Tannahill's store. Next we bought the Groveland Hotel. It was the second built in town, about '53 or '54. The builder's name was George Reid but he was no relative of ours. He sold it to Matthew Foote who ran it awhile in the '70s. There were other proprietors too, I think, J. D. Meyer for one. But we bought it in 1884. We didn't keep it long. My husband thought that operating a hotel in those days was too hard for a woman.

"The original Thomas C. Reid adobe house still stands just out of town and the orchard trees bear fruit. My son's name is Thomas also. For over one hundred years now," Mrs. Reid finished with some pride, "there has been a Thomas Reid in Groveland."

After the era of the placer mines much of the town's ready cash came from the payroll of the Mount Jefferson Mine on a hill just north of Mrs. Reid's house. Old-timers remember with a smile the white-faced sorrel horse whose responsibility it was to bring the ore from the opening of the mine shaft down to the crushing mill. This he did without benefit of anyone's advice, picking his way to the bottom, waiting with one ear cocked while the man in attendance dumped his load and then, slowly, making his way up the hill for more. He transported many thousands of dollars worth of ore, seemingly with a fair amount of pride in his job. The faithful (and unsalaried) animal took the place of several men who had previously brought the ore down in wheelbarrows held back by a sort of breeching strap around each man's shoulders.

Groveland, being well up into the mountains, was especially dependent upon its freighting business and particularly proud of the Garrote Teamsters—local ranchers and cattlemen with their sons, many of whom drove Egling wagons made in the Chinese Camp wheelwright shop. The list included: John and Michael Phelan, Daniel and Sylvester Carlon, John Sheehan, John Corcoran, Charles Schmidt Sr., and Jr., Robert Simmons Sr., and Jr., Martin Jones and son, Eugene, Daniel and William Sullivan, Dick

Meyer, Herman Gerken, John Hughes, Frank Goodnow, George Boitano and sons, George Pratt, George S. Brown, and others.

Teaming, as a business, overlapped the placer mining era in the Mother Lode and outlasted it.

Here, as in other places, the placers were soon worked out but the quartz mining paid well and kept the town full of hardrock men on Sundays clear into the '70s when the deep mines commenced to fade. By '77 Groveland was reduced to a population of about 100 rattling around in a settlement designed and built for many more. Two periods of rejuvenation came to all the mining communities, caused by the advent of modern machinery and the more favorable price of gold. In the case of Groveland the temporary prosperity of the short mining booms was materially assisted by the fact that beginning in 1915, the town was headquarters for much of the business connected with the building of the O'Shaughnessy Dam at Hetch Hetchy and that the Hetch Hetchy Railroad rendered it easily accessible for the duration of the project.

Groveland, being the supply center for a large back country, has not been in danger of fading into a ghost town at any period and now the constant increase of automobile tourists has brought a steady flow of outside money across the counters of the stores first patronized by the miners with their native gold dust.

* * *

Groveland's oldest structure is a cabin built in 1849 by Peter King, a miner. Around it has been built a two-story wooden house boasting an upper and lower balcony. King used both schist rock and adobe as you can see if you stoop to pry into the matter, for part of the old wall is visible under the back porch. Later Mr. Sheehan bought the property and added a second story which the Odd Fellows used for awhile as a lodge room. When the Mount

Jefferson Mine was producing, Sheehan's served as a boarding house for miners and was called the Elite Hotel.

The old trading post is at present known as the Red and White Grocery and saw the beginnings of business in Garrote. Recent alterations uncovered an adobe brick showing the imprint of a dog's foot and the date, 1849. The builder, Raboul, sold the business to Mr. Luigi Noziglia who operated a grocery and married into the Cassaretto family. In the course of a generation or two it became known as the Cassaretto store and retained that name through much of the town's history. Here came the Miwoks trading gold dust for broken chunks of sugar. Here the gambler, Hunter, died—stabbed by his own knife. This place more than any other has seen life in Garrote. Here the distribution of food has never ceased in one hundred years.

A sidewalk now runs in front of Hotel Charlotte and ends abruptly at the eastern wall of the building. Just beyond its termination, in any alley, stood the tree on which took place the hanging that so felicitously endowed Garrote with a name. When wheeled vehicles took the place of pack trains the tree was taken down and the stump sawed flat—even with the surface of the ground. Anna Reid remembered vividly running over the hard wooden circle as a child on her way to the store. It splintered after awhile and became a nuisance, so it was dug out and the hole filled in with earth. But somewhere down below the tread of work-a-day feet are the rotted roots of Garrote's historic oak.

Across the street is the "Iron Door." It is a bar now, squeezed into a row of buildings, but at one time was the Tannahill store where, for some years, that important pioneer family lived in the rear portion. Beside this business James Tannahill had large mining interests and nothing of moment took place in Garrote without his freely bestowed help.

The adobe butcher shop, owned for years in the past by Salvador Ferretti and in the upper story of which the Odd Fellows held lodge, is nearly opposite the Charlotte Hotel but often stands unoccupied.

The Groveland Hotel is conspicuous at the eastern end of the business section. Just beyond it, to the left and even with the road, is the low house, almost buried in vines and shade trees, which Mrs. Martin Jones built and occupied after the death of her husband. It is now the property of a son-in-law, John De Martini.

In less than a half mile two county roads come in from the north in quick succession. The first leads past the ancient frame house where Martin Jones raised his family, past the Thomas C. Reid adobe built in 1857 and various ranches. The second goes to the site of the Miwok rancheria on Big Creek, deserted long ago, which is on the property of A. B. McLellan and R. D. Dunn. It leads also to the old G. B. Boitano adobe rapidly disintegrating on the modern Gookin Ranch.

A mile from the edge of Groveland, under flowering locusts, are the remains of the Mueller (or Muller) Brewery—a famous and popular place in its day. Ferdinand Stachler built it in 1853. Twelve years later he sold it to Eugene Mueller who made and delivered ale to all the neighboring camps and even sent pack mule trains over ill-famed Bloody Canyon Trail to Bodie, east of the Sierra Nevada. The ale was in casks swung on each side of the mules and, should an animal get into loose rock at the trail's edge, there was little chance for rescue. The casks burst at the bottom of the precipice and caused a scandalous state of affairs among the otherwise sedate trout in the stream.

While the brewery was in operation long tables were set up where travelers might eat their lunches while enjoying steins of Mueller's best. The east end, or rear, of the building was constructed out of rock by Stachler. A big wooden portion with wide front doors was Mueller's contribution and was made of native timber with a heavy shake roof. Deep shade from drooping trees added to the enjoyment with which the customers consumed per-ambulatory mugs of ale while trying to walk the soreness out of backs and legs. Neither a stage nor a saddle trip was luxurious.

When Eugene Mueller died his brewery ceased to function and the farmers of the vicinity stopped raising barley. The only re-maining token of the business is the great kettle, bereft of its shelter and exposed to the elements. The vine-covered house close by was built by Mrs. Mueller after her husband's death. The present owner lives there and attempts, with the cooperation of the traveling public, to preserve what remains of the historic old ruin.

Second Garrote was the most easterly settlement of the mining area served by the Big Oak Flat Road. There were mines flung haphazard among the mountains farther to the east but not of sufficient importance to promote a town, and even Second Garrote had but three mines of any note: the Mexican, the Big Betsy and the Kanaka. Second Garrote Creek, however, boasted several arras-tras among its clustering azaleas.

The place was always small. The pay dirt really paid but there wasn't much of it.

Early in the history of Second Garrote its two most prominent citizens arrived in a two-wheeled cart, the only type of vehicle that could make its way along the as yet unimproved pack trail and to which they clung for the span of their long lives. We are assured, however, that these two citizens, although unassuming, did not arrive without fanfare of a sort as the cart could always be heard squeaking and groaning for a mile along the grade.

The two were young men. James Chaffee was about thirty, Jason

Chamberlain, twenty-eight. They had come around the Horn together in '49 and for two years had worked here and there in California, but at Second Garrote, the naturally beautiful little depression between the hills struck their fancy and held it. They were not changeable men. Around the sloping sides of the hollow, Miwok women squatted at the grinding holes preparing acorn meal while their solemn-eyed babies, hung from low branches nearby, watched contentedly. It was a scene of peaceful and pleasant activity. The partners never left it and the Miwoks became their devoted friends.

Neither placer mine nor shaft yielded enough to pay for full time effort but the two men did carpentering on the side and raised fruit and melons which they divided with the Indians. Apparently they were always known as "Chaffee and Chamberlain," in that order, and were greatly respected and loved by their neighbors; but their chief claim to general fame is the fact that their lifelong, faithful comradeship was the basis for Bret Harte's short sketch, "Tennessee's Partner."

This well publicized fact is hard to reconcile with the circumstance that none of the sordid details of the story match the facts of their blameless lives.

Chamberlain in his reminiscence wrote in explanation: "In 1866 Bret Harte was connected with the *Overland Monthly* & we had a friend & old partner that was secretary of the company. Bret Harte told our friend he was going to write a story and call it Tennessee's Partner Our friend said he knew a character that would just fill the bill for Tennessee's Partner & when Chaffee went to the City a year ago he was introduced by our friend as Tennessee's partner & was a big surprise to the partner as he never had heard anything about the matter before."

As Bret Harte became famous the partners grew very proud of this distinction.

So much the first citizens of Second Garrote were Jason Chamberlain and James Chaffee, that in the course of time, their words constituted full authority for all local history. The moot question of whether anyone was ever garroted at Second Garrote hangs, then, on their statement and, confusingly enough, two conflicting versions have come down from them to us.

The immediate sources of the contradictory statements are so impeccable that it leaves us no alternative than to believe that the two gentle old men changed their story after many years; probably without realizing that they had done so.

It was a constant irritation to them that the great oak on their property should be made an object of cheap curiosity by exaggerated legends. One, Ned McGowan, a stage driver, delighted in regaling his box-seat passengers with horrific tales. He once prepared two signs stating that seven men had been hanged from this tree, and nailed them on either side of a projecting limb. Mr. Chamberlain, usually the executive member of the two-some, then intercepted the stage in a state of high indignation and warned McGowan to remove his "cheap commercialism" from his (Mr. Chamberlain's) property.

It would be rather natural, after years of contradicting such unwelcome sensationalism, that they should lean toward denying altogether anything sordid in connection with their beloved home. At any rate that is just what they did. As they grew older they became more positive. A statement written by Chamberlain in the '70s is rather mild.[3] A similar statement written in 1901 (the year of his 80th birthday) expresses no doubt at all ". . . Second Garrote . . . had no reason to be called by that horrid name, for never a man was hung there in the world."

Mrs. Reid remembered that they gave that same denial to her husband. However, to the men who knew them when they were younger they had sometimes told the story of a lynching that had happened before their arrival. We heard it first from the Curtin family. Then, while looking up legal documents, we found in the archives of the museum at Yosemite a statement giving exactly the same incident in much the same wording and prefaced by the information that the writer had been told the story "by both the old gentlemen." The statement is signed by Paul Morris of Chinese Camp, one of the most highly respected men in the county in his day.[4] In brief it reads as follows: It was early in the Gold Rush. The Southern Mines were booming. The miners had begun to use sluice boxes. Water taken from Second Garrote Creek was allowed to run through them all night and they made their clean-up in the morning. The camp had always been honest and no one thought anything about the risk. Two or three dishonest men, observing the routine, decided to get there first some morning. They did so and were making a clean sweep of the accumulated gold dust when they were seen by two early risers. Unfortunately for everyone, during the ensuing melee, the early risers were shot. The criminals were caught and hanged at once by the enraged men of the camp. The statement is clean-cut and definite.

This is a perfectly usual affair to have happened, say, at the end of '49 or beginning of '50. As many towns along this road had lynchings, during that unsettled period before the law arrived, as did not have them.

Everyone is entitled to his or her own opinion, but the name, Second Garrote, is hard to explain away. We think it was well earned.

There is a modern trend toward calling the settlement "Bret Harte" and, in an effort to find out if the famous author had ever been there we divided between us a whole carton of diaries kept by Jason Chamberlain and read the story of their daily living from the time they drove up the mountain in their creaking cart to the day of the survivor's death. There was no mention of seeing the famous writer. Afterward we learned that he had never met Chamberlain.

He did his characterization from a distance, and we are grateful both to him and to them for a splendid bit of color in the mosaic of western literature. But it was not intended to be mistaken for history.

* * *

One does not enter Second Garrote on the old pack and cart trail of 1849. It wound along with the creek in the bottom of the hollow, and we were told that the grass along its course turns yellow faster than elsewhere because the earth is so packed.

In the uproarious beginnings of the settlement, a fandango house stood at the left and (quoting Charlie Schmidt) the men came down from the mountains "like ants—and had a time for themselves." Cochran's flour mill was on the right. A branch road leads up the hill to the garden-inclosed rambling home of the Schmidt brothers who lived here all their lives and died here in 1953. The main road passes beneath the shade of the blasted, arthritic-limbed giant now called "Hangman's Oak." Just across the highway from it lived the partners.

When Chaffee and Chamberlain erected their home they did not live on the main thoroughfare. Just when the road was moved so that it passed in front of their door is not clear, but by later staging days it did so. The partners were good carpenters and did not intend to live in a cabin. They built a house, quite a masterpiece. It was meant to (and did) last a hundred years.

Mrs. Robert Morse, who owns both the partners' house and the neighboring store, has managed to keep it in repair without unseemly patches or the use of new material and it has not been easy. The ceiling of their parlor was made of eight inch boards and had rounded wooden beading to cover the cracks. Mrs. Morse can show the wooden "grouter" used by the two men in turning out this architectural flourish.

They made their furniture too, and lived to wear it out most enjoyably. The mantel and shelves are jammed with old gadgets from the everyday life of the settlement and of the mines. Many of them were added in the later years of the partners' lives as earlier pictures show a more barren background; but the last pictures of the two old gentlemen sitting in this room show that they kept it gunnels awash with just such items.

Second Garrote was the scene of another lifelong comradeship and no doubt it was somewhat influenced by the memory of the famous partners. The brothers, Fred and Charles Schmidt, whose hilltop home is passed on entering the little community, were neighbors of Chaffee and Chamberlain. They were freighters and, for a time, Charles drove Mueller's brewery wagon.

At one of our many talks with them they sat on the shady porch where, through a century, the view has changed from pack-trains to stages and freighters and then to automobiles—all ascending Second Garrote Hill. Immediately in front of the vine-covered house was an inclosed garden full of tall, lusty flowers. Holly-hocks and golden glow elbowed each other away from the gate; a grape arbor shaded the walk. Split rail fences formed corrals around the blackened barn which shelters an Egling wagon. The first section of the house was built by a German miner named Kraft who had preëmpted Squatters' Rights on the property. Mr. Schmidt, Sr., bought it from him and enlarged it for his growing family of five sons and two daughters. The barn was built later, in 1862. Mina Schmidt, a daughter, married John C. McLaughlin, brother of Ellen Harper May. The early-day families were often connected by marriage.

In reply to a request Fred Schmidt told us of "Tennessee and his Partner." "We lived close to them," he said, "as you can see plainly enough; and, in those days, to be a neighbor really meant something. As boys we were in and out of their house day after day. They divided up their work, each one to do what he liked best. And they had a common purse. It was worth while to raise vegetables and melons and to cook and keep things straight because there were two of them to enjoy everything. Even after they were eighty years old they used to get good Christmas dinners and invite in the other '49ers. But finally," he went on, "Chaffee got sick. They took him to the hospital and he died. Chamberlain was alone. My brother Charlie had gone hunting and it was late in the afternoon. I walked onto Chamberlain's porch and there he sat with his head about shot off. The muzzle of the gun rested against his chin and stood between his legs. He had tied a string from the trigger to his toe and that's the way he shot himself. God, how I ran home!"

"I was back by that time," Charlie added, "and we got an undertaker from Sonora. There were only two months and a half between their buryings, but I was always sorry they weren't buried beside each other in the place they had picked out."

We never saw the Schmidt Brothers together again. Charles, who was 89 years of age, died and Fred mourned him for a little over a month before death claimed him also. "I just walk to the barn and then back to the house," he said, "but what's the use? Charlie isn't either place."

But two weeks later he took a longer journey to find him. As Bret Harte phrased it in the last line of Tennessee's Partner, "And so they met."

There must be some unusual quality in the air of Second Garrote—some element of love and fidelity. It is so quiet, nestled

in its hollow, so peaceful and unchanged! Weathered grey buildings, gnarled old oak, wobbling rail fences and fruitful corn
patches remain serene, while all around it climb the ever-lasting
mountains topped with pointing pines.

CHAPTER IX

ABOVE THE SETTLEMENTS

In freighting days one of the sections of road most frequently damned was known as Second Garrote Hill and, starting near the creek, led up and out of that inconsiderable settlement. Drivers considered it almost as bad as Moccasin Hill and added an extra span of horses to the stage before attempting it.

Near the summit of the modern grade the Golden Rock Ditch crosses the road and may be seen, perfectly dry, following the contours of the mountain. A short drive, over the crest of the hill and down a slighter slope, brings one to Sugar Pine Ranch.

The first settler built a cabin here in the '60s. He was called John Ratto. About 25 years later a French gentleman named Peri bought the land and planted at least some of the fruit trees. Between 1900 and 1902 two men from Boston, Benjamin Shaw and Lester Wiley, obtained the place from Mr. Peri and organized the Yosemite Power Company in order to use the greatly deteriorated ditch facilities of the Golden Rock Water Company. They built the present large white house as headquarters and apparently lived there also. For over a decade it was the scene of many a festivity. Mr. Wiley, who seems to have been the general manager, ceased operations about 1917 and the power company was abandoned but the Shaw family remained some twenty years longer. Two other owners made successive improvements. Then, in 1946, it was sold to Mr. and Mrs. Wesley Osborne.

They cleared out an amazing number of account books dating back to the 1860s; made the second floor over into bedrooms and built attractive cabins to act as a ranch-motel. Between hotel and cabins, bridged for easy crossing, runs the ditch. Between hotel

185

and highway ran the original Big Oak Flat Road. This is an excellent place to see both.

Down the highway just beyond the inn is the Church of Christ— a box-like rectangle with a red roof. It is on Mr. Osborne's land; he built it himself and officiates each Sunday. The traveler passing by during church services will find the road practically blocked with cars.

The orchard to the east of Sugar Pine Ranch was once part of the Watson acreage and, beyond it, was the Gravel Range School which educated 10 to 25 scholars.

Big Creek, fragrant with azaleas, flows north at the foot of the hill, crossing the highway and meandering off through its heavily wooded canyon. Manzanita grows to such size and in such profusion that signs designate the vicinity as "Manzanita Area." A rough and inadvisable road breaks away to the south going to Hell's Hollow. Investigation along its dusty miles discloses a saw mill and some nice stretches of the old ditch. Along the highway, one-half mile from its junction with Hell's Hollow Road, is a fine meadow. At first it was known as Sprague's Ranch and appears as such in *Scenes of Wonder and Curiosity in California,* by J. M. Hutchings, 1871. John B. Smith then homesteaded the flat and became George E. Sprague's partner. Smith's large two-storied frame house stood exactly where the the modern house is today, separated from the road by a picket fence. The open meadow is bordered with cone-shaped pines and cedars. The dominating feature is still a large and ancient barn which held the relays of stage horses, for Smith's was a change station and boarded the hostlers. When the Big Oak Flat Road Company was organized, construction started at this point and the first toll gate was temporarily located here.

Curving past the barn a crossroad leads south six miles to historic

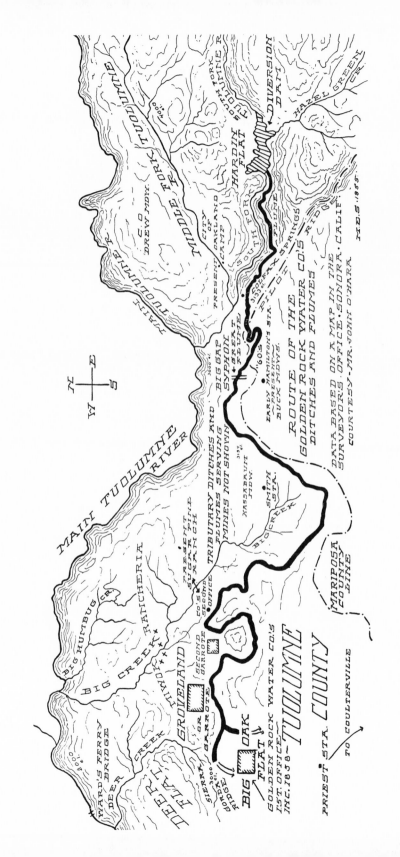

Dudley Station on the Coulterville Road where lives Mr. W. D. McLean, grandson of Hosea E. and Fanny Dudley, the founders of the station.

Smith's Flat, at about 3000 feet elevation, is gay in springtime but is too low for summer wild flowers. Across the hills to the north lies what was Charles Kassabaum's Meadow. Both are favored spots for deer. At dawn and dusk they may be seen grazing where formerly hay was harvested for the stage horses.

John Smith came to California in 1854 and eventually his wife, Charlotte, came out to join him with the son who was born in Maine the year that his father left for the west. Young John was seventeen and had never seen his father. A daughter, Mary, was born at Smith's Flat some years later. She became Mary Smith Lindsey of Stockton.

Smith's was one of the first of the isolated ranches above the settlements. In the summer they had overnight lodgings for stage passengers and served hot meals. Few of the travelers made any impression on a small girl but Mary never forgot Theodore Roosevelt. They also had a steady clientele among cattlemen, sheepmen and teamsters.

Winters were very lonely.

"When the snow fell," Mrs. Lindsey said, "there was no travel on the road and we were often shut in for weeks. When I was about ten the Gravel Range School was built and mother didn't have to hear my lessons while she sewed as she had always done before. Beside myself the Sutton, Meyer, Watson, Boitano and Hobron families attended.

"We had many pleasures. I remember going with my father to cut the snow-piled Christmas tree. I remember the red-throated linnets in the lilacs. And most of all I remember the great ten-horse freight wagons in front of the house which, twice a year, brought supplies all the way from Stockton.

"When I was thirteen father died.

"Mr. Sprague had sold his interest in the property to father and now he deeded an extra 160 acres to mother. So for a long time," Mrs. Lindsey concluded, "the place was known simply as 'Smith's Flat'."

The Flat was afterward sold to the Cassaretto family and had also other owners but was eventually purchased by Warren Burch who is still in possession so that, after the logical manner of the mountains, it is now called "Burch's" by most of the passers-by.

Just one mile from Smith's a dirt road leads north to the Lumsden bridge over the main Tuolumne River and goes on to the Jawbone country and to Cherry Creek Pack Station. The original covered bridge at this point, as well as several other bridges, trails and flumes, were constructed by James Lumsden and his brother, David. They were the sons of James and Clarissa Lumsden who settled in 1859 at Boneyard. It was never a village—just a small section on the connecting road between Priest's Station and Coulterville. James Lumsden, the younger, lived in Groveland for nearly sixty years and raised eight sons and a daughter. The brothers are best remembered as the pair who carved out the tunnel tree in Tuolumne Grove in 1878.

* * *

Somewhere in this stretch, between Smith's Flat and Hamilton's (Buck's Meadows), tradition has it that Nate Screech and his Indian helpmate set up permanent housekeeping.

The three Screech brothers, Joseph, Nathan and William, were well-known personages in the early days of the Southern Mines and hung out in the neighborhood of the Garrotes. They were always more notable as mountaineers than as miners and Joe has long been credited with the discovery of Hetch Hetchy, the fabulous companion valley to Yosemite and which lies to its northwest.

It seems almost useless to throw a monkey wrench into the smoothly revolving wheels of recorded history, but Alex Tannahill signed a written statement that the first discoverer was not Joe but Nate; and Alex Tannahill constituted the best informed and most creditable connecting link between the Screech brothers and posterity.

Tannahill has been dead many years but fortunately we have an authorized person to speak for him. Celia Crocker Thompson of Lodi was a close friend of Cordelia Tannahill, his sister, and was always a favorite guest in their house. In 1935 she asked that he write the story of the discovery of Hetch Hetchy Valley and received the following reply; which, as you will note in reading it, is the story told in the first person by Nate Screech and remembered later by Alex Tannahill:

"Once when I was hunting deer and bear in the high Sierras I saw about four or five miles ahead of me a very high mountain and as I had lots of time that particular day I put in the afternoon climbing to the top and after getting on top I had a wonderful view of the surrounding country, especially a passage way of the Tuolumne River from the San Joaquin Plains to far into the Sierra Nevadas and following a deep cut through which the river flowed was surprised to see a wide cut in the mountains that looked like it might be a deep wide valley although I could not see the bottom land or the river from where I was on the peak I had climbed. On getting home I asked the Indian chief the name of the valley and he said Nate there is no valley. It is only a cut in the hills through which the Tuolumne River runs but if you think there might be a valley keep looking and if you find such a place I will give it to you. The old chief claimed all the territory in that neighborhood.

"After hunting a couple of years I finally found the valley and entered it from the lower end and walked up toward the center and faced the Indian chief and his wives. He was surprised a little and said to his women pack up we are leaving. I promised this to Nate when he found it. To me he said I am keeping my promise to you. The valley is yours."

Mr. Tannahill's letter to Mrs. Thompson then continued in his own words: "Nate lived with an Indian woman and had a child by her named Jane, who when about 17 years old went to work at Savories Hotel . . .

"That's the way one valley was found. Who do they claim found it? also the Yosemite?

"I have written what Nate Screech told me of the discovery of Hetch Hetchy Valley as nearly as I can remember it. Ask the mother[1] if it checks with what she knows about it.

[Signed] Alex Tannahill."

Mrs. Thompson, born Celia Crocker, lived before her marriage at Crocker Station near the boundary of Yosemite National Park. Fortunately she always had a flair for interviewing and photographing the early pioneers of her vicinity. Her father gave her a good camera while she was still very young, and her interest never flagged. She developed the plates herself, washing them all night in the pure, running waters of Rush Creek, and they are still in perfect condition, completely captioned and indexed. Beside this collection she has several large scrapbooks of the newspaper clippings of her girlhood. The authors are indebted to her beyond measure for the use of these irreplaceable sources of information.

On being asked what she thought about the credibility of the statement from Mr. Tannahill, Mrs. Thompson replied readily that he was one of the leading citizens of the county, very reliable and remembered the past perfectly at the time the letter was written. She called attention to another item that adds credence to the theory that it was Nate who first glimpsed Hetch Hetchy. It was known to the Crockers (for whom he worked) and all up and down the Big Oak Flat Road that it was Nate who had the Indian wife.

A few more succulent morsels, discovered at odd times, may be stirred into the medley like raisins in a pudding. It would be just as much a pudding without them, but they add interest. Charles Schmidt of Second Garrote remembered the story of the naming of Hetch Hetchy Valley told to him by Alex Tannahill. When the discoverer finally obtained his first view of the valley floor, some Indians were camped there. It was not clear from his account whether these were the old chief and his wives or others. They were cooking a variety of grass covered with edible seeds. Screech spoke their language and asked what they were preparing. The answer was "hatch hatchy"—sometimes spelled "atch atchy" according to the hearer's idea of the sound. This chance occurrence, so various informants say, was destined to provide the lovely mountain valley with a name; and some of the old-timers, including the Schmidt brothers, continued to give that name the broader sound instead of the predominant "Hetch Hetchy" into which it has resolved.

Another bit was provided by James Ackerson whose meadows lay southwest of Hetch Hetchy. He told that *Joe* Screech and two others made the first visit *into* the valley and that he, himself, accompanied them on their second trip.

A simple explanation would be that both Joe and Nate Screech, with one other—possibly their brother, Bill, made up this first party of three; and that this was the occasion when Nate succeeded in his plan to visit the tempting valley glimpsed months before and searched for so long.

After the initial visit it was Joe Screech whose name became identified with that of Hetch Hetchy. It was he who cleared and blazed the trail to Hetch Hetchy later used by sheep and cattle men with their stock. J. D. Whitney states in *The Yosemite Book*, published in 1868, "This trail was made by Mr. Joseph Screech, and is well blazed and has been used for driving sheep and cattle into the Valley. The whole distance from Big Oak Flat is called 38 miles. Mr. Screech first visited the place in 1850, at which time the Indians had possession. The Pah Utes still visit it every year for the purpose of getting the acorns, having driven out the western slope Indians, just as they did from Yosemite."

* * *

South of Smith Meadow and consequently off the Big Oak Flat Road Douglas Hobron ran a mill almost entirely supplied by Smith's timber.

Beyond the Stanislaus National Forest Ranger Station .4 of a mile and on the north side of the road was the sawmill belonging to Caleb Dorsey, an early-day lawyer who had the peculiar distinction of representing Joaquin Murieta at court in one or two small matters—the same man who later identified the latter's controversial head. Dorsey had business interests spread about the county but lived and maintained an office in the county seat at Sonora. His mill was powered by a wheel run by water from the Golden Rock Ditch and sawed the lumber for the high flume which Mr. Smith then hauled with an ox-team.

The maneuvers of the county line will bear watching hereabouts. By reason of a bend in the watershed which the line follows, the highway at this point travels a couple of miles in Mariposa County.

Two miles beyond Dorsey's sawmill site another crossroad takes off for the Coulterville Road. Many privately drawn vehicles on the Big Oak Flat Road took a detour along this crossroad because there was a short period of time when they could avoid toll on both turnpikes and intersect their original road at Crane Flat; the Big Oak Flat toll gate being a few miles east at Elwell's and later at the South Fork of the Tuolumne and the Coulterville gate at Big Meadows far below Hazel Green. Later on it was changed to the latter place and thus in no way could toll be avoided by travelers on either route. This accounts for the fact that Bower Cave on the Coulterville Road is so often mentioned by early day travelers.

The circumstances under which the cave was named seem to be worth recounting: William Ralston, junior partner in the banking house of Fretz and Ralston, married Lizzie Fry in San Francisco. The whole wedding party was of the socially elect and a large part of the group accompanied the bride and groom on the Stockton boat. At Benicia many returned but a party of thirteen continued on their way to a "honeymoon frolic" at Yosemite. Miss Sarah Haight kept a diary of the trip which starts on May the 20th, 1858.

The next morning, not quite daring enough to put on her "bloomer," Sarah attired herself chastely in a traveling dress and a "great sunbonnet." At Mugginsville where the group ate breakfast they all added green spectacles. Staging by way of Murphys they reached Coulterville in the afternoon of the 23rd. The next day they left their horses and walked a short distance to the cave. Sarah wrote: "The cave at the top is partially open and the trees called boxwood elders[2] grow among the rocks and thrust their tops out of the opening so that the rays of light that come into the cave come through the green leaves and are chastened and softened to a proper degree." She describes the clear, cold lake on the right side of the cave with a boat on it, while up a flight of steps on the left one could enter "a spacious shantie which bears the name of the ball room." It was, she said, inhabited by pretty green lizards and swallows innumerable and a man called Nicholas Arni (or possibly

Arin) was the owner. Everything, trees, rocks and sides of the cave were covered with beautiful moss. Judge McRae of their party gave it the name—Bower Cave.

The next year, according to Catherine Coffin Phillips in her *Coulterville Chronicle,* John Becker, passing by on a prospecting trip, saw a flag flying. Investigation disclosed two young men whom she calls Arin[3] and Shaffer. They had found this strange and charming cave and had preëmpted the land surrounding it. Becker was struck with the possibilities of the spot; returned with his wife and little daughter and established a home at the cave site. He improved the property, using it as a picnic spot for tourists in which capacity it was famous as long as the road was traveled.

John Muir wrote of the cave in 1869: ". . . one of the most novel and interesting of all Nature's underground mansions. Plenty of sunlight pours into it through the leaves of the four maple trees growing in its mouth, illuminating its clear, calm pool and marble chambers, . . ."

Brewer gave a few more facts: ". . . and there is a pool of very clear blue water," he said. "It is 109 feet down to this water. The effect is charming."

The crossroad, just mentioned, which joined the two rival turnpikes to Yosemite, has not changed its course much in three-quarters of a century. At the spot where it leaves the Big Oak Flat Road stood Hamilton's Station. It is now called Buck Meadows but, when Alva Hamilton ran the stage stop, the large building stood on the north side opposite the dead end of the road to Bower Cave. It was opened for business when the Big Oak Flat turnpike was pushed through toward Yosemite in the early '70s. Previously Hamilton had maintained a rough sort of mountain hospice at Tamarack Flat where he served meals to saddle tourists and to pack trains. When it became possible to operate stages clear through to the floor of the valley the custom fell off. A fire destroying his buildings proved the deciding mischance and he moved down the mountain to this beautiful meadow.

Hamilton did some farming. For instance, he raised beans and used that succulent commodity habitually instead of currency. His wife was formerly Johannah Grayson from the Grayson Hotel, south of the river at Knight's Ferry on the elevation known as Buena Vista. She was invaluable as a hostess. In spite of a certain crudity of construction Hamilton Station was always kept inviting. The lean-to milk house stood *under* a large black oak and *over* an icy spring which provided a sort of cooling system for the food. Cream at Hamilton's flowed smoothly from a pitcher and dissolved instead of rising in chunks to the top of one's coffee as was the habit of the unrefrigerated cream of the period. Puddings were chilled and meat kept free from taint. One habitual traveler of the road wrote, "I could enjoy a meal there as well as at the Palace Hotel in San Francisco."

So many fine oaks grew in Hamilton's meadow that it was an annual event for the Mono Indians to cross the mountains and camp here until the women had gathered enough acorns for the winter. To save space they were husked and dried, then repacked in the large cone-shaped baskets and fastened to either side of ponies to be carried back over the summit.

At the eastern end of the Meadow just beyond modern Big Oak Lodge, was the location of what was by far the most amazing project ever to be consummated along the road—the great flume that brought the water of the Golden Rock Ditch across the depression of the "Big Gap." The company conquered this obstacle by walking a flume across the gap on legs 264 feet high (Brewer recorded them as 288 feet). These towers were as tall as a twenty-story building and built almost entirely of sugar pine. Their fearful and wonderful construction would make a modern engineer shudder. The flume was 2200 feet long and supported by eleven towers of which the two center units attained the height mentioned. It was the most magnificent flume in the state. It cost $80,000. It lasted seven years.

Its collapse was also colossal. A summer wind storm simply tore it apart and let the giant structure fall. Holt and Conrad, the contractors, had stated that its life would not be much over seven or eight years but the financial backers had gambled on getting somewhat more. It did not give to Tuolumne County a future quite as rosy as predicted but it *did* make mining possible for the span of its usefulness.

The Sonora *Union Democrat* of July 11, 1868, told the story: "The flume of the Golden Rock Ditch fell Thursday, the 9th inst., with a crash that was heard for miles. Being held on all sides by iron guys, it crashed right down on its foundation, leaving scarcely a beam erect, a vast heap of broken and rotted timbers. Just previous to the fall, a break had occurred in the ditch above which necessarily turned the water out of the flume. When it was again turned in, the increased weight coming upon the dry and absorbent timber brought on the collapse.

"The crashing timbers, cables and guys together with the air current, carried everything in their course, stripping the large pine trees adjacent and crushing to atoms the smallest growth."

Contemporary papers noted that the fallen flume would probably be replaced by an iron pipe which could be laid much more cheaply. J. M. Hutchings described the "Big Gap" in *Scenes of Wonder and Curiosity in California*, and concludes: "Now a large iron tube placed upon the ground answers the purpose of the flume. This only cost, we are informed, some twelve thousand dollars." It was purchased in San Francisco by Andrew Rocca in May of

Office of Golden Rock Water Company in the early 1900's.
This is now the Sugar Pine Lodge.

Lumsden

Flume of the Golden Rock Water Company at Hardin's Mill.

Perkins

Caleb Dorsey's Sawmill, about 1885. Water for the mill was purchased from the Golden Rock Water Company.

Celia Crocker Thompson

Covered Bridge over the South Fork of the Tuolumne River, 1906.

Lukens, courtesy of Pitts Studio

Stage on Big Oak Flat Road near crest of Hardin Hill, 1888. Ed McGowan, driver.

Stage "Yosemite" at Priest's Hotel, about 1900.

Crocker's Station, 1897.

1869,[4] just after gaining the controlling interest in the company. There were 2,500 feet of pipe weighing over 28 tons.

Today a small portion of the useful old siphon remains—all pushed out of shape. And who can wonder, remembering the construction crews, building first the Hetch Hetchy Railroad and later the highway, that have banged it around. To see it pace 180 feet east from the marker at the county line; turn right and cross the abandoned railroad grade. It is a disappointing and unimpressive piece of pipe, battered but big enough for a child to crawl within, partially covered with dirt and trash. But, at that, the simplicity and relative economy of the plebeian pipeline which answered the same purpose as the flume, points the difference between the grandiose effects of the golden age in the Mother Lode and the enforced common sense of later years.

The finest viewpoint on the road, short of Yosemite itself, is beyond Buck Meadows where the highway strikes the cliffs. There is an adequate turnout. The canyons of the South and Middle Forks of the Tuolumne open up below while, beyond, spread relief-map mountains molded in blue, forming a mighty barricade to the waters of the main Tuolumne River. The forested ridges and deep, mysterious gorges are usually enveloped in a soft haze. Only on an exceptionally clear day, such as comes in early spring with a north wind, may be seen the majestic white-topped peaks from which infant snow-trickles find their way to the beginnings of the Grand Canyon of the Tuolumne above Hetch Hetchy Valley. More often visible, to the right, are the twin falls of the Middle Fork glimpsed before it sinks from sight beyond the dark ranks of the ranges.

At modern Colfax Springs was a pioneer station. Charles Elwell probably came here in the middle '60s and built a modest stopping place patronized by teamsters at mealtime. About '74 it was enlarged and named the Eagle Hotel because of a large eagle shot by a proud small son. The patrons were still freighting men. To the stages Elwell's was simply a watering place by virtue of the unfailing cold spring which had its beginnings in the marshy area luxuriant with watercress south of the highway. The Eagle stood, in its new dignity, back from the road behind the site of the modern building. Through its ruined foundation were laid in 1916 the Hetch Hetchy Railroad tracks.

Elwell had been a sailor. His acreage on the side of a narrowing mountain canyon with rolling paths and stiff climbs presented no problem to him, and when the Big Oak Flat Road was completed in 1874, it was obviously the very place for a toll station. There was then no possibility in the rough and timbered canyon for even a horseman to circle the gate.

George E. Sprague, who had been surveyor and engineer for the upper reaches of the road, settled down as toll collector and ran a small store in connection with it, but Mr. James Ballentine, another '49er, is said to have handled the toll gate during the last few years it was located at Elwell's. Charles Schmidt said that the rates were high and that he had paid as much as $9.00 to pass his freighting outfit along the road.

Down the grade ahead there are indications of the old road snaking back and forth over the straighter course of the highway. Descending sharply one comes to the bridge over the South Fork of the Tuolumne.

Even in the era of the canny pack mule this crossing was not forded for very long. It was too dangerous to animals and too easy to bridge. A few logs felled across the stream at much the same spot served until 1870 when the Big Oak Flat-Yosemite Turnpike Road Company (no less) built the first covered bridge.

It has been difficult out of all reason to unearth the date when the toll gate was changed from Elwell's to Crane Flat and then again to the South Fork bridge but change it they did some time between 1894 and 1897 and a droll character named John Cox was, for about twenty years until the road became free in 1915, the one and only toll collector. He had been a Confederate bugler and teamsters leaving his place often heard the clear notes of his bugle sounding the retreat.

Cox had been a news reporter in San Francisco and it was generally (but wrongly) accepted that an unfortunate love affair had caused him to adopt the mountains. It was he who first felt the fascination of the waterfall below the bridge. A large rock overhangs it. He decided to build his cabin there. He was alone and must never get beyond earshot of the toll gate; consequently he had always to write for instructions. One letter asked: "What toll should I get from the new horseless vehicles that occasionally struggle by?" The reply set a price and defined an automobile as "A vehicle not used with horses."

John Cox felt that his small castle on the rock was perfect. Of course his sphere of action was limited to a hundred yards or so, but what matter? He had all the conveniences. A supply of fuel arrived daily, for so steep were the canyon sides sloping to the river that teamsters habitually cut young trees growing at the tops of the grades on either side of the bridge; tied them behind the wagons to serve as brakes and discarded them within a few yards of his door. Bathing facilities were readily available without the labor of filling and then emptying a tub. Cox just trotted a few feet from his threshhold and jumped in the deep pool below the fall. Paul Morris said, "In the winter he sometimes had several feet of snow to wade through but he never failed to take his daily plunge." During the spring flood season, though, one imagines that he made slightly different arrangements; especially as he was well into his eighties when the state took over the road and his job was abolished. The teamsters brought him all supplies, food, tobacco, medicine and his favorite long red flannel underwear. They always stopped to gossip. They were his companions and his safeguard against a lonely illness.

He liked to appear crusty but he had a soft heart just the same. One day a man carrying a pack plodded down the hill and turned his pockets out to show that they were empty. The river was in full flood. He asked Cox if it would not be possible to look the other way just for an instant; it was so dreadfully necessary that he get across the bridge and up the mountain. But John Cox was an honest man and didn't feel that he could wink at anything irregular. "I'll tell you what," he offered, "seeing that the rate is twenty-five cents for a man walking, suppose you run instead." So the man picked up his weary feet and loped across the bridge while John watched him with a clear conscience.

In 1924 Mrs. Nellie Bartlett and her brother William H. (Tug) Wilson leased the property and added room by room to Cox's cabin. It soon formed the nucleus of a popular resort. "At first we called our place Fall Inn," Mr. Wilson wrote, "but later we re-named it Cliff House. Many of our guests were nationally famous artists, writers or politicians and, when the O'Shaughnessy Dam was constructed at the mouth of Hetch Hetchy we boarded the engineers."

In July of 1939 it burned. Not to the ground—that was impossible, but to the rock on which it was founded. The whole structure blazed from rock to roof while the excited guests rushed outside doing what little occurred to them.

In a small shack nearby an inebriated character from the mountains was stretched on a cot sleeping off the effects of a week or two of indulgence. On him a helpful guest dumped the cash register which he had somehow rescued and with which heavy and abrasive article he had staggered across the road. The gentleman of leisure thus rudely awakened to the noise of crackling flames and many shrieking voices, leaped for the open and, being fortunately still able to use his legs, was seen for the last time running up the road toward Yosemite.

The proprietors started rebuilding as soon as the ashes cooled and had a successful party before the roof was on.*

A small modern bridge just above the fall replaces the old covered structure built at nearly the same spot by James Lumsden in the employ of the Big Oak Flat-Yosemite Turnpike Road Company. It was called Lower Bridge. Upper Bridge re-crossed the South Fork at what is now the Berkeley Recreation Camp farther up the mountain.

On the far side of Lower Bridge the highway and the old road are coincidental for about one-tenth of a mile when the latter turns to the right and proceeds steeply above the modern graded thoroughfare.

As the highway swings around the end of the mountain it connects with the private approach-road to the Oakland Recreation Camp. There used to be a fairly large Indian encampment on the Middle Fork in the area now partially occupied by the camp. Near the entrance are a few boulders having in them grinding holes used for making acorn meal.

The highway now climbs gently to where it is rejoined by the old road which has come straight over the mountain without benefit of grading. Opposite its point of entry a good road takes off to the north to Mather and Hetch Hetchy.

The more or less level ground at the top of the hill is called Sweetwater Flat, named from the spring now tanked and used by the Recreation Camp. Sweetwater Spring was anticipated by thirsty travelers all the way up the first long unshaded hill from South Fork.

---

* The Cliff House was again destroyed by fire in 1958.

Near James Hardin's fence line at the crest of the second (or Hardin's) Hill commenced the trail to Hetch Hetchy blazed by Joseph Screech.[5]

The top of the grade is barely reached before one goes down again—this time along heavily-timbered winding, steep Hardin's Hill. At the bottom lies Hardin's Flat.

The small eccentric Englishman, James Hardin, who owned the fence and the land just here, called himself "Little Johnny 'Ardin" and lived alone. Most of the road from the "Lower Bridge" to his ranch was personally wrested from the timber by Johnny himself with the aid of two tremendous oxen. It has been logged lately and a sawmill stands today in Hardin's Flat—the legitimate successor to a sawmill run single handed by Johnny and his capable brutes.

It was at Hardin's in the late '50s that the Golden Rock Water Company built the dam which supplied water for the great flume and ditch. It is best seen in September when the water is low. South Fork, released from its timbered prison, comes lazying through the sunny flat but deep-cut banks and whole trees piled like packstraws in its rocky bed attest the power of flood season.

At the west end, where the flat pinches out into a canyon, are the remains of the old dam—simply two heavy logs protruding from the far bank. The intake for the ditch begins just opposite what is (at this reading) the most westerly house in the flat. A fallen tree lies across the opening. It is possible to walk down the canyon which is heavily wooded on the south side and rocky on the north but the river must be waded. The water acquired by the Golden Rock Water Company was conducted, by ditch or by flume as proved necessary, along the south side of the river through the timber.

It is a good place to view the remains of this typical business venture of mining days. Although similar ditches were constructed all through the diggings it is doubtful if many paid interest on the money invested. Certainly this one in later years did not.

Hardin's Flat is now a hodge-podge of buildings—old and new, of piles of used lumber and the debris incidental to a logging mill. But the clean pitchy smell of freshly sawn boards makes it attractive.

When the Golden Rock Water Company was at its short-lived peak it was felt necessary to increase the water supply. To this end water was brought from the Middle Fork by means of a ditch, with the accompanying flumes, which conducted it into the South Fork at the Hardin's Flat dam. The *Alta California* of April 6, 1860, printed a paragraph about the project before its completion: "To insure permanent water, the year round, the Company intends soon to cut an additional ditch about three miles to the middle fork of Tuolumne River. Fifty men would do it in a month, as one half the distance is said to be a natural ditch, running through the 'Big Meadows' and, when done, the ditch will be likely to supply permanent water the whole year around."

Articles written after that time speak of the Golden Rock Ditch as taking its water supply from the Middle Fork instead of the South.

Modern hikers sometimes make inquiries about evidences of this abandoned and ruined ditch-line which they see to the east of Hardin's Flat, but the authors have found it impossible to follow in its entirety.

James Hardin was not responsible for, nor indeed much interested in, the ditch aside from supplying lumber for the flumes. The road was his concern. Having got it thus far by great exertion, he demurred at having it extended through his land. Above him only pack trains went on to convey supplies to the few settlers whose summer cattle range and rude cabins were located in the higher mountains, and to take sightseers and supplies to the hotels beginning to be established in Yosemite. To his disgust, in 1868, the more far-seeing citizens of Tuolumne County spurred on by J. M. Hutchings of Yosemite, commenced legal proceedings to provide a wagon thoroughfare. But Hardin had planned to open a stopping place for tourists and proceeded to do so. It was small but rated very well. He commenced a law suit to prohibit the extension of the road through his land.[6]

By June, 1870, the new road had been pushed up the mountain to Hodgdon's, just within the present Yosemite National Park boundaries. By August it had reached Crane Flat. In 1871 it was extended to Gentry's. The law suit was won by the road company.[7] Johnny, thereupon retaliated by putting up several gates and the stage drivers had to open and close them. Rumor has it that some of the gate posts remain.

When the infirmities of age overtook him and he could no longer live alone in such isolation his friends procured him a little place in Sonora; but a longing for his mountain home overcame caution; he wandered back and was found there dead by the same man, Fred Schmidt, whose neighborly instincts led him to look for and to find Jason Chamberlain on the day of *his* death.

At Upper Bridge, which used to be a covered structure, the road re-crosses the South Fork of the Tuolumne. Below, to the right, is the Berkeley Municipal Recreation Camp. Immediately beyond the bridge the old road proceeded up the canyon to the left, coming in to the highway again at the Santa Maria voting precinct.

When the Yosemite National Park was first established the western boundary ran hereabouts and a troop of cavalry was installed to enforce the rule concerning cattle grazing. Nearby Soldier Creek took its name from this circumstance.

A mile and seven-tenths beyond Upper Bridge was Stuart's Flat with the hotel run by Leo Stuart (or Stewart) somewhere on the south side of the road. The vicinity once maintained a small scattered population. It began with a group of Mexicans who worked the Santa Maria Mine less than a mile to the south, and gradually accumulated others who lived in cabins flung haphazard through the woods. Life for these men centered at the point where the road crossed their sphere of action—where they got their mail and made contact with the outside world. The community became known as the Santa Maria voting district and, much later, as Sequoia. The men of isolated mountain sections were jealous of their voting privileges and rarely missed an election.

Tuolumne County had special problems induced by the early advent of several thousand souls from France, Mexico, Central American and Chile who centered around Sonora and were no more guaranteed to be law abiding than were other camps. Few of these men spoke English and were lumped together under the slighting term "foreigners." The men from the States have been rightfully accused of drastic measures in dealing with them but no one will dispute the necessity of some sort of imposed discipline—imposed at once.[8]

Because of the early advent of the hard-rock miners from Mexico, Tuolumne County boasted several fine specimens of an ore-crushing device not often seen in this country—the arrastra. It was cheap, reasonably effective and practically indestructible. There were three or four within walking distance of Santa Maria.[9]

During the depression of the 1930s some of the old arrastras were repaired and put into use again and some were even moved to more convenient locations. However, the scattered and almost obliterated remains of one could be found five years ago in the bottom of a brushy gully about a quarter mile north of the Santa Maria Flat, and which was called Seavey Gulch.

Leo E. Stuart's hotel was actually a boarding house for the miners from the Santa Maria. It was never of importance to the stages which commenced to pass in the early '70s. They hesitated only long enough to throw off the mail. Close to Stuart's was a cabin whose joint occupants were his partners in a placer mine. These were a man named Seavey and the omnipresent Mr. George Sprague who seemed to have a finger in almost everything.

Less than one hundred yards from Stuart's, on the north side of the road, John O'Keefe kept, in the '70s and '80s, a store and saloon. One gusty winter the snug dwelling was completely demolished when a falling pine crushed it flat on the snow. Ten years later his son restored the business which was promptly wiped out by fire. Stuart's burned also—probably at the same time, and the flat gradually was left lonely.

The road to Babcock's soon turns off to the south. The sign now says "Sunset Inn." Franklin Babcock was best known as a shake maker. It is an art to split out shakes from big sawn sections of cedar or sugar pine, and Babcock was a real artist. Most of the nearby cabins had his shake roofs and some used them for walls as well.

Babcock is known to have had an arrastra. It was probably the one north of the highway and opposite his house site. It had been made too small and the mule pulling the drag-rock must be kept blindfolded in order not to become dizzy. One day the contents had been pulverized to an uncommon degree of fineness and all the unlikely bits of rock picked out. The mule had the blindfold removed and was allowed to graze on nearby brush while this was being done. Then it was decided to run the arrastra a few more minutes before the clean-up. In the excitement he was put back to work without the blindfold and, after a few rounds, became dizzy and fell into the rich, gold-bearing crushed ore. When they extracted him his shaggy winter coat was practically gold plated. Probably no mule was ever more carefully polished and manicured. It took them hours to be sure that he took no unearned increment to the stable at the end of the day.

This arrastra was replaced by a small Huntington Mill, almost as great a curiosity in its own right.

The private road to Crocker's Station leaves the highway three-tenths of a mile beyond the road to Babcock's (Sunset Inn). It formed a semi-circle to the north, encircling Crocker's Meadow. The buildings stood about midway. Crocker's vied with Priest's Station as the most important stop during staging days.

Henry Robinson Crocker of Massachusetts followed the sea and was due to become captain of a whaler when the gold urge intervened. He arrived in California by way of the Isthmus in 1853 and later built a cabin on this fine open meadow—the nucleus of the later stage stop. All the level, grassy land for several miles up the mountain was at that time known as Bronson's Meadow. Mr. Curtin informs us that the original Bronson maintained an early camp near what was later Crocker's, for the convenience of saddle travelers to Yosemite. Bronson Meadows sloped northward to the South Fork of the Tuolumne whence, on the far side of the river, timber meanders up into beautiful Ackerson Meadows. James T. Ackerson was a '49er who, from his vantage point in the high mountains, was in a position to know most of what went on along the Mono Trail and in the Hetch Hetchy and Yosemite Valleys. Before his time his land was known as Buckley Meadows. After his occupation it was purchased by T. C. Carlon and used as summer pasture by that well known cattleman.

Henry Crocker considered Ackerson a near neighbor.

Having acquired land and a cabin, the next need of Henry Crocker was a wife. He married pretty Ellen Hall, daughter of

Captain and Mrs. Perry Warren Hall who arrived in California in the '50s, leaving her in the east until her education should be complete. Her father died and Ellen came west in 1871 to join her mother who had remarried and was now Mrs. John Woodruff of Deer Flat. Ellen's brother, Charles, married Alice Mecartea of Big Oak Flat, the only daughter in that astonishing household of thirteen children. The pioneer families became, after two generations, pretty thoroughly related.

Ellen was a light-hearted girl twenty years the junior of her husband-to-be. Accompanied by her step-father, she happily rode horseback to Cutting's store in Chinese Camp to buy serviceable brown silk poplin for her wedding dress. After the wedding they went immediately to live at the cozy cabin in Bronson's Meadows where a son and a daughter were born. It is not likely that the elegant dress was taken out of the trunk very often in the next few years.

The wagon road to Yosemite was completed the year after their marriage and travel grew heavier each season. John Shine, superintendent of the stage company, became embarrassed at the lack of sufficient accommodations and, coming privately to Henry Crocker, asked that he build and operate a stopping place. Mr. Crocker agreed and, in 1880, erected fifteen buildings and named his inn "Crocker's Sierra Resort."

Ellen Harper May gave her remembrances of Crockers: "The meals were famous, family style, with the tables laid for six or more. Each table had a long white cloth, a castor set and spoon holder. They served great roasts or racks of venison or lamb chops, platters of crisp mountain trout, mutton, chicken and fine beef. They baked their own pies of course, mince, gooseberry, squash, cherry, peach and apple. Large pots of hot coffee topped the dinner.

"The land at Crocker's sloped down toward the canyon of the South Fork. There were tiger and leopard lilies on the hill and they used them to decorate the tables along with daisies and bleeding heart from the moist meadow. Sometimes spikes of snow plant were cut for the house, as that was before any law prohibited it.

"The paths were always raked. All the dry leaves were cleaned up at once as fire was about the only thing we pioneers really feared.

"Crocker's had a reputation to maintain and always lived up to it. Through the years the register showed many well-known names. I remember Joseph LeConte, Margaret Anglin, John Muir, J. M. Hutchings, Stewart Edward White, Edwin Markham, William Keith and Herbert Hoover. It was the showplace of the road."

Henry and Ellen Crocker had other guests, as interesting, if not as elegant—the Indians from the Miwok rancheria. They liked Henry and he liked them so they made the twenty-five mile trip on foot.

Old Grizzly, then head of the tribe, was a frequent visitor. Shoeless, clad in flapping, shapeless cast-offs (but *clad,* that was the important thing) horribly chewed and scarred as a result of slight miscalculations during his many bear hunts, Grizzly was a chief of distinction. Mr. Crocker always fed him. It was expected. To the best of everyone's knowledge he was about one hundred years old when he died in 1903.

The younger women of the rancheria confidently came to Crocker's Meadow for the choice herbs to be found there. They filled the finely made pointed baskets that were bound to their foreheads with deerskin thongs, ate the feast that Henry Crocker provided and carried their burdens back down the mountain.

The Indians of the Mono country also came to Crocker's, crossing the great Sierra nonchalantly to see their friend. "Where Henry?" asked one anxiously. He was told that Henry was away and was not producible. The dejected Mono sat on a rock by the wayside and waited a long time. When at last Mr. Crocker was seen arriving he jumped up in great excitement and cried, "Here Henry. Now hello."

The Miwoks of the rancheria could not be called neat by present standards, but the Monos were dirty beyond any power of that ordinary word to describe. They usually came bearing tokens of affection—fish. Fish caught on the eastern side of the Sierra Nevada and carried for a day or two tucked into some recess in their scanty attire. They brought also koo-cha-bee, made from the dried larvae of flies, nourishing and relished by them because it was salty. Hutchings spells it kit-chavi.[10] Henry Crocker received their largesse, gave them unimaginable amounts to eat in return, and did something suitable about the fish and other comestibles later.

In 1904 the founder of Crocker's Station died and six years later his widow sold the property. Subsequently it was turned over to the Yosemite Park Company and was for several years within the park, four miles from the western boundary. It was during this period that a detachment of U. S. Cavalry camped on Soldier Creek. Then the boundary was changed and the property fell into private hands again.

Under different managements Crocker's Station took guests as late as 1920. Then, in the next few years it began to disintegrate. Some of the smaller buildings were moved over the mountain to Carl Inn. Uncared for, the rest fell victims to the heavy snow.

A logging camp spread its ordered disorder upon the remains of the resort. The entrance road was rutted and gouged by the ponderous wheels of trucks. Trees were cut and underbrush crushed. Its beauty was completely despoiled.

Years went by and this, too, passed. Healing rain washed clean the dust-caked face of nature; grass grew; torn branches mended.

Patiently, its beauty slowly returning, the old place awaited quietly the coming of the new half-century.

* * *

The exit road toward the east led along the north fence of Crocker's Meadow. Their private road, taken as a whole, was a semi-circle leading off and then back into the main road. All that is left of the hostelry is a small portion of the foundation. There is some of the picket fence and a few orchard trees. In a deep gully down the hill from the hotel are the remains of a curious little two-stamp mill for crushing ore where Mr. Crocker did some mining on the side.

Leaving the western entrance to Crocker's it is three-tenths of a mile along the highway to where the eastern end of the private driveway cuts back in time to use the bridge over Rush Creek. From there the *old* Big Oak Flat Road kept to the right (or south) of the highway—going straight up and over the mountain to Hodgdon's about two miles away.

Beyond Rush Creek a road on the right turns sharply back at an angle. It leads through fine timber and giant lupine, over Crocker Ridge to Hazel Green. It is picturesque and rewarding but is not to be lightly undertaken by a driver unaccustomed to mountains. Just opposite it, on the left, a little thoroughfare starts north—the original "Tioga Road."[11] If one wishes to investigate, it is easy to go down two-tenths of a mile to a leaning black oak on the left, with a scarred blaze; to leave the road a few feet beyond and walk up the hill to the right to the cabin of Thomas Jefferson Quimby—one of the best relics of mining days. The cabin may be seen from the highway but not so readily reached. Down the hill from the blazed oak, to the left of the road are the remains of Mr. Crocker's arrastra, later used by Quimby. Instead of being mule driven it was powered by a water wheel operated by a flow of water ditched from Rush Creek. Very little is now left of it—not even enough to photograph. The ore was brought down here to water from a mine near Quimby's cabin.

It seems too bad that these sunny meadows which once housed hospitable families and teeming resorts should be, for the most part, lonely. But each year the prospect seems more hopeful and the timber shows the gradual but continuous obliteration of scars. Each year the promise is brighter that, at some not too distant day, the friendly little clearings may again be filled with homes.

CHAPTER X

ENTERING UNCLE SAM'S PROPERTY

Mules have never been much interested in scenery. The modern traveler on the highway dips down to the pebbled brown waters of the South Fork of the Tuolumne; the mule teams of yesterday continued to climb steadily over the mountain. Being up, why should a mule plod downhill and then laboriously pull up again? The change was made when the Tioga Road pushed through the timber and over the summit of the Sierra to this point. The river had to be crossed, so a bridge was built down in the canyon and approach roads slanted up in both directions, joining it to the Big Oak Flat freight route. The Tioga Road did not extend west of the bridge. At first no one went down unless he intended to cross the river but with the coming of the automobile the hills involved did not matter so much, traffic deflected down into the canyon and gradually the stretch of old road between the approaches fell into disrepair.

The modern Big Oak Flat Road to Yosemite (State Highway 120) does not cross the South Fork here; merely touches it. Within sight of the bridge it enters the boundary of Yosemite National Park and ceases to exist, becoming, from there on, a federal project.

On the boundary Carl Inn was erected in 1916 by Dan and Donna Carlon. It burned in four years; was rebuilt and again burned. In 1932 the Park took over their land but, during its short existence, Carl Inn was a popular resort.

The site of Hodgdon's Stage Station, 1.3 miles beyond the park entrance, is marked by a cottage set in the lower corner of a lush green pasture now known as Cuneo Meadows and facing on the

213

highway. Down the north fenceline of the meadow, to intersect the highway at the cottage, comes a ranch road. About halfway down the slope the old Big Oak Flat Road wanders around the shoulder of the hill and curves gently into the fenceline road, coming the rest of the way coincidentally with it. At the cottage the old road crosses the highway. The women often walked the two miles between Hodgdon's and Crocker's for they were near neighbors. The old road is now considered impassable for cars although traveled by Forest Service trucks. The barn that sheltered the stage horses stood on the downhill side of the road just before it merged with the fenceline road. An excavation marks the place. The two original Hodgdon cabins stood a few yards farther up the old road.

This is still part of the section called, originally, Bronson Meadows and is a tempting bit of mountain scenery. Here Jeremiah Hodgdon late of Vermont, settled in May, 1865, claiming it by squatters' title and later homesteading the land. In addition to his cabins here he owned a foothill ranch between Knight's Ferry and Keystone[1] and an interesting place in Aspen Valley on the old Tioga Road where he built, in '79, a two-storied log cabin which still stands—the only one of that description in or near Yosemite National Park.

Rough and rugged Hodgdon, always known as Jerry, had six children—a moderate family for the times. His buildings were all constructed of tamarack logs which withstood the extreme weather conditions of the elevation better than any other available wood and which might be found, courteously awaiting the saw and ax, in dense groves of uniform size.

Following the north fence up toward the crest of the rolling meadow, one finds a piling of large boulders shaded by cedar trees. They are pitted with Indian grinding holes. One smooth-topped rock has about forty shallow depressions where the women ground acorns. Another boulder, only slightly removed, has still more. Such out-sized mortar rocks suggest a large community and it is easy to picture the chattering women and children perched among the cedars. The squaws were gregarious and always worked in groups and, apparently, it never occurred to them to disengage any of their progeny.

According to Robert Curtin the remains of an Indian camp of cedar bark huts were to be seen here as late as the 1880s. It was near the meadow but on the left of the highway. A well defined Indian trail led from here to Hazel Green.

To add to the bizarre effect of the busy Indian women, the saddle-tourists headed up the mountain were confronted by Hodgdon's chief rider and factotem, a Chinese character named Ah Hoy who rode like a demon and made the family's welfare his business. It was (old-timers assure us) a practical education to hear him swear in pigeon English. He rode until he was old enough to go home to China to die which he then accomplished in spite of all arguments to the contrary. The presence of Ah Hoy, calmly informing them in unexpurgated cattle talk as to what they could and could not do, did not add lustre to the establishment in the eyes of the lady visitors.

Before the wagon road was completed to this point in June, 1870, Hodgdon's was simply headquarters for his summer cattle-camp. It was a matter of accommodation that the sightseers bound for Yosemite were housed and given meals. No mountaineer could leave tired strangers outdoors on a frosty night to nurse their saddle bruises but one can imagine what a nuisance some of them were. It was during this regime that Helen Hunt Jackson passed this way seeking the beauties of Yosemite and, in justice to that well-known writer, it may be said that it took a good deal to upset her. "Three, four, five in a room," she repined. "Some on floors, without even a blanket. A few pampered ones, women, with tin pans for wash bowls and one towel for 6 hands. The rest, men, with one tin Basin in an open shed, and if they had any towel or not I do not know. That was a night at Hogdin's.—Not in the wildest and most poverty-stricken little town in Italy could such discomfort be encountered."[2] Olive Logan contributed her bit about the same time, "The dinner was execrable," she wrote impolitely; and when after the noon meal they started out on saddle animals, she added, "Everybody is sick and sore. Poor idiots, wandering on horseback over these mountain fastnesses. We all get what we deserve for coming."[3]

But still they came and Jerry sensibly decided that he might as well prepare to deal with them comfortably. He built a mountain inn—still rough, but capable of housing sixty people.

He also inaugurated the staging business for his section of Tuolumne County and for some years he and his son, Tom, acted as drivers.[4]

The saddle trail, used before 1870 and for such time after that date as it took to complete the road to Crane Flat, crossed the highway near Hodgdon's and paralleled it somewhat to the left proceeding southeast. It passed over a rough and steep country, using a branch of the ancient Mono Trail which remains north of the road. The first telegraph line followed it because of its shorter distance and eventually it became known to its habitual users— guides and cattlemen, as Telegraph Way.

One-tenth of a mile up the road from Hodgdon's the Indian trail took off to the right, headed for Hazel Green and Bull Creek. From there the road continues to turn and twist steeply through dogwood and giant conifers. There are six miles of such slow progress before striking the new highway at Crane Flat. The road is surfaced but narrow. However as there are no cliffs and the little thoroughfare is safely inclosed in heavy timber most people simply take it as an interesting sample of what the road used to be. To make the picture complete one should visualize dust a foot deep in heavy ruts and every vestige of greenery hidden under its powdery grey coating. It is interesting what an uplift a little properly distributed "black-top" can give to scenery. As the modern traveler threads his way along the narrow, curving ribbon of black road the green gloom of the giant fir forest suddenly wavers into sunshine and the bright cinnamon-brown trunk of a *Sequoia Gigantea*, or Big Tree, shafts upward toward the open sky. Although the original trail had passed by to the north, the course of the wagon road was deliberately altered to allow the stages to drive through Tuolumne Grove.

For most of the travelers this was the first glimpse of what we now call "the oldest living thing." And, although the question has been long disputed, there is no doubt in our minds that Tuolumne Grove *Sequoia Giganteas* were the first specimens ever seen by white men—the Joseph Reddeford Walker Expedition of 1833. This always interesting controversy is dealt with later, in the last chapter.[5]

It is almost impossible to realize at first glance how large these Big Trees really are. They grow in groups of their peers and even the neighboring firs and pines seem bent on emulating their size and swell to amazing proportions. Joseph LeConte, nature lover of earlier days, wrote: "My first impressions of the Big Trees were somewhat disappointing, but . . . a sense of their immensity grew upon me. If they had stood by themselves on a plain, they would be more immediately striking. But they are giants among giants."

The trees of Tuolumne Grove seem particularly susceptible to this illusion of mediocrity, although the "Dead Giant" in its heyday is said to have measured more than 120 feet in circumference.[6] In order to force visitors to realize its size and to provide an additional point of interest, it was decided to tunnel the base of the trunk. The brothers David and James Lumsden were intrusted with the project.

The tree was charred into a black mass at the bottom where a large cavity had been used for years by the Indians as a shelter in which to build their fires and to cook. Lightning and forest fire had done their worst; two cathedral-like spires, shattered and scorched, topped the mighty trunk but the heart-wood was sound. This is attested by John V. Ferretti. As a boy of nine he went on the job with his father who supplied the team. He remembers a slab of wood weighing about one-half ton which was brought down to Priest's Hotel and made fast to one of the locust trees as a souvenir. The tree tunnel was completed in '78 and a branch of the road curved out to pass through the strange archway just as it does today.

Mr. P. Andersen traveled to Yosemite in a spring wagon in 1892. He wrote a description of his journey in Danish and sent it to his uncle in Denmark where it was published in a current magazine but never translated until a few years ago. "These trees are not small at all," he wrote. "Just think, we drove through one of them. This tree is 31 feet in diameter. It may make you think of the women in Copenhagen who jumped over the Round Tower. But this has to be literal when I say we drove through this giant tree with horse and wagon. The tree is dead and burned at the top. About 200 feet of the trunk is still standing and the road goes right through the base of it."

The archway in 1894 was ten feet wide by twelve in height.

The next point of concern, Crane Flat, shows at an elevation of 6130 feet after one very steep, crooked mile. It was visited and named in 1856 by George W. Coulter, Dr. Lafayette Bunnell and a small party from Coulterville, Mariposa County, who had made their way up the mountain from Black's on Bull Creek to which a wagon road had already been constructed. They were blazing a suitable saddle trail to join their settlement to the Big Oak Flat (or old Mono) Trail so that they might use its descent into Yosemite Valley. En route they had passed through a meadow boasting a thick growth of hazel bushes, named it Hazel Green, and pushed on to this point—a moist, springy upland. One of the party wrote: "Our next move was to 'Crane Flat.' This name was suggested by the shrill and startling cry of some sand-hill cranes we surprised as they were resting on this elevated table."[7] The junction of the two trails was accomplished on the near edge of Crane Flat and the joined trails went on together toward Gin Flat, keeping north of the marshy meadow. It is true that one of the two maps in J. D. Whitney's *The Yosemite Book, 1868*, shows the trails joining approximately at Gin Flat but John Muir, who traveled the trail and gave an account of his trip, states that they met at Crane Flat.[8] This has been corroborated by several of the old residents along the Big Oak Flat Road who habitually took that route to the valley.

The earliest known habitation in Crane Flat seems to have been a cabin mentioned (as being deserted) by Whitney in 1868.[9] There is some likelihood that it belonged to Hugh Mundy who ran sheep in the vicinity but no proof can be obtained.

From the time that naturalists and sightseers began to trek to Yosemite, Crane Flat was important. Animals and tourists alike needed food and shelter. Gobin's place supplied this need. In the '70s Louis D. Gobin, with his son, "Ed," summer-grazed here the cattle and sheep from their acres on the Rock River Road. At first they took in the oftimes unappreciative travelers simply because someone must do so. They served meals in their small log cabin which sat squarely on the county line so that one-half of the party consumed their dinner in Tuolumne County while those on the other side of the table ate theirs in Mariposa.

James Vick, who wrote "Vick's Floral Guide," was snow-bound at Gobin's in June of 1874. The road now extended to Gentry's on the brink of the north cliffs of Merced Canyon just below Yosemite Valley and in another month was completed to the valley floor. It was usually open by May but late snow evidently prevented further progress by stage and the party had sent a message to the valley requesting the services of the pack train. Vick was not comfortable but was able to see the viewpoint of his hostess, Mrs. Gobin. Thus: "In about an hour after leaving Hodgins we arrived at Crane's Flat, where a little mountain hotel is kept by Mrs. Gobin and here we were so near the clouds that our further progress was obstructed by banks of snow, and here we were compelled to remain until saddle horses and pack mules could be sent from the valley to carry us and our baggage over the mountains of snow. The accommodations were not equal to a first class hotel, but the good landlady apologized for the scantiness of her larder, stating that she had only just opened for the season, and her cows had not yet been driven up the mountain, and the chickens were coming with the cows, and the house had tumbled down on account of the weight of snow the past winter, and in the fall of the house the furniture had been destroyed or badly injured; and the accommodations were truly meagre.—We were compelled to remain, snow-bound in June, for more than 24 hours. Almost every hour the report came that the saddle horses were in sight, but they came not, and we remained anxiously awaiting their arrival until three o'clock of the day after our arrival."

Gobin's stopping place grew with its necessities and became a comfortable stage station. It burned in '86 and was rebuilt two years later.

Across from Gobin's, on the southside of the old road was Billy Hurst's saloon which served as warehouse, amusement center, address and home away from home to the solitary sheep herders from the camps far-flung on the steep mountain sides and in the aspen-clumped meadows. Billy was, each year, custodian of the supplies which were hauled thus far by pack mule or wagon, depending on how far the road had progressed. Billy stored them and later dealt them out piecemeal as needed. In his way he felt a great responsibility for these lonely men—enough so that he actually died in proof of it.

The little cabin was a popular place. Its owner was an admirer of Bret Harte and decorated his walls lavishly with illustrations of that noted author's "Heathen Chinee," cut from magazines. It was also a riotous spot much of the time; the men from the mountains didn't come down to play cribbage; they could do that at camp. Indians, although legally forbidden liquor, managed to get it at Billy's and went whooping up and down the trail in bands of twenty or thirty, giving the isolated ranchers cause for reflection, but never, to our knowledge, necessitating any more violent action.

Among the habitues of the establishment was "Smokey Jack" Connell who ran sheep high up in the rocky peaks and came down for an occasional forgivable bender. It was on one of these occasions that he dictated a letter to Billy to be sent to that tolerant lady, his wife, giving her such news as he was in condition to impart. As it was none of Billy's affair to rewrite the effusion, it was sent in status quo to the great delight of passing teamsters. The last two lines have survived: "The sheep are scattered and gone to hell Your affectionate husband, John Connell."

There is a specimen of Billy's flourishing handwriting at the museum in Yosemite. It probably was a source of satisfaction to the illiterate among the herders for whom he was always a faithful amanuensis.

It was while keeping Connell's herders under some sort of supervision that the naturalist, John Muir, found it possible to explore so much of what was later Yosemite National Park; and, incidentally, learned from personal observation the destruction that an earnest and persevering band of sheep can inflict on the beauties of nature.[10]

Billy Hurst's was a true democracy. Sharing the crude and limited space at the bar with these primitive characters were respected ranchers and distinguished visitors. Two lines from a simple and inoffensive doggerel have come down through the years commemorating a night at Billy's in honor of Lieutenant Governor Gobin of Pennsylvania who was visiting his uncle, Louis Gobin, in the '80s: "There's Cloudman full of music and Buchanan full of tune. We drank and ate and stayed up late, at Billy Hurst's saloon."

Well, said saloon was warm, lighted, full of cheerful company, whiskey, noise, music, poetry of a sort, and a riotous kind of good fellowship. There were worse places in Tuolumne County. In '88 it was prospering, but the winter of '89-'90 saw the end of it. Old-timers still quote that season as the worst snowfall ever known in the mountains.

Billy, a short but powerful, heavy-set man, always waited for the last straggler to come in from the camps before he closed up for the winter months and went below, traveling on snow shoes. This year he waited too long for some who never did get in. Terrible snowstorms followed, one on the heels of another. He tried to get down the mountain during the short interims when he could see to travel but never could make it and always had to turn back. Finally, his strength gave out completely and he became ill, alone in his cabin on the summit.

The people below watched for him and, when they were convinced that he was marooned, they banded together and went after him. He was taken straight to the hospital at Sonora and died there.

* * *

When automobiles were first permitted to enter the Yosemite Valley, various minor changes were made on the road at the higher elevations. Wherever possible, the sharpest turns and steepest grades were improved but the general route remained the same. Then in 1940, a new federal highway was inserted at Crane Flat connecting a brand new Ranger Station and entrance fee gate with the floor of the valley—a highway so insistent and so impressive that it is hard to keep in mind any theater of action in which it did not exist. To connect with this highway at the new gate the Big Oak Flat Road swerves to the right for the final few hundred yards, but the earlier route may be seen traveling straight up the hill through the trees to strike Crane Flat at the present Blister Rust Camp.

From the present Ranger Station one may drive a car 9.6 miles farther along what is approximately the course of the old road by turning left, taking the new Tioga Road for 1.3 miles and then turning off to the right at Gin Flat. But eventually the car will have to come back and go down the highway because the old Big Oak Flat Road has become "no thoroughfare" and winds up against a log barrier at the site of Gentry's Station.

In the meanwhile Crane Flat itself is a fertile field for study. Two-tenths of a mile down the Tioga Road is the Blister Rust Camp. Through it runs the pioneer road at right angles to the Tioga Road. Gobin's stopping place was about one hundred feet east of the present buildings. Although the land has been filled in order to level the road, the spot was identified by Mr. Curtin and is recognizable from old photographs. Portions of foundations, bits of crockery and glass gave further proof.

Immediately across the road was Billy Hurst's saloon where that faithful steward tried to outwait Death and failed. At present tiny pieces of old bottles and china may be found where Hurst threw his refuse to the rear of the kitchen. For a few years the early toll gate stood just beyond his dwelling.

A steep portion of the old Big Oak Flat Road winds its way over the mountain to the left; and roughly parallels the Tioga road, joining it again at Gin Flat.

Somewhere beyond the Blister Rust Camp, in the very early days, the Coulterville Trail curved into and merged with the Big Oak Flat Trail and went on together to the north cliff saddle trail (later the Zigzag) and thence down to the valley floor.

A detour on the saddle trail to Yosemite began here in Crane Flat near where the Coulterville and Big Oak Flat Trails merged. It was for use in the early spring season of heavy snow and cut out the higher portions of the trail through Gin and Tamarack Flats. Apparently when the Coulterville Trail was blazed in 1856, the exploring party did not encounter the heaviest snow until they reached Tamarack Flat. Bunnell wrote: "From this flat I blazed out two trails, the lower for early, the upper for later use; . . ."[11] But we know that in succeeding years the detour, always called "The Lower Trail," commenced at Crane Flat and avoided the climb up to Tamarack and down again. According to Whitney's map it proceeded down Crane Creek, to just above Big Meadows, thence due east to the regular crossing of Cascade Creek where it joined the upper trail again. It was blazed a full thousand feet lower than the regular trail and was difficult to find; the unaccustomed traveler needed the services of a guide.

The winters in Crane Flat were silent except for the howling of the wind. No human voice was heard. Business for the high mountain area was resumed in mid-spring. J. M. Hutchings' *In the Heart of the Sierras* gave a graphic description of the opening of the stage road one year in April.[12] Three men, known to be powerful and determined, left Crocker's early in the morning. They had with them sleigh and four willing horses on snow shoes made of one-inch ash plank fastened firmly to their hooves. By 2:00 A.M. the next morning they had progressed the six miles to Crane Flat but the buildings were completely submerged in 18 feet of snow. The men were forced to wait for daylight before they could locate where the door to the stable would be. They shoveled the snow away on an angle leaving a ramp-like approach to the barn door down which (with ropes fastened strategically to neck and tail) they slid the horses into the refuge of the hay-filled stable. By the middle of the morning they were again on the course of the road which lay far below them under the snow. They made two and a half miles to the top of the ridge and returned to Crane Flat for the night.

The next day they reached Tamarack Flat by 9:00 P.M. when the snow shoveling and horse tobogganing routine began again. It was past midnight when all were sheltered and by that time they were so hungry that they cooked and ate for an hour or two more.

They were now on the downhill stretch toward Yosemite Valley and Cascade Creek was the main obstacle ahead. Snow was piled on the little bridge house-high and roof-steep. They dug a path across which would accommodate one horse at a time and pulled the sleigh over by hand. They reached the snow line and the good warm earth three hours later.

These simply told stories relate difficulties such as we can scarcely conceive. Stories of responsibilities assumed one for another; of dangers faced for a neighbor with no thought of doing otherwise. Stories of the wild and fearsome romance of the lives of the Sierra dwellers.

CHAPTER XI

THE UPPER FLATS

The upper flats and the mountains surrounding them were the summer grazing lands both for sheep and cattle. Of the two, sheep were able to feed at a higher elevation, subsisting partly on the bunch grass that grows in almost inaccessible spots. The sheep owners, contrary to the habit of cattlemen, took up no land but moved their flocks from place to place in the unsettled areas.

The best known cattle owners of the county had an established technique. Each selected a high grassy location not yet preëmpted and obtained a government patent to as much as he was allowed. He fenced only a small portion containing some of the luxuriant grass and sufficient water. It then served as a corraling place.

By June each year the winter snows were melting and grass pricked through to the ten-thousand-foot level. Each cattleman, with his sons and his riders, started for the mountains driving all his beef stock—a man's size undertaking of about three days duration. When in the vicinity of his fenced enclosure the cattle were turned loose and allowed to graze all summer on the open lands. A rider remained somewhere nearby to keep an eye on the animals but herders never attained such a degree of chumminess with cattle as with sheep. It wasn't necessary to remain with them at night to forestall their inadvertently furnishing a dinner for a hungry mountain lion.

Of course, during the unattended period, various untoward events occurred. Calves running with the cows became unaccountably separated and turned up later marked with a different brand, or branded stock emerged from the mountains at the end of four months with an altered brand completely healed and incapable of

227

proof. If dirty work with a branding iron was suspected some likely calves were selected at the beginning of summer and a marked dime slipped under the skin just above the hoof. It quickly healed without a trace. These thin dimes were the means of hauling several unscrupulous rustlers into court.

At the end of the summer season the cattle belonging to each owner were collected from canyons and peaks and gradually driven into his fenced inclosure still lush and opulent with protected pasturage. They were kept there, inactive and eating happily, until fat and ready for market when they were driven slowly down to "the plains," as the San Joaquin Valley was then termed.

A list follows of some of the leading stockmen of the vicinity who operated during the last thirty years of the century: Tom and R. B. Kennedy who ranged at Kennedy Lake; William Cooper of Cooper Meadows; Dennis and John Fahey later succeeded by their sons; Joseph Lord; Colwell O. Drew of Drew's Meadows near "Hog Ranch," now Mather; J. S. and Joseph Rosasco; Bartholomew and Shippolite; Dick and Henry Meyer of Deer Flat ranging at White Wolf; John Wolfling and son Michael; Mark Crabtree and son Oscar; the Donahues; the Smiths from near Don Pedro; John Stockel of Crimea; Timothy H. Carlon of Deer Flat ranging at Ackerson Meadows; Louis Gobin and son "Ed" at Crane Flat; Jeremiah Hodgdon and son Thomas at Bronson Meadows; Jules and Jean Renaud; William Rushing from Willow Springs Road; John Grohl from Green Springs; the McCormicks who ranged at Eagle Meadows; W. A. Smith and sons; Armstrong who ranged the Jawbone country below Lake Eleanor; John Curtin and sons of Cloudman who ranged at Gin Flat; Rush and Miguel ranging at Miguel Meadows near Hetch Hetchy.

Their pasturage in the main extended between the Stanislaus and the Tuolumne Rivers.

Yosemite Museum

Stage on the Big Oak Flat Road.

Celia Crocker Thompson

Hodgdon's House and Hotel, 1901. Original log cabin in upper center.

The Dead Giant, Tuolumne Grove, 1894.

Crane Flat, 1901. Building with porch, Gobin's Hotel;
Billy Hurst's Saloon in front of team.

Curtin's "Cow Camp" at Gin Flat on the Big Oak Flat Road, 1901.

Wood's at Tamarack Flat, 1901.

"The Yosemite Flyer." Jerome Martin, driver.

The cattle industry, sheep raising and freighting gradually replaced mining as a source of income in the mountains of California. Our chief informant and advisor as to the intricacies of all three has been Robert A. Curtin of Cloudman who, from years of actual experience with cattle drives and jerk-line teams, has the facts at his command; and who, by reason of his long term as a special police officer in San Francisco, has learned the value of a plain fact left unembellished. His brother, John B. Curtin (Honest John), early elected a state senator, will long be remembered as the man who fought for over six years in the courts to protect the rights of the cattlemen, finally winning in the Supreme Court of the United States.

The summer grazing land of the Curtins was at Gin Flat lying just over the summit from Crane Flat at about 7000 feet elevation. In earliest days it was utilized as a sheep camp by one, Hugh Mundy. It remained part of the "open settlement country" and, in 1882, was filed upon by the elder John Curtin who obtained a government patent. In early days of mountain travel Gin Flat was not designated by any particular name. It acquired its title naturally through a more or less amusing incident. A freight wagon bouncing across the rough little flat lost a barrel of gin and rumbled on without missing it. Some men who were working on the road promptly rolled it into the shrubbery and knocked a hole in the top through which they inserted straws pulled from the grass. A few assorted sheepherders happily joined the party and the whole affair rapidly assumed an alcoholic flavor. When the men had been missing a day or so a search party was sent out under the impression that they had been attacked by bandits or wild animals and that a burial squad would be necessary—which latter was not far from the unfortunate truth.

The Curtins built a one-room cabin of tamarack logs which still stands as a sturdy ruin.

In a cow-camp duty was no respector of age. Before he was twelve Bob Curtin found himself more than once alone at the cabin to keep an eye on the place and on the cattle. A few warnings were spoken soberly and received in the same spirit: If you get lost give your horse his head, he'll take you back to camp. If you lose your horse as well as your way, follow the nearest creek to a river, then keep with the river. It will bring you, sooner or later, to where there are people. Above all never call out; it attracts the mountain lions.

Almost anything could happen at Gin Flat but seldom did. Most of the time the high country was peaceful enough. One morning very early in the spring the two young brothers, Bill and Bob Curtin, were sitting at breakfast when the door swung open and a party of Monos peered into the room. They were heavily painted which looked ominous. The boys moved to where their guns hung on the log wall; stood there motionless and presently the Indians padded off through the snow as silently as they had come. The boys found later that they had seen smoke and wondered who was there so early in the year. The paint was simply the custom during bad weather as a protection from icy winds and sleet.

The twenty year period ending in 1911 was hell in a hand basket for the local cattle industry. The bill creating Yosemite National Park was passed in October, 1890, and, beginning the next spring, stock might not graze on the lands included within the boundaries. Naturally, even those cattlemen whose patented lands were without the limits were affected because loose cows are no respectors of imaginary lines and no provision had been made to restrain their activities until the fall round-up.

The Department of the Interior sent out verbose proclamations in legal phraseology that restrained they must and should be. The stockmen's proclamations were equally verbose but the phrasing was quite different. The Department saw that it had acquired a problem child and decided that discipline must be maintained at all costs. The act had been passed for the express purpose of preventing the spoilage of the magnificent scenic area surrounding Yosemite Valley and no one denied that cattle ate the tops off of the new forest growth. If cattle were bad, sheep were devastating. They devoured the grass and (having a competent set of teeth in each jaw, which cattle do not) they ate it roots and all. They lunched off the blossoms of the beautiful tiger and leopard lilies and dined off the bulbs which they excavated for the purpose with their sharp hoofs. It took years for a meadow to recuperate from one season's grazing.

The Secretary of the Interior sent a troop of cavalry to see that no sheep nor loose stock strayed into the forbidden territory.

In the spring of '91 the trouble started. The stockmen drove their livestock up to their patented land; left them and went home to sit tight. The cavalry officers had to show results. Word was sent out that animals found on government land would be pushed across the summit by way of the infamous chute of Bloody Canyon. This stair-like descent was 3000 feet in less than four miles and was often fatal to animals. It had its outlet in the Mono Indian country.[1]

Robert Curtin was alone at Gin Flat awaiting developments when he heard that the cavalry had collected 200 head of stock and intended to start the drive for Bloody Canyon the next day. He rode down to Hodgdon's where they had camped.

Young Bob, then sixteen, and Jeremiah Hodgdon, seventy, were the only cattlemen in the mountains. During the evening they told the soldiers of the casualties that were certain to ensue if the cattle were sent plunging down the shelf-like Bloody Canyon Trail, so strewn with sharp rocks that the name came from the blood left by the cut legs of the pack animals. When the cavalrymen rolled in for the night, Bob rolled out—a determined lad on Jerry Hodgdon's best horse racing down the mountain. He reached Meyer's ranch and, by means of riders and the telegraph, sent word to the men whose cattle were threatened. These made forced marches through Sonora Pass; intercepted such stock as had been driven over the Sierra and started the long trek home. The soldiers had not put their hearts in the job and had managed to lose most of the cattle in the forests; still some were gone and some were dead. C. O. Drew's buildings which chanced to be on government land were burned with his hay, gear and supplies. The cattlemen were furious but it was made evident that they would have to go through the motions of keeping their cattle out of the reserve.

In 1905 Captain Harry C. Benson was put in command of the troops and undertook, with almost fanatical devotion to duty, to preserve the beauty of the park. His complete absorption in the matter was such that he acquired for the length of the Big Oak Flat Road and (privately) among his own men, one of the western nicknames that never can be shaken—"Batty" Benson. Benson (soon promoted to Major) did a splendid job but his methods were drastic and not always defensible. Among other things a stockman was not allowed to drive cattle from one piece of his own property to another by means of the general turnpike if it meant passing through a portion of the park. The cattlemen insisted that they were being deprived of the right of every American citizen to use his own land and the public roads.

The authors asked questions of available persons favoring both sides and finally took advantage of an opportunity to get the point of view of the cavalrymen themselves. The matter was put to Edwin Doel Hopkins, late of Mill Valley, California, who served in the 14th Cavalry under Major Benson from 1906 to '09. It

would be impossible to doubt his sense of duty for, during this
period, so we learned from another source, he responded to a
request from his superior officer for a volunteer to rescue the body
of a young man who had fallen about 800 feet over a cliff at
Union Point in Yosemite and was lying on a ledge some 1000 feet
above the floor of the valley. Hopkins went down the cliff on a
rope of which two strands cut through on a sharp rock and un-
wound briskly as he was lowered. The man was dead and he
remained all night on the ledge with the body while another adequate rope was brought from Modesto. It was lowered to him and
he made it fast; the body was swung to the valley floor and Hopkins then went down the rope himself—an exhibition of bravery
and physical prowess probably as outstanding as any in the annals
of Yosemite, done without reward at the request of his officer.
And yet he and his comrades were far out of accord with Major
Benson's methods of dealing with the livestock and softened them
when they could.

The affair came to a boil when Senator Curtin's cattle were
rounded up, funneled through Bloody Canyon and thence to the
four winds. The senator sued. First in the county court, then in the
U. S. Circuit Court in San Francisco where the earthquake and fire
of 1906 destroyed all the evidence and everything had to be done
over. He more or less patiently collected more evidence and lost
the case. Then he made appeal to the U. S. Supreme Court. The
case was delayed twice by reason of the deaths of Justices Brewer
and Fuller but finally arrived at the determining point and was
argued. The Sonora *Banner* for November 24, 1911, summed it
up. "Decision was in favor of the Senator. Senator Curtin contended that as the Government granted patents to his lands and
he bought and owned them and the highway leading to them was
a public road, he had the unquestioned privilege to travel and use

it in going and returning to his property. He challenged the Government, it was accepted and the fight made. The Senator was victorious and the troops had to retreat. He holds the fort at Crane Flat. The success of the Senator means much to all stockmen who have grazing rights in reservations."

This decision gave no excuse to the cattle owners to allow grazing beyond their own holdings but it was a sweet victory to many residents along the Big Oak Flat Road.

It must be remembered, however, that Major Benson, although grandly, unbendingly wrong on this point, stood immovable between the natural beauty of the mountains and despoilage; impressing on the public mind the necessity of protecting our national parks at all costs. He later received the rank of colonel and has become one of the permanent names remembered in the history of Yosemite.

The inquiring traveler who investigates historic spots on foot will find the disintegrating walls of Curtin's cow-camp sturdily resisting the weather in the center of Gin Flat. According to Mr. Curtin, who lately re-visited the spot, the barn was between the cabin and the present road where the symmetrical young tamarack now grows. The old road passed between the barn and the cabin.

Due east of the flat is Lightning Ridge containing a group of three peaks of which only one can be seen from this location. They are named Jot's Peaks because of a sheepman, Jot Jones, who long ago ranged his flocks high on their rough slopes.

* * *

Tamarack Flat, three miles down the grade toward Yosemite from Gin Flat, is a labyrinth of overpowering chunks of granite—heaps and heaps, tons and tons of them. The trees are big but are dwarfed by the boulders. Through the level section runs modest little Tamarack Creek. The place is quite grown up with brush but, in the days of the annual grass burning, used to be fairly open.

Alva Hamilton (later of Hamilton Station) is credited with being the first settler at this high mountain clearing and conducted a small stopping place called Tamarack House. However, John Muir, passing through the flat in July, 1869, found a log house occupied by a white man with an Indian wife.[2] Probably, as it is known that Mr. and Mrs. Hamilton came up the next season, the man was either employed by them, or they purchased his house with the idea of establishing a stopping place. The flat, then infested with grizzlies, was named by Coulter and Bunnell in 1856 while hunting a suitable saddle trail from Coulterville to Yosemite.[3]

Johannah Grayson Hamilton presided over the rough accommodation of Tamarack House with as much poise and capability as she later displayed at Hamilton Station. Although small and retiring she had a mind and a will of her own and a large, enveloping hospitality. In October, 1870, Ellen Harper May, then sixteen years old and accompanied by Mrs. Hodgdon, was coming out of Yosemite with a pack train. She had been all day on a side saddle and was stiff, tired, cold and terribly afraid of bear. As a final blow, just at dusk it began to snow. Apparently they were passing Tamarack House without stopping when Ellen began to cry. Out marched Mrs. Hamilton and stopped the cavalcade which had intended to make Hodgdon's before putting up for the night. Shamelessly she delayed them with a roaring fire, hot biscuits and venison and finally delivered the ultimatum, "This little girl shall not go on tonight. The woods are *full* of bear." And she didn't. Almost seventy years later Ellen said gratefully, "I shall never forget that kind lady."

With the best will in the world, though, Johannah Hamilton had very little room in which to display her hospitality. The irrepressible Olive Logan gives us one of her vinegary word pictures: "At Tamarack Flat the experienced Hamilton is ready—he is ready every time every saddle train arrives, for he knows the state the arrivers will be in—and he lifts poor tourist women off their horses. Our limbs are paralyzed. Some of us are barely alive. The bride from Chicago has swooned. The good wife Hamilton does all she can for us. She offers wine—she rubs us with whiskey —and at last all of us, men, women, and children, married and unmarried, friends and total strangers, lie down in the one only room which composes their cabin, and pass the night in blissful disregard of civilization and modesty at once. A propos, lest the reader might forget it, I wish to again remind him here that this is a pleasure trip."[4]

In the middle '70s, not long after the road was completed to Yosemite, the house burned and the Hamiltons moved permanently to their place at what is now Buck Meadow. David Woods rebuilt Tamarack House and erected the large stage barn seen in later years. There was no well. Water was always obtained from the clean little creek. Within a few years he erected also a store and saloon. After his death in 1884 his wife and son continued the business. Probably the heavy winter of 1889-90 which ended the career of Billy Hurst took its toll of the buildings; rumblings of the imminent "cattle war" were beginning to be heard and the government put the U. S. Cavalry in charge of the country. One thing taken with another discouraged them and in 1891 they moved away.

Tamarack House stood lonely for more than two decades and then, in 1914, it was moved up the mountain to Gin Flat and placed against the left wall of the Curtin cabin, making that solid edifice twice as large as formerly. But apparently it had suffered too many vicissitudes. It commenced to weather away and disappeared many years ago, while the original portion of the Curtin cabin is still an interesting ruin.

The old road was more curving through Tamarack Flat than the one now in use and the house stood to the right or south of it, between the road and a huge pile of boulders. Just beyond the site, on the left, is a telephone box on a post. Here the old road swung toward the creek and passed between two large tamarack trees studded with spikes. Southeast of the second tree stands another large tree which shaded the saloon and store of David Woods' regime. Beyond the telephone box a road leads to the right toward an abandoned C.C.C. camp. The large barn which sheltered the pack animals on occasion when, for a few months, Tamarack Flat was the terminus of the road, used to stand in the farther angle of this side road with the main road.

Near the saloon the old road crossed Tamarack Creek and proceeded toward Yosemite in back of the rocks on the opposite side of the current.

A generous two-tenths of a mile past the present bridge over Tamarack Creek brings one to a well-marked gully leading up on the left. Along this small gulch went the Mono Trail joining Tamarack Flat with Yosemite Creek as indicated in "the map of a portion of the Sierra Nevada adjacent to the Yosemite Valley" in *The Yosemite Book, 1868,* by J. D. Whitney, State Geologist. It was exceedingly rough and steep even after being cleared out and blazed in 1857 but had the advantage of water and shade. Now it is impassable. Other portions of the Mono Trail have been maintained by the government for modern hikers but this branch has been forgotten and is only recognizable by the blaze marks about six feet up on the large trees. Many of them have fallen and disintegrated but such marks as are left are always to be found on trees standing to the right of the trail no matter in which direction one is traveling. About a mile up the hill the trail goes through "Split Rock" which looks as if it had been divided for the purpose.

Along its steep footway the ill-favored Mono Indians came to see their friend Henry Crocker.

The famous naturalist, John Muir, once met a portion of the tribe on their way to Yosemite to feast on acorns. They were sketchily covered, at least in spots, by the skins of sage rabbits; were revoltingly ugly and inexpungibly squalid. He was impressed by the inhuman faces of the older individuals which he described as "strangely blurred and divided into section by seams and wrinkles that looked like cleavage points, and had a worn abraded look as if they had lain exposed to the weather for ages."[5]

A fraction of a mile beyond the Tamarack Creek crossing, the automobile road passes Coyote Creek and ascends a hill. In plain view to the right is Balancing Rock. It used to be known as Pivot Rock and the precariously poised tons of granite have always been considered one of the sights of the trail. One-tenth of a mile beyond Pivot Rock, very close to the road on the right, is what was pointed out by the stage drivers as "Elephant Rock." It is simply a pile of boulders the top of which resembles slightly an elephant's head and trunk.

The telegraph line to Yosemite followed the road and at this point both plunged down through small, precise, silvery fir trees to cross Cascade Creek. A keen observer may be lucky enough to spy one of the rare dull green insulators still fastened high on a tree.

Cascade Creek was steep, rocky and hazardous for animals. A crossing was soon contrived. It was the bridge over this stream that had to be traversed with such care by the first vehicle over the road each spring. Snow packs the short span to such height and weight that it is a wonder it survives. In fact, snow in the upper Yosemite region is a miracle of beauty lasting from October until June. At first it is scattered sparsely under the dark conifers as if some slovenly gardener had sprinkled his beds with lime. A month later it extends in billowing curves like white and shining Christmas plastic. After a fresh fall everything is covered but tree-trunks the color of blackstrap molasses, the uprights of the fences and the darkling little creeks stealing between encroaching snowy banks. Later, as warm weather melts the more exposed portions, the all-enveloping white blanket dwindles to hard heaps in sheltered spots. Heaps whose rounded upper surface is untidy with droppings from the overhanging trees and etched with blackened tracings from the tiny feet of squirrels and other small householders of the forest. And so it stays until well into July.

For all the years of vehicle travel to Yosemite by way of the upper flats, snow was the great natural barrier, unpredictable and not to be underestimated. The early users of the road partially solved the problem for the pack mule by blazing the "Lower Trail" from Crane Flat to the Cascade Creek bridge.[6]

* * *

The last station on the road was Gentry's, down the mountain from Tamarack Flat at an elevation of 5627 feet. It was on the brink of the tremendous cliffs overhanging the canyon of the Merced just below Yosemite Valley but was so hemmed in by timber that the precipice was invisible.

Colonel E. S. Gentry settled there while the travelers over the high ridge where his stopping place was located were still riding a rough trail on horse and mule back. The wagon road with its appropriate concomitant of stages and freighters was so slow in arriving at his door that he was but little known to the dwellers on the lower portions of the turnpike. Tamarack Flat was the last destination to be discussed with familiarity by the cattlemen and, until 1872 when the final miles of the road were under construction, only the determined sightseers headed for the wonders of fabled Yosemite or owners of supply trains plodded into Gentry's on tired horses or mules.

Colonel Gentry believed whole-heartedly in a great future for the valley and was willing to rise or fall with its success as a resort. Sawed lumber was difficult to obtain and his buildings were of logs and hand-split shakes. The main dwelling was a stark, two-storied, porchless affair with a steep roof to shed snow and stood on a tiny flat to the right of the road. It was a self-respecting little hotel whose tidy sitting room held the outstanding luxuries of lace curtains and a melodeon. The proprietor and his wife were well liked and did everything possible for their guests' comfort but the place did not vie with Priest's and Crocker's where they had almost metropolitan service. One of the sights at Gentry's was the noisy string of sore-backed mules, belonging to J. M. Hutchings of Yosemite, that carried the weary and often frightened tourists from whatever stopping place was the current terminus of the stage line. Going down the cliff to the floor of the valley they sometimes found their heels higher than their heads on the precipitous trail.

It was Colonel Gentry's great ambition to see a stage road built past his hotel and on into the confines of the Yosemite Park grant. Even though it entailed a difficult piece of construction he was confident that it could be done.

How difficult it actually proved to be he had no conception but his main idea was correct. It could be and was accomplished.

Although no one had foreseen it, the wagon road which he had anticipated with such pleasure was his undoing. When it was no longer necessary to leave the stages and to go down the steep descent on horseback most of the passengers bowled right on into the valley. Soon the little hotel was no longer a paying proposition. After many years of serving the public at this strategic spot Colonel Gentry moved out.

In 1885 Joseph Hutchins took over the location and built a saw-mill near the house. This is obviously easy to confuse with the sawmill run by James Hutchings on the floor of the valley but neither men or mill had any affiliation one with the other. The small cabins of the workers were across the road; the whole group of buildings, as evidenced by debris, stood some 500 yards north of the log barrier that ends the present road.

Hutchins took a contract to supply lumber for the $40,000 government-owned Stoneman Hotel in the valley and used two strings of ponderous oxen to haul the logs in from the woods. Horse teams drew the lumber down the Zigzag. The place (still known as Gentry's) was enlivened with a group of mill hands' cottages; families lived in them during the working season of the year and children played among the trees. The Hutchins family was popular and, during the years that the mill was in operation, gave some of the gayest parties the mountains had yet seen. Dances lasted all the hours of darkness with a chicken dinner at midnight. It was not considered appropriate to serve breakfast to folks who had postponed every tentative advance of hunger by a steady bombardment of pickles, stray chicken gizzards and huge wedges of cake all night so, after daylight, the "neighbors" drove home to recuperate.

Neighbor was an elastic term. According to Celia Crocker Thompson, a neighbor was anyone who lived near or along the Big Oak Flat Road or on its age-old termini, the various branches of the Mono Trail. Even Mr. Farrington of the Mono Lake Ranch was considered to come under that heading though his visits were always sparing.

When the *raison d'etre* of the mill had vanished into the past— Stoneman Hotel was complete and the salable timber worked out—Hutchin's sawmill was dismantled. Down toward the settle-

ments came the freight wagons carrying the family and its posses-
sions; the two mighty bull teams holding the tempo of the whole
procession back to their plodding amble. But it didn't actually
make progress any slower than the farewells from every ranch
and stopping place—a parting of old friends who did not expect
to see one another again. At Gin Flat John B. Curtin sat his horse
and waved as long as the women's handkerchiefs could be seen
fluttering. It was twenty-seven years later at a political rally while
he was campaigning for governor that he saw them once again.

Family and neighborly bonds were strong but goodbyes in the
mountains were apt to be final.

And all through the years the slow, steady freighters plodded
up and down the mountain carrying food, drink, household goods,
clothes—everything that the householder could not raise for himself. Even with their invariable accompaniment of noise and dust
they were always welcome. It was they that made life interesting.

CHAPTER XII

COMPETITION

Beyond Crane Flat, and from 1856 to 1874, the rival communities of Tuolumne County and Mariposa County used a common terminus to their thoroughfares to Yosemite Valley. It followed more or less along the old Mono Trail and led through Gin and Tamarack Flats, Gentry's (in later years) and down the cliff to the floor of Yosemite Valley. A peculiarity which did not interfere with practical usage was that one contingent called the entire length the "Big Oak Flat Trail," while the other group spoke of it as the "Coulterville Free Trail." About the middle sixties the normal course of progress spelled the end of this amicable agreement. There were now hotels in Yosemite depending on tourist trade. They needed stage roads in order to promote custom. J. M. Hutchings, the main hotel owner, decided to make an appeal. He put the proposition first to his friends in Mariposa without result; he then proposed the matter to the citizens of Coulterville who also were uninterested. As a last resort Mr. Hutchings approached the settlers between Chinese Camp and the Garrotes and was met with cooperation.[1]

A group of local men of influence in Tuolumne County caused a declaration of intention to be placed in the newspapers of both counties as a preliminary to a business meeting to be held September 19, 1868. On that date they met according to plan and organized a road company. Surprisingly George W. Coulter of Mariposa County was elected president. Charles B. Cutting and Martin Bacon, merchants of Chinese Camp, Tuolumne County, were secretary and treasurer respectively. In the Declaration of Intention it was outlined clearly that the route was to extend from the east end

243

of Washington Street, Chinese Camp, "running south easterly to Jacksonville Hill, thence to the Tuolumne River south of Woods Creek to a point known as the canyon, thence by Bridge to south side of said river thence up said river to Moccasin Creek, thence up Moccasin Creek to Newhall and Culbertson's Ranch, thence up Big Oak Flat Hill through Big Oak Flat, First Garrote and Second Garrote to Big Gap. Thence up the ridge to Pilot Peak Ridge, thence through Hazel Green to Crain (sic) Flat, thence on South side of the ridge to Tamarac (sic) Flat, thence to head of the YoSemite Trail."[2]

A franchise was granted the company by the State of California on February 20, 1869, to run for fifty years.

Not quite a month later, on March 19, 1869, the group met again "for the purpose of organizing permanently" and reëlected the same officers, with the notable difference that Coulter was replaced as president by Abraham Halsey of Chinese Camp, Tuolumne County, and that Mariposa County was not represented among them.[3] They then moved ahead with their project, beginning work on that portion of the road immediately above Sprague's Ranch.

On September 3, 1869, George Sprague, L. E. Stuart and J. B. Smith, all living above the settlements, wrote to the Commissioners of Yosemite Valley requesting exclusive permission for this company to build a road into the Yosemite Park grant entering the valley from the north side.[4] Permission was granted provided that they would undertake to complete the project by July 1, 1871. They went at it doggedly and by June of 1870 the road had reached Crane Flat.

On January 20, 1871, the company incorporated under the title of Yosemite Turnpike Road Company,[5] thus changing their status to that of a stock company.

The people of Coulterville had by this time begun to realize that they, themselves, would be compelled to have a road reaching into the valley or lose the patronage of staging tourists. They held a meeting. A document was filed,[6] almost the duplicate of that of the Tuolumne County group, Dr. John T. McLean being listed as president. They began extending the road up toward Crane Flat in 1870. Apparently they intended to connect with the Big Oak Flat Road at Crane Flat and use its facilities on into the valley. Later the Yosemite Commissioners stated that they had so understood.[7]

It is true that J. M. Hutchings, on page 287 of his *In the Heart of the Sierras*, states that "... 'the Coulterville and Yosemite Turnpike Company' was formed in 1859, and the road extended, by this company, to Crane Flat, some eighteen miles distant, at a cost of about $15,000." But facts to fit in with this have not come to hand. The earliest road company, which constructed a rude passageway for wagons as far as Bull Creek, was in existence prior to 1856 when the Coulterville Trail was blazed. It is possible that this early organization was incorporated in 1859 but it certainly did not spend $15,000 extending a road to Crane Flat for, as late as 1870, a usable road did not exist beyond Bower Cave, many miles short of that objective. Later in the same volume, on page 335, Hutchings writes, "... it becomes my pleasant duty to chronicle the historical fact, that the Big Oak Flat and Yosemite Turnpike Road Company was the first ever organized for the purpose of extending wagon road facilities beyond the settlements in the direction of the Yo Semite Valley." The last-named company was organized on September 19, 1868, and incorporated January 20, 1871. The Coulterville and Yosemite Turnpike Company was incorporated in June, 1871.[8]

Whatever their reason or objective the Coulterville crew went to work, hammer and tongs, determined not to be left out of the picture.

Meanwhile the Tuolumne group was having trouble. In July, 1871, the time limit specified in the franchise arrived and the Big Oak Flat Road had only reached Gentry's at the edge of the Park grant and at the top of the stupendous cliff. Money and time ran out. The Park Commissioners extended the time six months but this only gave them five, or more likely four months during which, at this elevation, they could work. They were faced with building three miles of zigzag switch-backs down cliffs so precipitous that they must be walled up with masonry—and without the necessary money. On January 1, 1872, they unavoidably forfeited their franchise and apparently did not immediately ask to have it renewed.

The Commissioners then stated that, as the Tuolumne group had not carried the Big Oak Flat Road into the park boundaries, which was the portion specified in the permit issued to them, they felt themselves justified in giving said franchise for an exclusive entrance on the north side of the Merced River, to the rival Coulterville Road group. When this franchise was granted, July 16, 1872, *their* thoroughfare had already been completed almost to Crane Flat. A proviso stated that the work must commence at once and that a right of way suitable for a stage and four horses must be completed to the floor of the valley within the year 1873.⁹

This put a different face on the situation. It would be the Mariposa County group who were to operate the profitable toll gate. Coulterville would be the over-night stop for tourists. The Tuolumne communities were left with a stage road that ended at the end of a cliff and nothing but a saddle train to take the tourists down. It was probable that very few travelers would come their way.

While surveying their road thus far the Coulterville men had rediscovered and named the Merced Grove of Big Trees.[10] In the wave of excitement that followed acquisition of the new franchise they abandoned six miles of roadway between Hazel Green and Crane Flat and made an expensive detour to include the new-found attraction which they felt would equal or excel Tuolumne Grove. At this time they gave up any plan to join the Big Oak Flat Road, leaving that frustrated organization with no possibility of a staging entrance for tourists into the valley.

The Big Oak Flat Road group were badly upset. Through their secretary, C. W. H. Solinsky, they asked, on August 29, 1872, for a franchise to be allowed to build a road—not an exclusive right of way—but just another road into the valley. The following month they were officially refused because the Commissioners had given the exclusive privilege to their rivals from Mariposa County.[11]

In the spring of '73 weather conditions in the mountains were so unfavorable that the Coulterville contingent, in its turn, was unable to begin work until July. Lack of money further handicapped their efforts, making it impossible to meet their deadline. An appeal was made and granted for an extension of time to December 31, 1874.[12]

Along in the fall the Tuolumne group shot another bolt. On November 17, 1873, at a meeting of the Commissioners which the Governor attended, they again requested a franchise permitting them to build a road connecting their district with the valley and were refused. The Commissioners explained reasonably that the road from Mariposa County would cost a large sum and that its supporters were counting on having the exclusive rights in order to pay for it. As a last resort C. B. Cutting of Chinese Camp presented the Executive Committee of the Commissioners a petition asking for the right to construct a wagon road "from Gentry's Station to the Yosemite Valley, which shall be forever free of tolls." The reply sent read in part: "Owing to the peculiar conformation of the Valley, the Commissioners have thought that one road on the north and another on the south side of the Merced would be amply sufficient for the requirements of the public during several years to come. . . ." Among the eight Commissioners were three whose names are familiar to us: J. D. Whitney, the famous geologist; Galen Clark, Guardian of the Valley, and G. W. Coulter, of Coulterville, who at this meeting was suitably excused from voting.[13] In spite of this correct gesture the Tuolumne people, having no one from their county on the Board, were sure that the Commissioners were biassed in favor of the rival road; assured them that they had spent just as much money as had the Coulterville contingent; and accused them of partiality which, in the light cast by future events may have been true. Seven weeks after the last application for permission to extend a toll-free road to the floor of the valley the secretary of the Board of Commissioners wrote a letter to John T. McLean,[14] reading in part: ". . . Mr. Sprague and his associates accomplished nothing, and the Commissioners, hearing nothing from the Yosemite Turnpike Road Company, from the time Sprague and others appealed to us in 1869, until the application of the Coulterville and Yosemite Turnpike Company came, in the Summer of 1872; and being thus ignorant of any intention on the part of the first-named Company to continue their road from Gentry's into the Valley, but supposing they were content to have passengers over their road use the Coulterville trail to enter the Valley, as they had been doing since the completion of their road to Gentry's in 1871, the Commissioners, in accordance with their policy to improve the means of access to the Valley were ready to make and did make the agreement under which the Coulterville and Yosemite Turnpike Company is now constructing its road to and upon the level of the Valley."

Sprague and his faction still contended strongly that the Commissioners knew perfectly well that they wanted to build that road and reminded them that the extension of time was given them in July of 1871 proving that their intentions were a matter of public record. But they didn't have a legal leg to stand on—or did they?

Sprague, Newhall and the other Tuolumne directors were desperate. They had backed the venture strongly, urging their neighbors to put money and time into the project. The impending fiasco was crushing. They began to reason that, as Governor Booth had been elected as a "non-monopoly" man, there might be a chance to appeal to the Legislature for an equal opportunity. But that body did not meet until spring. Meanwhile they had to prove that their projected route from Gentry's down into the valley was feasible.

They appealed to Galen Clark, Guardian of Yosemite Valley, for permission to build a new and improved saddle trail down the cliff. Clark, intensely independent and an individualist, gave the requested permit.[15] They commenced work in earnest on the lower stretches and wherever the snow allowed access. Coulterville had twelve miles to build. They had only three—but such miles! On a two thousand foot precipitous mountain side covered with scrub and loose rock and unprotected from sun or storm. The horse trail was supposed to be only four feet wide but they were allowed passing places and, as the Sonora paper remarked sagely, no one could help it if a pick slipped now and then and made the footway a little more ample.[16] There surely had never been such a saddle trail constructed in the state—graded and smoothed and with strangely wide and flowing curves.

It must have been a fairly mild winter and snow did not cling to the steep mountain side down which the trail zigzagged. It was a big improvement on the previous terminus to the combined Big Oak Flat and Coulterville Trails which had been in its beginnings greatly modified from the original Mono Trail to the valley. Each had used the track of its predecessor where practical and digressed where necessary. The builders needed to take every slight advantage for the grade was so uncompromising that the chainman of the survey crew had to be suspended over the edge of the cliff on ropes. The workmen made the passageway through the loose and rolling rocks as nearly like a road as they dared.

As soon as practical the legislators from Tuolumne County were invited to inspect the horse trail and to pass on the feasibility of widening it to a stage road. Every nerve was strained to make this a successful occasion and the men went back to Sacramento pleased and approving.[17]

At the opening of the Legislature in 1874 a measure was introduced to grant to the Tuolumne group the permission requested and in effect, to overrule the Commission decision. The measure was hotly contested before the committee, the Coulterville group contending that the act was unconstitutional whereas the proponents insisted that the Commissioners had illegally created a monopoly.

On February 17, 1874, the Legislature issued the ultimatum that the Yosemite Commissioners had made an error in granting an *exclusive* privilege to any road company and that both thoroughfares might enter the valley on equal terms.[18]

Andrew Rocca of Big Oak Flat came forward with a $16,000 loan; men were hired and the work, under the enthusiastic leadership of Daniel Newhall, began to show form. George Sprague called into consultation five Italians among the road crew who were adept at rock work. It was amicably agreed among them (with apparently no attempt on either side to get the better of the bargain) that the road company should put up $5000; the Italians should supply a sufficient number of trained men and should finish the cliff-side stretch as expeditiously as possible for a total of $16,000 to be paid later out of tolls collected. In five months of working time and under the supervision of Surveyor Beauvais and Mr. J. Conway the "Zigzag" was completed by these skilled artisans.[19]

Using the beautiful technique learned in their mother country the Italians cribbed up the steep side of the twisting roadbed with solid rock walls, for a stone unseated on one portion of the road might roll down on the switch-back immediately below it or an unusually heavy storm might start a landslide that would wipe out enough of the thoroughfare to make it impassable. No mortar was used. The rocks were simply cut and fitted—a Herculean undertaking.

It was a jubilant crew that wielded ringing picks and shovels on the Zigzag. It was a disappointed but dogged Coulterville group that swung axes against timber between Hazel Green and the valley floor. Determined (and pardonably so) to finish first, the men from Mariposa County rushed their twelve miles of twisting roadway through the forests; the last portion, almost within sight of the valley, at "the Cascades," being considered a worse grade than Priest's Hill and without any saving curves or turns—a straight, steep stretch that frightened women travelers and caused various accidents.[20]

Spring came in 1874 and the switch-backs were not quite finished. The Coulterville roadmakers were victorious by a month and, in June, the first wheeled vehicles came into the valley by way of that route. It was a disappointment to the Tuolumne people but they had given up hoping to be first. All they desired was the equal chance for tourist travel into the valley. Whenever their long-anticipated road should be completed they intended to have a festivity and a parade unequalled by anything yet celebrated in the mountains. That it should be built at all was a triumph. John W. Bookwalter who traveled the route when its wagon terminus was Tamarack Flat had written: "I doubt if the engineering skill of this or any other age will be equal to the task of constructing a road from the last-mentioned point into the valley." His opinion was shared by J. D. Whitney, State Geologist, but its promoters and backers were ethically obligated to face the problem of finishing it. They were now certain of success.

Choral societies and the Sonora band practiced for weeks. Ladies had new dresses made and rushed the final fittings. Men polished their boots until they were like black glass and emptied the stores of shirts, silken ties, pomade, cologne and gloves. As a final gesture many went to the barber, each selected his own shaving mug from the row prominently displayed on the shelf and indulged in a two-bit shave—a comparatively recent luxury as during early mining days only the man with plenty of dust could afford to have his whiskers removed. Both men and women owned voluminous dusters to cover their new haberdashery.

Blacksmiths all through the county were busy setting brakes and putting various conveyances in perfect order. Horses were curried and many a plump work animal had her tail braided to produce the wave that was just that added touch of elegance.

Much thought was given to precedence and Andrew Rocca who had loaned the money to bring the project to completion was given a seat in the first stage driven by Rice Markley and carrying the Sonora band.

July 17th dawned, a fine blue-eyed morning with promise of noonday heat. A caravan assembled, beginning at Gentry's and trailing a mile back along the road.

Mr. C. H. Burden of Sonora who had traveled two days by

stage to attend the celebration gave an eye-witness account of the excitement: "We reach Gentry's and halt for dinner and to decorate our horses. In my mind I see the six-horse team decorated with flags, rosettes and ribbons, and Rice Markley proudly viewing the artistic work. Dan Newhall and George Sprague gave the command, 'Forward march!' and those 52 teams commenced to descend the grade. The writer will never forget the sight."[21] One by one the wagons lowered themselves over the shoulder and down onto the breast of the great uncaring mountain.

Across from them and beyond the small blue ribbon of the Merced River were the cliffs of the south wall a mile or so west of Bridal Veil Fall—raw and seamed and fissured. Before them thousands of wild pigeons wheeled in vacant miles of sun-washed emptiness.

Within a few yards of Gentry's this first breath-taking view from the cliff was entitled "Prospect Point"[22] but when the general public began to travel this way and to express their surprise the early stage drivers soon dubbed it "Oh My! Point." From it the descending parade could see the final miles of the Coulterville Road and, far to the Southwest, the hazy top of Mount Bullion on the edge of the old Fremont Grant.

Most of the occupants of the parading wagons had never been confronted with this startling view. Practically none of them had any idea of the stark steepness of the cliff.

The heat increased. The Zigzag was obscured by a cloud of dust. But nothing could daunt the wildly happy crowd who sang, sweat, flirted and admired the horsemanship of the selected men who spaced the procession to give instant help if a team should become frightened or if a brake should fail.

The fine, energetic girls and women of the mountain country, capable of an enormous amount of either work or enjoyment, were all there, basking in the holiday gallantry of the opposite sex, preening in pride of the new clothes that were rapidly becoming too warm beneath their dusters. It was an age when the much touted womanhood of America kept itself covered with yards of unnecessary cloth from neck to heels. Even the few who dared the descent on horseback rode side saddles and wore immensely long full skirts made heavy to prevent a possible breeze lifting them above the ankle.

A fashion note in the Sonora *Union Democrat* described the ladies so carefully tucked into the polished but already dust-covered buggies: "Between her ruff and the white frill inside her hat, the fashionable belle peeps out like a chicken coming out of the shell."[23]

At the foot of El Capitan and in the welcome shade of the timber on the valley floor the triumphant procession was met by James Mason Hutchings in the capacity of host. Hutchings was one of the first to settle in Yosemite; to build a home and raise a family.

Among the residents of the Big Oak Flat Road the valley was most frequently referred to as "Hutchings' Place." Mr. Hutchings was exuberant that his dream of a practical stage road to the Yosemite Valley hotels had been twice fulfilled within the month.

The caravan proceeded, led by him. Mr. Burden continued: "As we reached the floor of the great wonderland we were met by a procession of campers and residents of the valley. Such cheering, shouting and singing! It was deafening, but the music of it all was even as pleasing as that rendered by our band. The great throng, with continuous cheering, moved on, and 512 persons passed over the Ira Folsom bridge that evening. Our first stop was at Black's Hotel, where the band was most royally entertained." They then started a round of the hotels which were all on the south side. Feasting, dancing and entertainment by the amazingly costumed Indians completed a notable day.

The Sonora papers proclaimed that the festivities were an immense success; (quoting the same authority) "the road as a success is still 'immenser'." All the Tuolumne people were positive that between their new entrance and Mr. McLean's there could be no parallel. We beg to quote again: "McLane's road as compared with it, is the sinuous winding of a broken-back eel, to the gentle curves of a majestic boa."[24]

In spite of the fact that the trail was quoted as being ". . . as steep as it is possible for your animal to keep his feet, where a single false step would hurl both horse and rider on the jagged rocks a thousand feet below. . . ."[25] there were no untoward events during the procession. In fact, there were but few accidents on the Zigzag, for its very nature counciled caution and one could see a long distance over the empty slope. Before a control was established any encounter between vehicles, however, meant time wasted and usually plenty of hard work. Charles Schmidt, who freighted to the valley, said: "In the '70s there was no control system and many a carriage I helped to lift off the Zigzag so that we could pass. Bells on the leaders helped a lot. They could be heard a long way and gave a chance to stop where there was room to pass." In the case of light buggies they sometimes tied ropes to them and dangled them over the edge but Mrs. Case and her party recorded that (even though the control was supposed to be functioning) they suddenly came face to face with a de luxe camping wagon belonging to the Charles Crocker family of San Francisco and were obliged to dissect their own small vehicle and pass it by hand over the top of the big van.

The only notable casualty was in 1902 when J. M. Hutchings was the victim of a run-away team and was thrown from his buggy almost at the foot of the grade. He and Mrs. Hutchings had visited the Crocker family where they posed for a photograph before leaving. He never reached his valley home. Before Mrs. Hutchings could return with help her husband was dead.

On July 19, 1915, Tuolumne County bought the Big Oak Flat and Yosemite Toll Road for $10,000 and shortly after deeded it to the State of California which proceeded to improve it as far as the boundary of the National Park. Here, of course, the state's jurisdiction ended.

After the Zigzag became a control road the checking station was at Gentry's. There was a similar station on the valley floor. Down traffic was allowed to proceed at stated hours. Up traffic was checked out of the valley in the intervals. For forty years, from 1874 to 1914, only horse-drawn vehicles traveled this stretch and two miles an hour was a fair average speed. Nor, especially on the up grade, was there much one could do about hurrying it. It was, we have been told, about 1905 or '06 that a professor of the University of California was part way down the descent when he and his party were held up by a masked bandit. They were told to get out of the vehicle and hand over their valuables which they wisely did, being all the while enlivened by the unhelpful sight of a troop of cavalry riding slowly up the steep, short turns below them. When the road agent had obtained what he wanted he scrambled up the mountain side to where, doubtless, he had a horse waiting. The victims were free to do anything they wished which amounted to nothing. It wasn't safe and would have been ineffectual to follow him on foot. A horse could not get up the boulder-studded mountainside. They could not turn the vehicle around to return to Gentry's. And it would take half an hour at the best for the cavalry to arrive. They simply continued their journey.

In 1913 automobiles were permitted to enter the park via the Coulterville Road; a year later by way of Big Oak Flat. This was in a great measure due to the efforts of Senator John B. Curtin.

Apprehensive motorists zoomed down or chugged up the Zigzag at a maximum allowed speed of six miles per hour; experience in the previous year having proved that ten miles was too fast. This could not be called mercurial but was faster than the two miles per hour of private horse-drawn vehicles. The stages, of course, made better time. One of the three spans of stage-horses was usually taken off going down grade as there were no uphill stretches and the turns were short.

The new highway from Crane Flat to the valley superceded the Zigzag in 1940. Very few then used the old route but it was kept open, for down traffic only, until 1943 when a major rock slide obliterated a portion and rendered it impassable. It was not considered worth while to clear it.

The difficulty between the Big Oak Flat and Coulterville Road Companies was never overcome. Each one felt, with some justice, that the other had taken advantage of a period of low ebb but that only the future could decide which one would reap the most benefit. Meanwhile the rivalry was keen and sometimes bitter. After completion the two turnpikes were always competitors.

As time passed it became evident that the Coulterville Road, although courageously managed by its owner, Mr. McLean, was not getting enough travel to prosper. It became deserted and lonely but is still a notable landmark, and, with its attendant town of Coulterville, is well worth the time and attention of any visitor in the Southern Mines who is thoroughly accustomed to rough mountain roads.

The Big Oak Flat Road had better luck. For forty years horse-drawn vehicles and, later, automobiles by the hundred ventured over the edge of the cliff at Gentry's and crept down the one-way road that followed in the main a pathway worn by the padding feet of long-dead Indians—the unbelievable Zigzag that, until 1940, was the shortest route between Stockton and Yosemite.

CHAPTER XIII

YOSEMITE—ITS INTIMATE STORY

Yosemite, miracle of grandeur! Rendezvous of beauty unimaginable! Hidden for three and half centuries, wrapped in folds of fir-napped mountains, while explorers—Spanish, Portuguese, Norse, Dutch, English, Russian, French—probed here and there throughout our continent.

But it was not always lonely. Within the deep smoke-scented hollow lived an almost lengendary tribe who called their home "Ahwahnee."[1] Generations passed and the Ahwahneeches were decimated by wars and epidemics. The survivors scattered.

Then the valley waited uninhabited. But it was not forgotten.

A young warrior, Ten-ie-ya, of the blood of the Ahwahneeches, had spent his life among the Pah-Utes living in the foothill country eastward of the peaks. Ahwahnee called to him. With some two hundred souls gathered from the Pah-Utes and other peoples the warrior journeyed west over the mountains and down into the valley. He grew to be an old man and was still chief of this motley tribe which was called "Yo Semite," meaning perhaps Big Grizzly Bear.[2]   *   *   *

Ten-ie-ya and his people were there when, in 1833, Joseph Reddeford Walker and his party of mountain men passed along the Mono Trail north of the great gorge of the valley, crossing Yosemite Creek some two miles above the brink of the falls.

Whether Walker or his men detoured close enough to the valley to see any of its features, except possibly Half Dome and the tops of the surrounding peaks, is one of the open questions that add spice to the study of Yosemite. There is no doubt but that they were the first white men entitled to say their eyes had gazed in disturbed awe upon the Yosemite country; but actually to look into the gorge, to see its breath-taking cliffs and waterfalls, is another matter. Although it will probably always be a point having strong arguments for and against, we personally think that they did not.

Dr. Lafayette H. Bunnell gives this account in his *Discovery of the Yosemite:*

"The topography of the country over which the Mono Trail ran, and which was followed by Capt. Walker, did not admit of his seeing the valley proper. The depression indicating the valley, and its magnificent surroundings, could alone have been discovered, and in Capt. Walker's conversations with me at various times while encamped between Coulterville and the Yosemite, he was manly enough to say so. Upon one occasion I told Capt. Walker that Ten-ie-ya had said that, 'A small party of white men once crossed the mountains on the north side, but were so guided as not to see the valley proper.'³ With a smile the Captain said, "That was my party, but I was not deceived, for the lay of the land showed there was a valley below; but we had become nearly barefooted, our animals poor, and ourselves on the verge of starvation; so we followed down the ridge to Bull Creek, where, killing a deer, we went into camp.""

Bunnell was correct. The country through which runs the Mono Trail gives no intimation of the tremendous drop-off into Yosemite Valley only a couple of miles south, although the conformation of the mountain peaks indicates a depression. The timbered plateau allows but few viewpoints and does not begin to incline and form a mountainside until west of Ribbon Creek (or Virgin's Tears).

If Bunnell quoted Walker with anything approaching accuracy, Walker did not see the valley. If the quotation is suspected of inaccuracy (for which Bunnell's character gave no justification) it is best to ignore it and turn to the other source always quoted in an attempt to solve this puzzling question of what white men first saw Yosemite: the account written by Zenas Leonard who traveled with Walker and kept a record of the expedition. From it we learn that the party spent almost a month in crossing over "the mountain," as they called the Sierra Nevada Range. Their route has

Opening of the Big Oak Flat Road into Yosemite Valley, July 17, 1874.

Mr. and Mrs. J. M. Hutchings at Crocker's Station, 1902. Mr. Hutchings was killed a few hours later when his frightened horses ran uncontrolled down the zigzags of the Big Oak Flat Road.

First automobiles over the Big Oak Flat Road.
Locomobiles at Crocker's Station, 1901.

Down into Yosemite Valley. El Capitan in background. About 1907.

Boysen

On the zigzags above Yosemite Valley. These were obliterated by rock slides in October 1942.

always been a mystery except that they used "the Mono Trail" north of Yosemite which then forks into many branches, but by combining field and library research it seems capable of analysis.

It was October. Where they at first thought they had struck the summit they found old snow left from the winter before, topped by about eight inches of fresh snowfall. They could find no trail, no feed for their horses, no game for themselves. The rebellious men wished to turn back although to do so meant probable death. Walker stemmed the tide by having a couple of horses killed for food.

We can be certain that they had no Indian guide.

Zenas Leonard wrote:

"We travelled a few miles every day, still on top of the mountain, and our course continually obstructed with snow hills and rocks. Here we began to encounter in our path, many small streams which would shoot out from under these high snow-banks, and after running a short distance in deep chasms which they have through the ages cut in the rocks, precipitate themselves from one lofty precipice to another, until they are exhausted in rain below.—Some of these precipices appeared to us to be more than a mile high. Some of the man (sic) thought that if we could succeed in descending one of these precipices to the bottom, we might thus work our way into the valley below—but on making several attempts we found it utterly impossible for a man to descend, to say nothing of our horses. We were then obliged to keep along the top of the dividing ridge between two of these chasms which seemed to lead pretty near in the direction we were going—which was West,—in passing over the mountain, supposing it to run north & south."

If the creeks that "precipitate themselves from one lofty precipice to another" are to furnish evidence that Walker's party looked down into Yosemite Valley it is plain that they must be proven to be the creeks that fall over the north rim instead of the south or the men could not have attempted to descend along their courses. Passing over the fact that all the falls flowing over the north wall of the valley would probably be dry by the middle of October we will take them in order: Snow Creek does not have such falls near the top of the mountain. Indian Creek does not fit the picture as down its canyon and beside the falls was a well-worn Indian trail, their accustomed exit from the valley to the north rim. Yosemite Creek and Falls might be considered but it would hardly be possible to be in a position to see them and still to miss the easily accessible Indian Falls trail so close by. Walker's men were trained mountaineers—the very best. The spectacular, uninterrupted drop of Ribbon Falls, said to be the longest in the world, does not match the description. And it is hardest of all to believe that anyone could have looked down into Yosemite Valley for the first time, no matter how tired and hungry, and not have given a word picture that would apply to it alone and to no other place nearby.

It is easier to reason that the creeks which "precipitate themselves from one lofty precipice to another" were Cascade and Little Cascade Creeks, Tamarack, Coyote and Wildcat Creeks which the Mono Trail crosses west of Ribbon Creek after the plateau has ended and the mountainside angles sharply more than a mile down to the canyon of the Merced River west of the valley. Their progress is a series of cascades and falls—some of several hundred feet in height. The descent of this mountainside, so old-timers tell us, is impassable; the Indian trails detour around it. The "valley below" into which the men were so anxious to arrive would be either the invisible terrain at the foot of the heavily timbered, snow-covered mountain or (using another and broader interpretation) simply the San Joaquin Valley which was well known to them by reputation as filled with herds of deer and elk. It was late in the year; the winter snows were falling and the men were living on the flesh of exhausted horses which had died or had been killed on the trail. The San Joaquin Valley to the west was their objective. Any detour would be unwelcome.

Some authorities suggest that the word "chasms" refers to the great gorge of Yosemite to the south and that of Hetch Hetchy to the north; but Leonard has already used the word to indicate the canyons of small creeks. We believe that "the dividing ridge between two of these chasms" along the top of which they "were then obliged to keep" and which led west is undoubtedly the ridge running west from Crane Flat on which is the Crane Flat Fire Lookout. A branch of the Mono Trail rode the crest of this hogsback and from it one may see the Tuolumne Grove of Big Trees to the north and a few miles farther along, look down on Merced Grove to the south. A bird's-eye view of the peculiar dome-like crowns of these trees is like nothing else and would certainly lead to investigation by the hunting parties who wandered far afield in any case. During "two days' travelling" they saw these trees and measured some specimens "16 to 18 fathom round the trunk." Now the *Sequoia Gigantea* grows only in more or less compact groves, never scatteringly through the forests; and the only groups in this particular portion of the country, Tuolumne and Merced Groves, are small, numbering about two dozen trees apiece. It has not yet been suggested to our knowledge that more than one grove was seen by Walker but it would be unnatural to write that they saw two dozen trees growing close together in "two days' travelling." The logical reasoning is that the party saw first the grove fartherest east—Tuolumne; then having bivouacked on the trail, strung along past Merced Grove the next day. From no other ridge would they have seen both groves.

After passing above the Big Trees the ridge becomes precipitous; they had difficulty in making the descent from the hogsback. A rocky, steep declivity, impassable for horses, extends for miles, growing worse toward Pilot Peak which climaxes the end of the range.[4] Anderson Flat and Deer Flat lie temptingly below, each at an air-line distance of about a mile. Old-timers say that an

Indian foot-trail led to Anderson's Flat on Bull Creek and that it was the logical termination of the trail along the hogsback. On being questioned they say that Walker could have and probably did go that way. It fits Leonard's description perfectly and one can imagine the weary horses being skidded down the last few hundred feet as Leonard describes. Here the party left the snow and found forage.

The country to the west of Pilot Peak, rather lightly timbered now, was at that time a magnificent forest dwindling down to the foothills. Leonard's description is too long to quote but fits the topography of the lower hills in every respect. Here, beyond any reasonable doubt, lies Joe Walker's route.

Referring again to the discovery of Yosemite and discounting the proposition of its being seen by Joseph Reddeford Walker's men in 1833; the question arises as to whether any other person of white blood viewed the valley before the year 1851 which history has tentatively selected as the date when its amazing vista came to light. The answer is a definite "yes." The proof is the diary of William Penn Abrams who came to California by the Chagres route in 1849; progressed from San Francisco to Stockton to the Southern Mines, giving an almost daily account of himself as he went along; returned to San Francisco and wrote on October 15, 1849:

"Returned to S. F. after visit to Savage property on Merced River prospects are not too good for a mill   Savage is a blaspheming fellow who has five sqaws [*sic*] for wives for which he takes no authority from the Scriptures   While at Savage's Reamer and I saw grizzly bear tracks and went out to hunt him down getting lost in the mountains and not returning until the following evening found our way to camp over an Indian trail that lead [*sic*] past a valley inclosed by stupendous cliffs arising perhaps 3000 feet from their base and which gave us cause for wonder. Not far off a waterfall dropped from a cliff below three jagged peaks into the valley while farther beyond a rounded mountain stood the valley side of which looked as though it had been sliced with a knife as one would slice a loaf of bread and which Reamer and I called the Rock of Ages."

The described view from the old Indian trail on the south cliffs is known to thousands: El Capitan to the left, Bridal Veil Fall pouring from beneath the three Cathedral Rocks on the right, while, beyond, the almost unique silhouette of Half Dome arises. Yosemite Falls are invisible around the curve of the valley. To conjure up this scene without seeing it, especially to place it within one day's trek of James Savage's trading post, would be a coincidence beyond our credence. William Penn Abrams *saw* Yosemite in 1849 but evidently did not descend to the valley floor.

Could it be possible that no white man invaded its granite corridor during the three years between the discovery of gold in the spring of 1848 and 1851? Even though it lay beyond the gold belt such a thing seems unlikely with swarms of amateur prospectors roaming the mountains. J. M. Hutchings, whose book *In the Heart of the Sierras* is one of the standard sources of Yosemite information, had his doubts. "It is true," he wrote, "the writer has heard of various persons having visited it, when prospecting for gold, as early as 1849, but no responsible data to establish the fact has yet come to his knowledge."

Who was the first white man to tread the meadows of Yosemite is still an open question and waits for more definite information to be turned up, but scattering bits of information point toward James Savage, a wild and romantic character whose well-known habits render such a conclusion very possible. It is a fact that the honor *was* accorded to him as leader of the Mariposa Battalion, of which Bunnell was a member, and which entered the valley early in the spring of 1851 to chastise the mysterious Yosemite Indians; but these indefinite stories and rumors hint that he was there at least as early as 1849. One such incident was recorded by Robert A. Curtin in his notebook, the material in which has unfailingly proven to be truthful and correct. He wrote that James Ackerson, who lived in the high mountains, told him of a party of four who were on an "exploration tour" sometime before the Mariposa Battalion entered the valley ". . . they," wrote Mr. Curtin, "upon seeing the big valley from Eagle Peak country drifted down into it. They soon found a white man there with the Indians. He approached them and told them they would have to get out as the Indians didn't want any white men there. 'Then what are you doing there,' asked one. He gave an evasive answer, and was quickly told by the spokesman, 'If any trouble starts you will be the first man I will kill.' Not knowing what the odds might be, they went back the way they came and told of the discovery upon their return. I always regretted that I did not learn their names, but at that time history meant nothing . . . so a priceless heritage slipped through our fingers."

Backing up this vague story of a lone white man in the valley is another, more definite statement, signed by a participant in the scene of action and provided with names of the actors. The Modesto *Stanislaus News* of January 22, 1875, printed this article: "Editor News:- There has been much written and published concerning the first discovery of the great YoSemite valley by the white man, and no doubt the writers believed they were correct in what they have written and published. But there is one great error in their statements, and which, with your leave, I propose to correct.

"In the latter part of the month of June, 1849, the writer of this article, in company with six others, whose names are here given, viz., Remington of New York, Hayyerd, N. Y., Taylor, N. Y., Doctor Clements, of Winchester, Virginia, Goff, of England,

Stevens, of Wales, started on a prospecting tour south from Sonora, Tuolumne county, and crossed the Tuolumne river at the place now called Don Pedro's Bar, we then traveled in a north-easterly direction between the Merced and Tuolumne rivers, till we found the camp of James Savage near Pino Blanco. At this time Mr. Savage was acknowledge [*sic*] the Chief of the Indians from the Mokelumne river to the Merced river on the south, and embracing all the territory from the San Joaquin river on the west to the summit of the Sierra Nevada Mountains. We staid in his camp three or four days and got all the information we could in regard to the country south of his camp.

"Now, Mr. Savage was married according to the Indian custom, and I must here state that his wife was not what would be considered a beauty on Fifth Avenue, . . . I asked Mr. Savage where he found her, and who she was. He answered that she was the daughter of the great Chief of the Yo Hamete Valley, that is what the Indians called it. We then asked where the Yo Hamete Valley was. He told us that it was high up on the Merced river, and entirely out of the gold belt. We asked him if he was ever there. He said that he was. And he then went on with a description of the great valley, its waterfalls, etc. Some of the falls he said were 18 hundred feet high. So the reader will see that Yo Semite Valley was known to at least one white man as early as the month of June, 1849, for James Savage was a white man and an American. . . .

"If the foregoing should meet the eye of any of my companions who were on the prospecting trip, they can testify to the correctness of what I have written. . . . Respectfully yours, Huge Paw."

On the second page of this same issue of the *Stanislaus News* the editor, a 49er in his own right, expressed his views and incidentally corrected the spelling of the name of the author of the foregoing item as follows: "Yosemite Valley:- On the fourth page of to-day's issue, 'Huge Paw' gives us an article on the discovery of the Yo-Semite Valley. The writer, we think, very clearly shows that the old mountaineer, James Savage, was actually the first white man that ever visited that wonderful valley. From our own personal knowledge of Savage, and his peculiar roaming habit, we cannot see how he could have well failed in coming across the YoSemite in his many travels among the Indians of the great mountain range of California."

As might have been expected L. H. Bunnell, who was pardonably proud to have entered the valley with the Mariposa Battalion, wrote clear from his new address in Minnesota to refute this statement. His article appeared in the *Mariposa County Gazette*, March 13, 1875, stating that Savage personally told him that he had never been in the valley before the advent of the Battalion. Dr. Bunnell's character for veracity does not permit us to doubt his words but the doctor, himself, says in the article: ". . . the Major was an inveterate quiz and given to romancing . . ." so skeptics merely wonder in this case of conflicting stories just which man he was deceiving, Dr. Bunnell or Hugh Paw. It is not irreconcilable that Savage should possibly have been both the leader of the Battalion and the son-in-law of Chief Ten-ie-ya. The company was committed to the job of chastising and changing the marauding policy of the tribe with as little bloodshed as possible and was assembled and practically on the march when Savage was elected commander. In what other position could he have accomplished as much honest good for both races. Students of this small but interesting campaign will note many incidents that point toward this solution: Ten-ie-ya's calm arrival alone at camp, the escape of the Indian village up the cliff while the Battalion delayed attack and other incidents of clemency—marred by the unplanned shooting of Ten-ie-ya's two sons by a guard as they attempted escape—total a record of Indian fighting as innocuous and devoid of bloodshed as any one is apt to find in history.

Every reader must form his own opinion, and possibly someone will have another item of information to add to the collection.

* * *

When gold was discovered in California Ten-ie-ya was old and firmly resolved that the ant-like columns of miners should not enter his stronghold. The arresting figure of Savage was also well established among the Indians on the western slope of the Sierra. It was his habit to take a wife from each of the more influential tribes and the estimates of those writers who mention him vary from five to thirty. He possessed some trading posts but his biggest profits came from his numerous in-laws who more or less industriously panned out gold dust and nuggets for his benefit.

There is no need for this volume to treat of the details of depredations by the Chowchilla, Yosemite and other tribes that led to the formation of the Mariposa Battalion of Volunteers which Savage commanded by unanimous vote. Farms and trading posts had been ravaged and men killed for the length of the lower San Joaquin Valley by Indians who were determined to halt the advance of the white men. The subject has been competently handled in other volumes. For source information read Hutchings' *In the Heart of the Sierras*, Bunnell and Kuykendall. To find the information in one volume read *One Hundred Years in Yosemite* by Carl Parcher Russell. It is enough to say here that, after a couple of bloody skirmishes, the Battalion entered the valley—supposedly the first white men to do so—toward the last of March, 1851. Previous sources have said March 25th. Eccleston's daily diary says the 27th.

The foray was not successful. The tribe had disappeared up the Indian Canyon trail, leaving but one feeble old woman behind them. In May another attempt was made and this time the Indians were brought out and many of them installed on the Fresno Reservation. They were disconsolate and, on solemn promise of good behavior, were soon permitted to go back to their beloved valley.

In May of 1852 they attacked a party of prospectors. Soldiers were dispatched to the valley; found five Indians with articles known to belong to the murdered men and shot them. The rest of the tribe, including Ten-ie-ya, took refuge in the Mono country. Almost exactly fifty years later a reminiscence by Stephen F. Grover came to the authorities at Yosemite showing that this outrage was probably instigated by a white man. It sums up briefly: A party entered Yosemite consisting of Grover, Aich, Peabody, Babcock, an Englishman whose name Grover had forgotten, and three partners in an existing mine, Rose, Tudor and Sherburn. None of the party wished to enter the valley except the partners but were finally persuaded. While encamped they were attacked by Indians. Rose fell first at some distance from camp apparently with a death wound. Sherburn and Tudor were killed but the rest received superficial wounds and escaped to the cliff where with two rifles they kept the Indians at a distance. When one of the leaders of the Yosemites was disabled the Indians withdrew, enabling the prospectors to creep away and return to their camp at Coarse Gold Gulch and their friends. A burial party led by Aich met with no resistance but they found only the bodies of Tudor and Sherburn. In a few days Rose turned up, unhurt, at the partners' mine about five miles west of Coarse Gold; reported the attack and said that the whole party except himself had been killed. When he heard that he was mistaken and that the other five had escaped he disappeared at once without permitting them to see him and they came to believe that he had egged the Indians on to the attack in order to fall heir to his partners' share in the mine.

In the summer or fall of 1853 the Mono Indians and the Yosemites quarreled. Ten-ie-ya and several of his braves were stoned to death; the old people were ignored but the women and young children were absorbed by the Monos. The Yosemite tribe was effectively dispersed. Ten-ie-ya's remains were carried over the mountains to Hite's Cove on the South Fork of the Merced where they were disposed of according to tribal custom.

* * *

Yosemite became known. Dr. Lafayette H. Bunnell of the Mariposa Battalion should be thanked for most of the scant publicity but, although none of the glory of the surroundings nor the pathos of the events were lost on him, he did not publish his book *The Discovery of the Yosemite* until 1880. So, at the end of four years although the existence of the amazing valley was noted by the public its features were still hazy and it was still inaccessible. In 1854, so Luella Dickenson wrote, five women and four men visited Yosemite, finding the Indians friendly.

The next man who was to figure in publicizing it was however in California, having arrived inconspicuously in '49 walking behind a pack mule.

There is an unusual amount of data on James Mason Hutchings, the "father" of the valley, unofficial host to early visitors. His life and his personality were known to all the mountain families for he was a person of prominence in the far-flung community. Helen Hunt Jackson described him as "an enthusiast, a dreamer, a visionary." His voluminous diary is extant and old-timers will talk of him at length but the most intimate information came from his daughter, Gertrude Hutchings Mills—always called "Cozie."

This lady, white-haired and frail, is permitted to set her camp anywhere in the park and, between the years 1940 and 1949 she frequently availed herself of the privilege. It was necessary to drive to her secluded tent in Tuolumne Meadows to obtain an interview. It had been raining but the sun was struggling out from behind the clouds. Her fireplace was at the base of a great rock and the space about it was floored with natural flat slabs of granite, wet and shining; but the pitch pine and chunks of dead bark were dry and the energetic blaze leaped and crackled. She was glad to talk of her father and the interview covered a good deal of territory. Only the most significant items or details not apt to be found elsewhere are given here.

"My father lived for awhile in Placerville," she said. "It was in the early '50s. He wrote a weekly column for the town's paper. He always liked to write. It was while he was there that he became the author of the "Miners' Ten Commandments." It was amazing how many copies were sold.

"About that time he met Joseph Reddeford Walker who captained the first party of white men ever to set eyes on the Yosemite country. They had approached it by way of Bloody Canyon, the only trail that crossed the Sierra in this vicinity. I think the two men talked about the high Sierra country for, from that time, my father was bound and determined to see it."

While she talked Cozie Hutchings Mills continued to feed crumbs of bread to three white-crowned sparrows who ate cautiously from her hand.

"In 1855 father made the journey to Yosemite Valley and took an artist with him to sketch the cliffs and the waterfalls. From that time on Yosemite was in his blood. He brought mother here to live in 1862. They built a house south of the river for no one realized at first that the north side is much warmer in winter—gets the sun longer each day and also the heat reflected from the cliffs. On August 23rd of 1864 the first white child was born in Yosemite—my sister, Florence. Mount Florence, that magnificent peak in the park, was named for her. She dearly loved the woods and all animals and died when she was seventeen.

"I came along later. My real name is Gertrude although no one ever uses it. Father named me for the ship that brought him over from England. My people kept a sort of hotel for it was practically impossible not to take guests with scientists, naturalists and travelers beginning to arrive and no place for shelter. What we had we shared."

Straight from James Mason Hutchings' own diary comes the following information: He was not, it seems, exempt from the lure of the gold camps but lost the proceeds of several years' work in the diggings due to the failure of a private bank and of Adam's Express Company. He undertook to recoup by traveling through the gold camps selling "letter sheets" to the miners who seldom had anything suitable on which to write home. One variety had a letterhead decorated with supposedly the first picture ever made of a "Mammoth Tree" in Calaveras Grove. Others had pictures of mining processes or of Indians. Some had the Miners' "Ten Commandments." Of the latter he sold enough to supply one-fifth of the population of the state.

He did this profitably for a year when he decided to get some sketches of newly-found Yosemite. An Indian guided a party of four, including Hutchings and the artist, Thomas Ayres. These four named Mirror Lake and Bridal Veil Fall. On the way out, while in Mariposa, Hutchings wrote an article for the Mariposa *Gazette* featuring the scenic wonders of the valley but the notable success of Hutchings' publicity campaign was greatly aided by the accomplished Ayres, whose pictures were the first likenesses of the beauties of the valley to be circulated and created a sensation. Ten of them are now in the Yosemite Museum. An immediate result of their appearance was a succession of small parties who trekked to the beautiful gorge before the year was out, hiring the same Indian guides.

Yosemite became an obsession with Hutchings. It possessed him. He had always wanted to publish a magazine. Now it became an obligation. He went to San Francisco, rented an office, made arrangements with engravers and printers, acquired a "Daggnerean machine" (whatever that may be), hired an assistant and was then free to dash off to the mines again at the top speed of his horse and wagon.

Famous *Hutchings' California Magazine* came off the press for the first time July 18, 1856. The opening article extolled the unique features of "Yo-ham-i-te Valley." The magazine was only published about five years but is still known in the historical libraries of the nation as an exponent of the old west.

About that time illness in the family made it expedient to leave the foggy coast. Hutchings at once visualized a home in his ideal valley but, as ridiculous as it now sounds, no one was sure at that time but what, in a heavy season, Yosemite might fill a hundred feet deep with snow slides. To disprove this disconcerting theory he had to see it in winter and set out again with an Indian guide; but, when the going got rough, the Indian vanished. Hutchings pluckily kept on alone and the effort did not fall far short of costing his life. He approached the valley from the south cliffs, as was then the custom, and the happiest sight of his journey was the irregular black ribbon of the Merced River showing through the snowdrifts of the valley floor.

There were at that time Indian trails entering the valley from many directions.[5]   *   *   *

The exact progress of events in the valley is difficult to chronicle because the main recorders of those early years, Hutchings, Galen Clark, Whitney, Bunnell and others, do not always agree and statements must be weighed one against another and against known facts. Russell's *One Hundred Years in Yosemite,* gives a splendid chronological history of the building program and of historic happenings. This will be a more casual but (we hope) enlightening story of the coming of civilization to Yosemite Valley and the comedies and tragedies of the daily lives of the first settlers.

As might have been expected the very first rude shelter to be thrown together was erected in 1855 by some men (including Lafayette Bunnell) who were considering ditching water down to the Mariposa mines; but it was a temporary affair and soon disappeared. The first building intended for permanence was put up the next year, crushed by snow and rebuilt in the spring of 1857. Galen Clark wrote with open disapproval that it was, during its first season, a saloon and gambling place but it soon came under the management of Mr. and Mrs. John H. Neal and was conducted suitably as a simple mountain inn. It was known as Lower Hotel.

Eighteen fifty-seven was notable for the advent of Galen Clark and the establishment of Clark's Ranch in the lovely opening in the forest later known as Wawona. At once it became an important stopping place on the Mariposa-Yosemite Trail. On May 25th, 1857, Clark was startled by a party in which were five women, the first ever to arrive as tourists. One of their number, Harriet J. Kirtland, tells the story in a journal which makes light of the extreme neighborliness of the grizzly bear in the vicinity but appears to be approaching disaster in the matter of an unironed chemise which, however, she fully intends to launder properly before wearing. Final results are not obtainable.

Galen Clark, retiring and exceedingly independent but much beloved, was a member of the first Board of Commissioners of Yosemite Valley and Mariposa Grove and was more than once appointed "Guardian of the Valley." As in the cases of John Muir, the famous nature-lover, and James Hutchings, Clark identified himself completely with the stupendous mountain area that he loved and to many is best remembered as the accredited discoverer of the Mariposa Grove of Big Trees. He was a silent man and once, when beseiged for information by a lady visitor, told her expressively that his supply of words was not of the artesian type (by which we fear he was referring to John Muir) but that, if she would keep on trying, he could be pumped. He lived in the valley or in its vicinity more than fifty years.

In the spring of 1858 Upper Hotel came into being at what is now the south end of Sentinel Bridge and across the highway. Mr. and Mrs. Neal moved up from Lower Hotel and managed it until 1864 when James Hutchings became the proprietor. It was then known as Hutchings House and, for five or six years, was the stopping place most frequented by particular travelers. Not that it had much to offer but the travelers couldn't afford to be choosy.

Helen Hunt Jackson, writing under the initials "H. H.," arrived at Hutchings' place in the '70s when the road was only a "sandy path." There were four buildings, she said, three of which made up the hotel. Two of them were cottages for lodging only: the Cottage by the Rocks and the Cottage by the River, the latter being precariously closer to the full, strong current of the Merced than she "deemed" quite safe although there was always the recompense of viewing Yosemite Falls through a back window while lying in bed. The floors were of rough pine, the walls of thin laths on which was stretched white muslin (far from sound or shadow proof), the mattress a sack filled with fern, the wash bowl a shallow tin pan, while the water was obtained from a barrel in the hall and was merely on a slight detour from the river whence it came and to which it would eventually drain back. Mrs. Hunt mentioned that one window had no curtain, and if she didn't see an aboriginal nose flattened against the pane during her stay it was because the Indians hadn't as yet found out that the blind was gone. H. H. had no complaints, however, and had a poor opinion of any dim soul who would put personal comfort above the appreciation of nature's beauties.

Another building was the Cosmopolitan Saloon, respectable and respected. H. H. was undoubtedly glad to see it as, at that time, it was the only place in the valley where one could get a comfortable hot bath. It had five fully carpeted bath rooms, equipped with pin cushions and bay rum, and a private sitting room for ladies. Nor were the gentlemen neglected. Two fine tables for the billiard room had been brought in miraculously on mule back. Culture had come into the valley with the first families; comfort was arriving. Of course they had always to reckon with the four or five villages of Indians scattered against the cliffs. No resident of the valley objected to their age-old habits but visitors were sometimes disenchanted. Olive Logan, arriving at Hutchings House via saddle train and thoroughly disgruntled, had a few words to say.

"There is an Indian camp beside Hutchings'. A vile stench greets us. These filthy wretches found a dead horse yesterday, and are now eating some of the carcass. Its entrails and other parts are strung out in the sun to dry for future eating . . . Indian men loll under the trees playing cards for silver coin. They glare at us as we approach."

There was probably something to be said both for Olive's point of view and that of the Indians. Olive went home at the end of three days leaving Mr. Hutchings "deeply chagrined."

Meanwhile Yosemite's first horticulturalist, James C. Lamon, arrived in 1859 and helped to put the finishing touches on Upper Hotel before preëmpting a claim about where Camp Curry and the park stables now are. Under the large pines to the right and in front of the present stables he built the first log cabin home in the valley and, according to pictures in the museum, it was made of trees about eighteen inches in diameter. Near what is now the Camp Curry parking lot he planted four acres of orchard of which the trees still bear fruit. Lamon was the first person to live in Yosemite the year around. During the winters of 1862-63 and 1863-64 he remained entirely alone and, as the first named was one of the heaviest seasons ever recorded, he must have witnessed rare sights. Of the more than 1100 acres in the valley floor Hutchings and Lamon held 160 acres each. Other claims were made but became invalid as the holders failed to maintain permanent residence.

In 1862, so said Cozie Hutchings Mills, her mother came to the valley, but evidently not as yet to remain for the winter season. By '64 she was permanently installed and the first white baby was born in Yosemite—her daughter, Florence, whom, when she was six, John Muir called "a little black-eyed witch of a girl, the only one in the valley."[6] A good portion of her short life was spent regretting that she had not been born a boy but that slight miscalculation on the part of nature did not prevent her from hiking and even camping in the high mountains alone. She used tobacco, because she liked it, as women do now; was impatient of social usages and of any restraint and was not afraid of anything. Her death at seventeen was directly attributable to her refutation of any form of caution.

According to her father, by the year that Florence was born 653 tourists had managed to arrive undamaged in the valley and Yosemite was granted by act of Congress to the State of California as a recreational reserve or park. It was two seasons later before the Legislature met, officially accepted the gift and appointed Galen Clark "Guardian." Governor Low at the proper time appointed the Board of Commissioners and announced that claimants to property within the grant must relinquish their title. As was to be expected Hutchings and Lamon resisted this ultimation and litigation began.

And in this year, 1866, Lamon acquired a partner. Fred Leidig with his wife Isabel trekked in from Coulterville.

The intimate story of Yosemite from that time on has been obtained in a large measure from their son, Charles. His fund of information is remarkable and, under test, proves accurate. His father and mother, so he told us, came with pack animals by way of Jenkins Hill and down into the Merced Canyon.[7] At the foot of Jenkins Hill was McCann Flat where the Irish McCanns raised goats and kept a small eating place. Isabel had two little children and was using a side saddle. She was glad to rest there before proceeding by saddle trail up Merced Canyon.

Fred Leidig and Jim Lamon farmed 160 acres on both side of the Merced River which flows, deep and silent, through the level valley. The Leidig home was a two-storied log house possibly 150 feet south of the present Ahwahnee Hotel. They weren't expecting trouble but, just as a precaution, it had a breastwork thrown up all around. Port holes in the cabin were even with the top of the breastwork. There was a spring in the cellar. They lived upstairs but Isabel cooked down by the spring.

Here the Leidigs buried the first to die, their small daughter, Agnes, and a little boy whose name may have been McCoy. It was in the middle of a heavy winter. No one could get out to buy provisions and the family was on short rations although they still had flour and turnips. If a man could work his way as far down the valley as Bridal Veil Fall (so Charles Leidig affirmed) he could usually get through to the settlements but in this year no one succeeded. The hungry children, happening to find some spoiled peaches which had frozen, ate them and died. They were buried, side by side, beneath two oaks near the present Ahwahnee Hotel.

Three months later Isabel's third child came into the world— our informant, Charles Leidig, first white boy to be born in Yosemite Valley.

Years later the body of little Agnes was removed to the cemetery.[8]

John Muir made his initial appearance in this small cliff-bound society in 1868. The name of the great naturalist is possibly the most famous to be inextricably associated with Yosemite. He arrived without fanfare and was permitted by Hutchings to build for himself a cabin of sugar pine shakes near the foot of Yosemite Falls and right in back of the Hutchings' home. While there he was employed by Hutchings to build and operate a sawmill adjacent to his cabin.

There has been much adverse criticism against Hutchings and Muir, both nature lovers, for sawing up quantities of the large pines from the floor of the valley. An entirely different light is thrown on this activity by the reading of Muir's unfinished memoirs in which he tells that he was hired to build a sawmill to cut lumber from pines blown down by a violent wind a year or two before he arrived.[9] He constructed from them his cabin with which he was completely charmed. He wrote:

"This cabin, I think, was the handsomest building in the valley and the most useful and convenient for a mountaineer. From the Yosemite Creek, near where it first gathers its beaten waters at the foot of the fall, I dug a small ditch and brought a stream into the cabin, entering at one end and flowing out the other just current enough to allow it to sing and warble in low, sweet tones, . . . My bed was suspended from the rafters and lined with libocedrus plumes, . . ."[10]

In a few months Hutchings took back the cabin which, being built on his land and with his lumber, he claimed was technically his. Muir moved to Black's Hotel but apparently often slept in the mill. He wrote to his sister:

"It is hard to write here, as the mill jars so much by the stroke of the saw, and the rain drips from the roof, and I have to set the log every few minutes. I am operating the same mill that I made last winter. I like the piney fragrance of the fresh-sawn boards, and I am in constant view of the grandest of all the falls. I sleep in the mill for the sake of hearing the murmuring hush of the water beneath me, and I have a small box-like home fastened beneath the gable of the mill, looking westward down the Valley, where I keep my notes, etc. People call it the hang-nest, because it seems unsupported, thus: [a simple sketch is inserted] Fortunately, the only people that I dislike are afraid to enter it."[11]

It seems quite probable that listed under this heading was James Hutchings with whom Muir, by this time, was decidedly not en rapport. Without attempting an explanation, which we are in no way qualified to give, we simply note that the Valleyites who heard their parents discuss the feud predominantly favor Hutchings.

To hear of a quarrel, especially one in which he may not have been one hundred per cent right, makes the famous naturalist seem more human. We honor him as the greatest exponent of the valley. His untiring efforts in its behalf were of two sorts: an unshakeable determination to preserve the alpine sublimity of the high mountain area by having it set aside as a national park (only one, Yellowstone, having preceded it in attaining that status) and an equal determination to prove the glacial origin of Yosemite. The State Geological Survey under the direction of J. D. Whitney did not subscribe to this theory having decided that in some terrific convulsion of nature the bottom of the gorge had simply fallen out. But Muir's ability to be everywhere and to see everything that pertained to the area, even at continued risk of his life, combined with his meticulous field notes, finally convinced the scientists. We also honor John Muir as the man whose personality and eloquence persuaded the governor, the president of the nation and others in positions of prominence to use their influence toward the preservation of the magnificent country surrounding Yosemite and, possibly most of all, we think of him as the gifted writer whose works make us feel the splendour of the mountains he loved. Yosemite preserved Muir's name to posterity and John Muir performed a most devoted service to Yosemite.

The building of Leidig's Hotel in 1869 seems to have been Jim Lamon's idea. The land he homesteaded was no longer his. "By the goblins," he told his partner with his favorite expletive, "you'd better get yourself a hotel for tourists." So it was erected at the foot of Sentinel Rock—farther west than any of the valley inns—and ran for over twenty years. About the same time Leidig put up a cabin north of the river in the woods at the edge of Leidig's Meadow where the family lived in the winter when there were no travelers.

While the epidemic of construction lasted A. G. Black tore down historic but unprepossessing Lower Hotel and put up Black's Hotel on the same site, where it remained until 1888. And, in a perfect eruption of hostelries, Charles Peregoy built Mountain View House on Bridal Veil Creek about four miles above the falls on the Mariposa-Yosemite Trail. Practically all dates for early Yosemite construction can be found in Hutchings' two books.

Now that they had provided accommodation for the tourists the people of the valley took thought to render the noted landmarks more accessible. In 1870 Albert Snow built a much-needed trail to Vernal and Nevada Fall, giving visitors their first easy view of the two great falls of the Merced River. Harriet Kirtland recounted that in 1857 the men of her party had worked, standing in icy water to their chests, trying to make a safe crossing over the river so that the women might ascend the stream and see Vernal Falls. At first they failed, but succeeded on the second day in felling a tree across the current on which everyone crossed. She added that some of the men had then gone on to see Nevada Fall which, up to that time, but two women had visited. From other sources we learned that the first woman to do so had been Mrs. John Neal. Frances Pool (now Emerald Pool) was named for her. According to the Mariposa *Democrat*, August 5, 1856, Madame Gautier, hostess of the Union Hotel in Mariposa, was the second woman to make the trip. Lady Franklin, wife of the Arctic explorer, for whom was named Lady Franklin Rock beside the trail, did not visit the falls until 1861. Even after Snow had constructed the trail it was so narrow that it was customary for the afternoon party to wait at this rock until the group which had gone up in the morning came back. Through the years three trusted guides, Sol White, John Murphy and Nathan Pike, became fixtures in the valley and it was a brave tourist who disobeyed their mandates.

Before reaching the first view of Vernal Fall the climber of the '60s and '70s passed Register Rock where were painted names of previous passers-by. Sometimes John McPeters sat by the trail with brush and paint and charged for this service. After the first view the climber arrived at the foot of "the ladders" where Snow had contrived a steep ascent. Underneath a large overhanging rock was a shack where a toll keeper slept, ate and separated tourists from 75c apiece.

Snow's hotel, Casa Nevada, was built in full view of the magnificently overwhelming Nevada Fall. "As near the base of the Fall as the Fall will let it stand—in fact," said H. H., "so near that in some winds half the piazza is drenched with spray."

Hutchings had meanwhile built a house for his family on the sunny north side of the valley. Yosemite Creek splits into three parts at the base of the falls and their cabin poised at the very edge of the most easterly branch. Back of the cabin he planted an apple orchard which still bears lustily. Back of the orchard, and also on the creek (probably under the first cottonwood trees) was the cabin of which John Muir was so proud and, still farther up the creek (definitely under a couple of frowsly old cottonwoods) was the sawmill. The sawdust is now overgrown with hop vines gone wild and spaced with vigorous young cedars.

Hutchings' cabin was across the Merced River and the width of the valley from his hotel. The two were connected by a board walk laid across the meadow starred with evening primrose and by a sturdy log bridge placed about as Sentinel Bridge is now. Bridge and walk were free to all. To give his hotel guests a better view of Yosemite Falls Hutchings cleared a lane through the trees on the north side that focussed directly on them. Many a camera enthusiast takes advantage of it today with no knowledge whatsoever of the kindly and visionary man who made it possible. As the hotel needed more room he added a lean-to, which encircled a giant cedar, on the right rear of Hutchings House. Soon the whole building was known as Cedar Cottage. The tree still stands and bears the slanting mark of the roof. The lean-to was large and became the gathering room of the vicinity. All dignitaries were entertained here; parties given; funerals held. Hutchings himself was laid out in it for burial in October of 1902 and a picture showing the coffin exists at the museum. It also shows a crude electric light globe which served to correct an error in the date of his death—first given as the year before electricity came to this cliff-bound and sometimes snow-bound community.

A cable ferry was installed in '71 by Ira B. Folsom. It was on a distinct curve in the river, about one-half mile west of the foot of the Four Mile Trail, where the Merced most closely approaches the south cliffs. The place is marked on old maps as Ferry Bend and, during the low water of early autumn, one can see the dead trunks of trees swept down during flood season and dropped at this relatively slack stretch. Later Folsom built a toll bridge not more than fifty feet up from the old ford at the mouth of Eagle Creek. The approach to the ford cuts down through a high bank on the north side; the bridge took advantage of its elevation in order to keep above high water when, of course, the ford was impassable. A convenient pine tree plainly shows cable marks about six inches up from the ground. This was the bridge used by the excited crowd of 500 people at the opening festivities of the Big Oak Flat Road.

Bridges were extremely handy articles during a great part of the year but visitors in the dry season, who would have forded without question had the bridge never been built, couldn't bear to do so in plain sight of such an easy crossing and complained bitterly: Charles Nordhoff wrote in 1875:

"Moreover, abuses are creeping in already. A lease has been granted to a person who has bridged the Merced River, and charges fifty cents per head to all who choose to pass over it—which you need not do."

Sometime before the winter of 1866-67 a bridge for saddle horses had been thrown across the Merced River near the present Pohono Bridge and another one above Vernal Fall but they lasted a disappointingly short time and went booming down the river in the high water of '67-'68. The incomparable viewpoints of Yosemite were not attained easily.

In the same year, 1871, that Folsom built his ferry Charles Peregoy erected a tiny inn on the top of Glacier Point. It took so long to get there and to get back that shelter was sometimes necessary. James McCauley decided to expedite matters and, still in the same year, hired John Conway who had superintended construction on the Zigzag to build what was, and is, called the Four Mile Trail. Helen Hunt Jackson wrote that it took eleven months to finish and cost $3000. The toll was $1.00 which she considered reasonable. At the time she went up McCauley was living "in a sort of pine-plank wigwam" with an American flag on top about half way along the trail at Union Point. However, his son, Jules McCauley, says that the trail-side shelter was probably for convenience in constructing or repairing the trail and that the family lived in the toll house just to the east of the foot of Four Mile Trail near the gigantic rock that has apparently fallen from the cliff. In 1878 McCauley built Mountain House at Glacier Point and it still stands.

It may be that these huge boulders at the foot of the trail are the result of a cataclysm of which John Muir wrote and about which Charles Leidig told: A tremendous earthquake shattered Sentinel Rock and sent a portion thundering down the cliff mowing trees like grass before a sickle. It bounded and burst; skidded and came to rest within a few hundred yards of Leidig's Hotel. Impalpable dust filled the air like fog and took hours to settle after which the entire landscape seemed to have been whitewashed. It was possibly the next year that McCauley built his house among these titanic fragments.

Two uproarious festivals set the valley by the ears when, a month apart in 1874, the rival Coulterville and Big Oak Flat Roads made successful entries to the valley floor. Stages could now unload sightseers at the hotel doors—tired, yes, but probably with a nominal amount of bruises and able to dine comfortably from a table. In this year the State of California commenced to get the park affairs in order and business enterprises which had been in a rather anomalous position began to be run as concessions of the government. The Wawona Road was completed the following season so that the old Mono Trail pack-route was practically abandoned southwest of the park and travel arrived easily. A measure of prosperity arrived also. The Sentinel Hotel was built, squeezed in between River Cottage and the bridge and opposite Hutchings House. This was the stopping place remembered so affectionately by our parents and grandparents and was managed for about twelve years by J. K. Barnard. The stretch lying west of Sentinel Bridge, now known as the "Old Village" was beginning to fill.

According to Charles Leidig life in the valley ran an accustomed routine: Summer and the tourists were undergone on the cool south side of the river; then came a glorious but short period of autumn with its crystal clear sky and flaming colors leading to the inevitable time when snow finally cut them off from outside help or contact and the resident families withdrew to their northside cabins. Excitement then centered around the coming of mail once a month. John Muir wrote to his sister:[12] "A grand event has occurred in our remote snow-bound Valley. Indian Tom[13] has come from the lower open world with the mail . . ."

Mr. Lawrence Degnan told us that a cabin stood just below what is now Pohono Bridge—a tiny place but equipped with food, bed and a fireplace for the mail carrier and warm shelter for his horse. Sometimes he met the snow farther down the canyon but it was always possible for the knowing horse to keep on to the desired objective. In the morning the man went on alone into the valley with snowshoes. One of the last thrills of the fall season, so Mr. Degnan said, and especially so for the children, was the coming of the freighters with the winter supplies—great creaking wagons crammed with molasses, rice, beans, flour and other food that would keep the full six months that must elapse before the road would again be open.

The Leidigs, who ran a hotel before a single road came into the valley, bought their supplies from Taburg and Gulcher's store in San Francisco and had them delivered by a pack train of from thirty to forty animals. Hooper and Jennings of the same city was another favorite firm. After the wagon roads were completed in '74 and '75, Charles Schmidt of Second Garrote freighted in with a jerkline bell-team of mules. He told his own story:

"Most of the supplies I hauled went to Black's or Barnard's Hotels or Angelo Cavagnaro's general store. It used to take me five days to make the trip up into the valley and two days to come back with an empty wagon. That wasn't bad time though. J. G. Skinner from Jacksonville brought fruit from the orchards around Knight's Ferry and peddled it from there to Yosemite. He began his business in the '70's. It took him eleven days to make the round trip with four horses and a thoroughbrace wagon. James Ackerson brought in timothy hay from Ackerson Meadow.

He drove his own four horse wagon. Unless it rained the freight teamsters threw their blankets on the ground and slept wherever night caught them."

During the open season Chinese brought eggs from outlying ranches in bobbing baskets slung at either end of carrying poles.

Mosquitoes were an almost unendurable pest. During the spring months of melting snow when they were at their unspeakable worst, the Leidigs built smoking fires and pulled their beds as close to them as possible. After the local snow had gone melting drifts in the high Sierra often flooded the meadows making it impossible to pasture the stock or even to cross the valley. Bridges (when at last they came) were most welcome. By the month of June most of the adult population were busy again with duties centering around the entertainment of sightseers, starred now and then by a visitor of distinction.

The large Leidig family, scrubbed painfully, were sent out to feast their infant eyes on ex-president Grant and returned disillusioned to tell Isabel that there was nothing on the porch except men.

Four or five Indian villages under the cliffs made the valley Indians a part of everyday life. Charles Leidig played with them as a child and his remembrances are supplemented by those of Eunice Watson Fisher whose father found work in the valley and brought his family there to live when she was small. Eunice and her brother made the descent down the Big Oak Flat Trail tied in saddle bags and hanging on either side of a steady pony. The small Indians were good companions. Dolls made of bundles of sticks amused the girls. They played "rancheree" with forked sticks for people, acorns for bear and pebbles of assorted sizes and shapes for cattle, horses and sheep. Boys made traps and other more or less workable gadgets, ran and swam.

It is worth noting that, although the name for an Indian village is almost always spelled "rancheria" as designated by the Spaniards who first had occasion to write the word, it was seldom pronounced, by anyone familiar with Indian customs and conversation, anything but "rancheree." Eccleston spells it "rancheri."

The rancheria nearest to Leidig's Hotel was strung out along the base of the south cliff from Sentinel Rock eastward; the village nearest their winter cabin was under the sunny cliff just east of the Three Brothers where the modern Indian village may be found today. There was also one at the foot of Indian Canyon and one near Hutchings House.

Young Charles often watched the Indian women with their babies. In the early morning each mother bound her infant's arms and legs lightly so that it lay wrapped like a mummy. Then she placed it in the specially shaped papoose basket; secured the baby carefully and swung it to her back where it hung whenever she left the village. On grasshopper drives, carrying home the game the men had killed, traveling over the mountains, in almost every activity the baby was a passive spectator but always facing the rear. Like the much-quoted goofy bird who flew backwards, he only knew where he had been. Charles spent many idle moments trying to coax a smile from these taper-eyed infants and says that he was never successful. An Indian baby was born solemn.

But, at the end of the day, the mother gently loosened her tiny papoose; waited while it squirmed and stretched and then bathed it with icy water from the creek. The baby shrunk spasmodically as the cold splashings struck its body but never whimpered. If a child was more than a year old the mother was apt cautiously to lower it into a pool and take her hands away, for these children of nature could often swim as soon as they could walk. From the evening bath to the coming of the dark it was loved and fondled and slept against its mother's breast.

Isabel Leidig, who had through the years eleven children of

her own, was especially kind and patient with the small Indians. She had such simple home remedies as were available and was always willing to share them. They learned to go to her for help. A young lad, half Indian, half white whose name was Sam Wells, came to her one day with his foot swelling rapidly from a rattle-snake bite. It happened that a cow had just calved and the first milking stood nearby in a bucket simply because they had not as yet thrown it away. The ingenious woman heated the milk and placed the boy's foot in it, keeping it the right temperature by dropping in hot rocks. Either because of, or in spite of, the treatment the lad recovered and became devoted to her, always call-ing her "Grandmama." The Mariposa *Gazette* of June 8, 1867, credited his recovery entirely to incredible quantities of straight brandy.

Sometime after this incident the Bull Creek Indians, a tribe of mixed blood living along the Coulterville Road, decided to make war on the nondescript Indian villages in the valley. It was not difficult to imagine that the white families would be in trouble once the war paint was on. Sam Wells was now sixteen. Fred Leidig was in San Francisco buying supplies so Sam warned Isabel of the danger and advised her to take her children and make camp under a rock near the foot of the Four Mile Trail; he also promised modestly that he would do what he could to turn them back. As Leidig's Hotel on the south side and their cabin north of the river were the most westerly houses in the valley and would be the first in the path of the marauding Indians, Isabel followed his advice. With her children huddled beside her she held vigil under the rock for several nights and nothing happened so she shrugged it off and moved back into her house. Investigation disclosed that Sam had taken an old rifle with what ammunition he possessed; had gone down to the Big Meadows on the Coulterville Road and concealed himself in a hollow log. The Bull Creek Indians came along on schedule but Sam Wells banged away so efficiently that they lost the carefree spirit of battle with which they had started and went home. They carried their dead with them. Sam was a good shot. The story goes that they carried eleven. It has probably grown with the years. At any rate they left Sam just where they killed him when his ammunition ran out.

There was, Charles Leidig told us, about one-half mile west of the rocky bluff near El Portal, an old and respected Indian chief who lived high up on a bluff. About 1000 feet below him lived his son. Every day they communicated in sign language but no one was allowed to approach the upper ledge where the old man stayed alone. Boylike, Charles disregarded the embargo and, one day, climbed the cliff. The chief patted him on the head and after that he went several times to sit in companionable silence and to admire the unerring skill with which the old Indian could shoot an arrow straight up into the air and have it come to earth near his feet. The boy was fascinated by the success of the chief's clever quail trap. By following a trail of dropped grain, the quail were lured into a long, narrow passage leading to a compartment of coarsely woven reeds. They squeezed along with heads down, pecking at the seeds. When they emerged into the box-like compartment the seeds disappeared and their heads went up to look around. Never again could they find the low passageway out. This provided quail dinners with no expenditure of effort.

As an Indian grew older he did not usually care for effort. Oh he would, so Mr. Leidig said, load the firewood on his squaw's back, if he had one, and pull her to her feet. Otherwise she never could have risen. He would even start her toward camp with an unbegrudged kick. But, as a regular thing, an old buck did little more than breathe for himself and only ate what his wife handed him. The young men kept themselves occupied. They fished daily and sold trout and "dog salmon" to the hotels. In past years they had, Mr. Leidig told us, stocked the waters of Yosemite with trout, bringing them alive in baskets from the upper watercourses and moving them quickly from stream to stream.

To catch ground squirrels the Indian women turned snow rivulets into one end of their underground runs, making a strainer of a flat cedar bough so that dirt wouldn't wash in. Then they sat patiently with sharpened sticks at the other opening of each run, where the little animals would have to emerge, and speared them. To prepare a squirrel for cooking they removed the bladder and gall bladder and wrapped the rest, au naturel, in wet grass. This bundle they coated thickly with mud and placed under a bed of coals. Spouts of steam showed that it was still cooking pleasantly. When the steam ceased they dug it out, cracked off the mud, peeled off the grass and loosened the skin at the head. One skillful pull and the cook had skin and entrails in one hand and clean white meat in the other.

The social slip during which the Indians of the Mono country had wiped out their friends the Yosemites had not interfered for long with the visiting proclivities of the former. At least once a year they descended on the villages which housed the hybrid successors to the Yosemites. By the time that Mr. Leidig knew them the Monos respectably wore overalls. Out of them their broad, separate-toed feet hung like bell-clappers on either side of their bony horses. They begged horribly of any white person but had come particularly for acorns, apples and wild pigeons. The acorn-bearing black oaks were mainly in the west end of the valley so the local villages set up a deadline, Yosemite Creek, and insisted that the Monos stay up by Mirror Lake unless invited down to visit.

There was a large "sweat-house" a half mile down the river

At the "Gates of the Valley."

Taber

Approaching the Stoneman House, Yosemite Valley, 1895. Yosemite Falls at left.

from Leidig's Hotel which would have located it close to Ferry Bend. It was at the edge of the current—a pit roofed with a dome-like mound made of poles and bark. The squaws spread mud over this and then thickly coated it with earth. A small fire heated it to an almost unbearable temperature and in it the braves steamed until red hot, then ran quickly to the bank and plunged into the swift river only a few miles from its glacial-ice beginnings on the peaks. Therapeutically this was considered sound practice by western Indians but, in the case of the diphtheria epidemic that raged through the Southern Mines, it was usually fatal; so that, when the measles broke out, Galen Clark (at that time Guardian of the Valley) put a complete stop to the custom with but little opposition. Meanwhile the sweat house was a suitable place to entertain various brown-skinned dignitaries. They omitted the icy plunge but could work up quite a festivity by smoking "Indian tobacco" in little wooden pipes. A few puffs, said Mr. Leidig, "made 'em like crazy chickens."

The Monos were not the only tribe who came to visit and to trade. The Mariposa and Chowchilla tribes, the Bull Creek, Bear Creek and Big Creek Indians all came. The latter being none other than the residents of the Deer Flat rancheria near Big Oak Flat.

Many of the Indians contracted tuberculosis from the whites and, when this happened, they gave up all activity and sat chanting "Chum-ha, chum-ha," meaning I am ready to die. And death usually arrived promptly. Young Charles saw the last ceremonial burning that took place in the valley. The funeral pyre was between their hotel and the river but he was not sure that the cremations always took place at the same spot.

The funeral customs of the Yosemites, especially in later days, were different from those of the Miwoks. We are indebted to Mr. Sell of Ahwahnee, Madera County, for his remembrance of a "cry" that he attended which lasted several days. A large quantity of food, including a whole steer, was provided and all the mourners with their numerous children slept and ate in the dwelling of the deceased's family. The crying, or wailing, took place at stated times, especially when the body was removed from the house. After final disposition had been made of it the mourners were taken outside and water poured on their hands and heads to "wash away the memory," after which they settled down to games of various sorts as long as the food lasted. This reaction was also far removed from that of the Monos who burned their dead; mixed pitch with their ashes and smeared their head and arms with the horrible concoction. As a widow was exempt from labor as long as evidences of the pitch remained, no effort was made to remove it and the black gummy mixture often remained in the hair for months.

It was necessary in old Yosemite to take thought ahead for one's family and also, so Isabel Leidig believed, for one's neighbors. In order to have clothes Isabel kept a dressmaker by the year. To have a school she, at first, kept the teacher, May Anderson. The earliest schoolhouse was only a few yards from their hotel and almost within the uncertain bounds of the small rancheria against the cliff. It had about twenty-five pupils. The little Indians were welcome although no real effort was made to stimulate their interest. Anything that they cared about they learned easily enough. One bright small boy came at the beginning of each year and stayed until he had seen all the pictures in the text books when he absented himself until more pictures were produced at the beginning of the next term.

The chapel, now at the old village, was first situated right next to the school. It was built in 1879 by the Sunday School Union and was later moved to its present location where it has the honor of being the oldest building left on the valley floor. The bell was donated by Mr. H. D. Bacon of Oakland. The organ by Miss Mary Porter of Philadelphia in memory of Florence Hutchings.[14]

Times changed. The park authorities began to be more and more conscious that the public had a right to see the wonders of a state park and to return home in a state of pocket book enviably short of stony broke. The land that had been James Lamon's was leased to Mr. A. Harris who managed it as a camp ground and sold supplies to campers from the first real store. Something was done about flood control; obstructing boulders in the river were blasted out and the old El Capitan Iron Bridge was built in 1879.

The year 1884 was marked by the arrival of John and Bridget Degnan with three small children. John maintained a dairy herd and Bridget, to fill a crying need, tried her hand at baking bread and providing meals for travelers. Her equipment was simple— just a Dutch oven and an open fireplace, but Bridget was a natural cook and business woman and the public appreciated what she offered. The business she started so simply grew steadily; so did the family; and the one is still managed by the other at the same site in the old village.*

In the '80s Mr. Angelo Cavagnaro also founded a store that was destined to be a part of valley history and, quoting J. M. Hutchings, had on hand "almost any article that may be desired, from a box of paper collars to a side of bacon."[15]

Mr. Lawrence Degnan remembers the terrible winter of 1889-90 when his father, who was working for the park, shoveled snow from the stable roofs both day and night in a successful effort to keep them from caving in on the animals. Meanwhile his own stout little house was buried completely under fourteen feet of snow and the children were agog with excitement at having candles in the daytime.

* Following the construction of a new Degnan's restaurant in Yosemite Village in 1958 the old store was razed (March 1959).

About this time Stoneman Hotel was built at what is now Camp Curry with $40,000 of government money. It was leased to J. J. Cook and a comprehensive gesture was made to get rid of the privately built concerns that had served the public in past years. Leidig's and Black's Hotels were ordered torn down by the board of park commissioners. Stoneman Hotel lasted eight years and burned to the ground; some say because green lumber was used and its shrinkage caused a fault in the chimney.

In 1890, to the great joy of the valley dwellers, the high mountain area surrounding them was created a national park.[16] True the valley which was its nucleus remained a state park for a disturbed period of fifteen years until the necessary legislation had undergone its tedious course when it was receded to the national government. The government accepted it with due formality in 1906 and thus one of the wonderlands of the continent was placed safely under the nation's wing. The next year after the national park came into being, 1891, began the period of Army control. For awhile headquarters was at Camp A. E. Wood (now Wawona) but was moved into the valley on August 1, 1906, by Major (later Colonel) H. C. Benson.

Charles Leidig remembers the coming of the 14th Cavalry on their tired black horses. They were quartered at Fort Yosemite where Yosemite Lodge now is. In fact the lodge is nothing but the barrack buildings pushed together. The employees' cottages now across the road from the gas station were then the officers' homes and were never called anything but "soapsuds row." The horses were exercised in beautiful Leidig's Meadow. Fred Leidig had borrowed a bull team from Wawona; grubbed out the willows and planted rye. Its green expanse waving in a soft breeze is lovely and a perfect complement to the rugged cliffs. Toward the western end may be seen the small circle surrounded by the larger oval where the horses were put through their paces by men in uniform with flashing swords.

With the cavalry Gabriel Sovulewski came as supply sergeant and remained until his death. Like Hutchings, Galen Clark and certain of the old guides, he identified himself with the area that he loved and never left it. He moved his family into Hutchings' old cabin and later rebuilt it. Superintendents came and went but, between times, Mr. Sovulewski acted in their stead and, at all times, kept the mechanics of the park operating smoothly.

In 1899 David A. Curry founded the famous "Camp" that bears his name. He arrived in his beloved valley, where he was to be so impressive a figure, in time to see the turn of the century. Many can remember his powerful voice signaling each night to Glacier Point 3000 feet above him "LET THE FIRE FALL." He was an unforgettable character and a host par excellence.

The firefall consists of glowing embers from a huge pile of bark fragments which are ignited several hours in advance. At a given signal they are pushed over the edge of the precipice in an even stream of fire falling several hundred feet down the night-shrouded cliff. The spectacle, which nightly holds thousands spellbound and is the spectacular climax to each day of wonder in the park was originated by James McCauley. Just once it was tried from the north cliff and started a conflagration which burned for several days and endangered nearby property.

Theodore Roosevelt came to the park in 1903. If Mr. Leidig remembers the coming of the cavalry, how much more does he remember each day and hour of this visit! The president wished to camp and for three days Charles Leidig was guide, cook and companion—a memorable and prideful experience.

But few landmarks survived into the new century. The hotels had been torn down. Lamon's cabin was razed. Even Register Rock was painted over by order of Major Benson. The old village was built up solidly, tapering off to the west with a row of studios where famous painters and widely known photographers had their headquarters. Among them were J. T. Boysen, George Fiske and Harry Cassie Best with his sweet and beautiful wife. Major Benson's home was included in this row. Chris Jorgensen the artist, lived elsewhere in the park. The center of interest had moved eastward from the area around the foot of the Four Mile Trail which had for years included three resorts and Galen Clark's headquarters as Guardian of the Park.

At the beginning of the new century arrived the automobile with whose advent this intimate chronicle ends. The mountain miles leading to Yosemite were a continual challenge to the more daring drivers, but as yet Yosemite National Park was a stronghold into which the horseless carriage might not legally venture.

But just they same they came.

A. E. and F. H. Holmes of San Jose drove their Stanley Steamer over the Wawona Road in July of 1900 and are acknowledged to have brought the first car into the valley. Mr. Lippincott and son claimed the honor via another road. The museum has a picture of the peculiar appearing vehicle and also of a couple of Locomobiles with their occupants, the first who came by way of the Big Oak Flat Road, in 1901. All three cars made the trip under their own power. Celia Crocker Thompson photographed the Locomobiles as they stopped at Crocker's Station and says that, having reached that point, they were allowed to go on as the lesser of two evils but that they were fined and "immobilized" upon reaching the valley floor.

It was, of course, a useless gesture. The response of the traveling public to faster transportation was so swift and complete that the hotels and camps where automobiles might not come felt the drop off in custom. The Yosemite Valley Railroad which was completed in 1907 helped the valley but the freight business immediately slumped on the upper roads. Of all the miles that had re-echoed to the creaking, pounding and clanking of the great wagons only the section of road between the railway terminus at El Portal and the valley hotels lay under a perpetual cloud of dust raised by the freighters and the big horse-drawn carryalls that brought goods and passengers from the train to their objectives under the shadow of El Capitan.

In a great measure through the efforts of Senator John B. Curtin, the law was changed and motorists were permitted to enter and to spend their money in the park. In 1913 the big carryalls began legally to be crowded off the road by sizzling and snorting little cars arriving by way of the Wawona route. The horses lived through the shock and even began to get used to the process. Motor stages appeared; the Indians, balanced happily on running boards, rode free. In the next year automobiles were permitted on the Big Oak Flat Road and the Coulterville Road. They even swarmed up the Zigzag and the conquest of the park by gasoline was complete.

For a quarter of a century the old roads deteriorated while a new low-level highway up the Merced River in time replaced even the railroad, causing it to be abandoned in 1945. When the need became desperate, the Park, in 1940, constructed the fine highway from Crane Flat down to the valley floor, eliminating the difficult Zigzag section and enabling travelers to enjoy the fascinating country through which the old freight road had wormed its way— mile after mile, year after year—and, at the last steep descent, to enjoy safe conduct down the mountain.*

The Big Oak Flat Road at last combines comfort with its beauty. Still the shortest way to Stockton, San Francisco and all of Northern California, thousands of visitors either enter Yosemite or leave

---

* After the opening of the new Big Oak Flat road in 1940 the old road was maintained for down travel only until October 1942, when rockslides destroyed the zigzags. The National Park Service plans a history trail down this historic route.

through its historic vistas. To thousands the name is synonymous with adventure, excitement, youth. To some it spells the uplift of anticipated vacationing; to others the deep-seated love of childhood home. It is a part of early California, landmarked with century-old houses and still traveled by many of the original families. It has character and authenticity, an individuality all its own.

Notes

CHAPTER I

1. A History of California—the Spanish Period. Charles E. Chapman. pp. 418-420. Building the Heart of an Empire. Harry D. Hubbard. pp. 35-41.

2. The Travels of Jedediah Strong Smith. Maurice S. Sullivan. p. 151. Jedediah Smith and his Maps of the American West. Dale L. Morgan and Carl I. Wheat. Introductory paragraphs.

3. History of San Joaquin County. F. T. Gilbert. pp. 11-12.

4. Narrative of the Adventures of Zenas Leonard. Written by himself. pp. 46-47.

5. The full name, Charles Marie Weber, furnished by his granddaughter, Helen Weber Kennedy.

6. History of San Joaquin County. Pen Pictures from the Garden of the World. p. 441.

7. Ibid. p. 441.

8. The three Mexican pueblos in Alta California were San Jose, Los Angeles and Branciforte (now Santa Cruz). Chapman, op. cit., p. 391.
   Dr. Cleland expresses it less definitely: "Los Angeles and San José were the two principal pueblos in California, although Branciforte, or Santa Cruz, also laid claim to the title." *The Cattle on a Thousand Hills*. Robert Glass Cleland. p. 7.

9. Information from History of the French Camp Settlement to 1853. Elton Fletcher.

10. Information from Rancheria del Rio Estanislaus. Margaret Gaylord Ruppel.

11. Information from Helen Weber Kennedy.

12. Two other facts must be dovetailed into this sketchy picture as best one can: A reference slip from the Original Archives of California, Departmental State Papers, Naturalization, Tomo XX, states that Peter Lassen was granted naturalization as a Mexican citizen on July 24, 1844, at which time he would presumably be present in Monterey. Also he did not receive his land grant until December 26, 1844. Reports of Land Cases. Ogden Hoffman. p. 26 in the Appendix. None of these facts are necessarily mutually contradictory.

13. Article in Stockton Record. Feb. 2, 1935. Inez Henderson Pond.

14. History of San Joaquin County. Pen Pictures from the Garden of the World. p. 30.

15. History of Amador County. J. D. Mason. p. 36.

16. Information from "The Black Binder," Calif. State Libr., Sacramento.

17. Fletcher. op. cit.
18. Information from Helen Weber Kennedy.
19. Ibid. Also life in California Before the Conquest. Alfred Robinson. p. 269.
20. Information furnished by Helen Weber Kennedy.
21. Information from History of San Joaquin County. Thompson & West. Also from Memorial and Biographical History of Merced, Stanislaus, Calaveras, Tuolumne and Mariposa Counties, California. p. 39.
22. "Isbel" is the accepted spelling used in the counties where this prominent pioneer was best known. It is found (among many other sources) in the History of San Joaquin County. Pen Pictures from the Garden of the World; appears on the Map of the Mining District of California by Wm. A. Jackson which is found in Carl I. Wheat's Maps of the California Gold Region 1848-1857, and is listed as Map No. 161. However, in the same volume a French edition of a portion of this same map is shown, listed as Map No. 162. On it the name appears as "Isabelle." James H. Carson, in Recollections of the California Mines, refers to the same man as "Dr. Isabell."
23. Personal Adventures in Upper and Lower California in 1848-9. William Redmond Ryan. Vol. II, pp. 48-49.
24. Life in California. James H. Carson. p. 14.
25. Recollections of Pioneer Work in California. Rev. James Woods. p. 15.
26. From the "Binder of Miscellaneous Statements." Bancroft Library.
27. Diary of Wilton R. Hayes. Bancroft Library.
28. Woods, op. cit. p. 91 and p. 232.
29. Information from Map of the Survey of Stockton, Calif., 1849. Major Richard P. Hammond. In poss. Helen Weber Kennedy.
30. Fletcher. op. cit.
31. Item in Alta California, San Francisco. Dec. 19, 1851.
32. Article in Stockton Daily Independent, by George H. Tinkham. Feb. 24, 1894.
33. Letters of Dexter H. Hutchins, 1853-4.
    Express and Stage Coach Days in California. Oscar Osburn Winther. p. 66.

CHAPTER II

1. A Memorial and Biographical History of the Counties of Merced, Stanislaus, Calaveras, Tuolumne and Mariposa, California. p. 134.
2. The route of the freighters through Stockton has been worked out by interviews and by comparison of old and new maps.

3. The Exploring Expedition of the Rocky Mountains, Oregon and California. J. C. Fremont. p. 359.

John Charles Fremont and his men, in the year 1844, had great difficulty in selecting a place to cross the Stanislaus River, traveling twenty-five miles up and down the stream before coming to a decision. The splendid drooping oaks, gorgeous poppies and abundance of elk and antelope demanded attention even though they were tired and annoyed. "But," he wrote, "the stream was flowing by, dark and deep, swollen by the mountain snows; its general breadth was about 50 yards." At last they encamped in an oak grove and, killing several cattle, ferried the baggage across the river in a boat made of their hides sewed together and dried over a willow framework after the manner of the mountain men.

4. Interview with Elsie Wilhoit Hodgkins, Stockton, Calif., whose father, Roley E. Wilhoit, commenced a freighting business between Stockton and the Southern Mines in the fall of 1852. Also Seminar Report, Elton Fletcher.

5. Stories of the Stanislaus. Solomon P. Elias. p. 242.

6. The M. J. Dooly Company ran a scheduled four-horse stage line between Stockton and Knights Ferry. When Dooly died Chas. V. Sisson who had been a driver continued the line.

7. Information concerning William Knight contained in Bancroft's History of California. Vol. IV (1840-1845) p. 702. Also in the Illustrated Atlas and History of Yolo County, Calif. (1825-1880). Also in the Western Shore Gazetteer and Commercial Directory for the State of California—Yolo County. Also in the Historical and Biographical Record of Sacramento Valley, Calif., J. M. Guinn. Also in the "Black Binder" at the California State Library, Sacramento, Calif. Under headings William Knight. Also from: Roster of Fremont's California Battalion, Mexican War, 1846. Muster roll of Capt. Richard Owen's Company (A). Also from interviews.

8. El Rancheria del Rio Estanislaus. Margaret Gaylord Ruppel.

9. Information from the "Black Binder." op. cit.

10. California '46-'48. Jacob Wright Harlan. pp. 142-143.

11. Historical and Biographical Record of Sacramento Valley, California. J. M. Guinn. p. 1532.

12. Sonora Union Democrat. May 7, 1910.

13. The Black Binder. op. cit.

14. The Stockton Journal. Aug. 24, 1850. "At the Ferry House a Restaurant and Boarding House, has just been opened, where the traveler will always find the

best accomodations, and the most attentive consideration of his wants. (Signed) Dent, Vantine & Co."

Elias. op. cit. In connection with the ferry was a tavern called "the Knight's Ferry House." It served dinner at $1.00, boarded the stage company's men for $10.00 per week. There were also stables which the stage company rented for $200.00 per month. p. 242. Quoted from a letter Gen. U. S. Grant to his wife, the former Julia Dent; dated Benicia, Calif., Aug. 20, 1852. Allowed by the courtesy of Major U. S. Grant, III, grandson of the former president.

15. Ibid. p. 242.

16. The date and manner of arrival of the Dent brothers, Lewis and John, were supplied by Mrs. Samuel Baugh whose father, William Göbel, accompanied them.

17. A Memorial and Biographical History of the Counties of Merced, Stanislaus, Calaveras, Tuolumne and Mariposa, California. p. 134.

18. Elias. op. cit. p. 225 and p. 240.

19. Personal Adventures in Upper and Lower California. William R. Ryan. Vol. II, pp. 46-47.

20. Stockton Journal, Nov. 6, 1850. "A pontoon bridge has been constructed across the Stanislaus at Emory's ferry, and we understand that the Messrs. Dent, Vantine & Co. have entered a contract for building a suspension bridge at their place on the same stream."

Bancroft Scraps of California Counties (Volume begins with Solano Co. and ends with Stanislaus Co.) An undated newspaper clipping, data evidently furnished by William Grant, a driver in the employ of M. J. Dooly & Co. of Sonora: "The wire foot-bridge at Knight's Ferry was carried away at noon on Friday after sustaining an immense pressure from the logs and drift which came down and lodged against it." p. 113.

Elias. op. cit. Containing statement of John Edwards (son of Thomas Edwards, pioneer): "My father was part owner in the Knight's Ferry bridge which was washed away in the flood of 1862. He helped place the footbridge across to Buena Vista. Tom and Harry Pentland were with him on the job. The Lockes were prominent at this time and one brother always had charge of it." p. 239.

21. Alta California. Mar. 22, 1856.

22. Stockton Argus, Stockton, Calif. Nov. 27, 1850.

23. Dent Bar is shown on the Topographical Map of the Mineral Districts of California. John B. Trask. 1853. Contained in Maps of the California Gold

Region, 1848-1857, by Carl I. Wheat. Map No. 247.

24. San Francisco Bulletin. May 7, 1856.

25. Keeler's Ferry, later acquired by the Dent brothers and still later by Locke, was built by G. W. Keeler. An advertisement appeared in the Stockton Journal, Aug. 24, 1850: "Keeler's Ferry. The undersigned respectfully informs the public that he has just completed a large and commodious ferry boat on the Stanislaus, just above the big hill, known as the jumping off place. This ferry, from its position, recommends itself to the traveling public, being 32 miles from Stockton, by way of twelve mile house and lone tree, and thence direct to big hill." (signed) G. W. Keeler."
Keeler's Ferry is also shown on the Silas Wilcox Map of 1855.

26. All the papers for the use of which we are indebted to Mr. Ed. Whitmore are listed in the Bibliography under "Documents."

27. Information contained in Oakdale Leader, Oakdale, Calif. May 22, 1930. Article on Knight's Ferry Celebration.

28. Elias. op. cit. pp. 241-242.
(This gentleman's signature was "A. Shell." Scrapbook of Calif. Counties—Solano to Stanislaus.)

29. Alta California. San Francisco. Nov. 23, 1851.

30. Memorial and Biographical History of the Counties of Merced, Stanislaus, Calaveras, Tuolumne and Mariposa, California. pp. 138-139.

31. Elias. op. cit. p. 245.

32. Corroborated by granddaughter, Miss Elsie Flower.

33. Oakdale Leader, May 22, 1930. Article on Knights Ferry Celebration.

34. Ruppel. op. cit.

35. Old Knight's Ferry Post Office records in poss. of Mr. and Mrs. Roy De Graffenreid, Knight's Ferry, Calif.

36. Information contained in Dictionary of American Biography. Ed. by Allen Johnson and Dumas Malone. Vol. VII. See under heading "Ulysses S. Grant."

37. L. T. Remlap. General Grant's Tour Around the World. p. 575.

38. Mattie V. Reynolds. Interview with Alex Locke.

39. Harlan. op. cit. p. 142.

40. Remlap. op. cit. pp. 575-576.

41. Oakdale Leader, Oakdale, Calif. May 22, 1930. Article on celebration in Knight's Ferry.

42. Information concerning the mill ruins, road to Copperopolis, the dams and sawmill given at the site by Mr. David Tulloch.

CHAPTER III

1. The information in this chapter is from original sources: interviews, questionnaires and letters, carefully compared and checked.
2. The spelling in use at the time was "O'Byrne" according to a certificate of sale, dated Mar. 15, 1864.

CHAPTER IV

1. Letter from Charles V. Gillespie to Thomas O. Larkin.
2. The name "Campo Salvador" and the reason for its use is found in a written statement by William Solinsky but, for many years, it has been locally known as Camp Salvado.
3. Quotation from an undated clipping contained in the scrapbook of Eugene Mecartea.
4. Full name of Count Solinsky vouched for by grandson, Edward Solinsky.
5. Information about Garrett House from Helen Cutting Stratton and Robert Curtin.
6. Information from The Pioneer. Vol. 13, No. 5. May 15, 1898.
7. Information from Recollections of Pioneer Work in California. Rev. James Woods.
8. Gleason's Pictorial Magazine. Feb. 18, 1854. Statement that a large amount of gold was shipped back to relatives in Ireland by these emigrants.
   The Illustrated London News (beginning Jan. 7, 1854). No. 662. Vol. XXIV. Jan. 21, 1854. p. 63. Gives date of potato famine in Ireland.
9. The last land owner to develop a large section of roadway along the Big Oak Flat Turnpike was James (Johnny) Hardin.
10. Information about lynching at Chinese Camp from an undated newspaper clipping in the scrapbook of Eugene Mecartea.
11. History of Tuolumne County, California. Herbert O. Lange. Vol. I, pp. 210-216. Dorsey had been involved in a legal matter where he met Murieta at close range. It is also recorded that, while riding up a steep hill above Moccasin Creek (probably Moccasin Hill) he met Murieta, magnificently mounted; recognized him; exchanged a few wary sentences and proceeded.
    History of California. Theodore H. Hittell. Vol. I, Part 2. p. 721.
12. Ibid. pp. 725-726.
13. Gold was also found in the adobe bricks of a building on Maxwell Creek near Coulterville, according to Mr. John Vigna, late of that town.

CHAPTER V

1. From—The Statutes of California.
   An Act of the Legislature subdividing the state into counties and establishing Seats of Justice therein. Passed Feb. 18, 1850. p. 63.
   Also, in the county records at Sonora, California, the first deed recorded in Vol. I—"Deeds." On April 2, 1850, Manuel Castillo to Walter Taylor and Chas. Bruce, a deed in the town of Stewart.
2. From The Statutes of California, passed at the Nineteenth Session of the Legislature. 1871-1872. p. 61. An Act of the State Legislature, approved Feb. 2, 1872, appropriated the sum of $200 a month for the relief of James W. Marshall for the period of two years. Marshall was not successful financially and the Legislature expressed the people's gratitude thus to the discoverer of California's gold.
3. History of Tuolumne County. Vol. I. Herbert O. Lange. p. 52.
   Also History of California. Hittell. op. cit. p. 130.
4. From Narrative of David S. Smith, taken from the MS diary of Byron N. McKinstry.
5. Todd's Statement. Contained in The Binder of Miscellaneous Statements. The Bancroft Library.
6. Stockton Journal, Stockton, Calif. Nov. 6, 1850.
7. Bits of Travel at Home. Helen Hunt Jackson. pp. 141-142.
8. Information from Up and Down California in 1860-1864. William H. Brewer. pp. 241-244.
9. California Notes. Charles B. Turrill. p. 187.

CHAPTER VI

1. See pp. 264-269.
2. Letter dated Dec. 19, 1849. Printed in a New Orleans newspaper. Name and date of paper unknown.
   Personal Adventures in Upper and Lower California in 1848-49. William Redmond Ryan. Vol. II, p. 42. Speaking of the Indians along the Stanislaus River "The squaws were finely-proportioned women, but their features were somewhat coarse." p. 42.
3. West Point to California. Erasmus D. Keyes. pp. 12-13. "I had in my camp an excellent man named Vinconhaler for guide. We called him 'Captain Haler.' He had crossed the continent twice with Colonel Fremont, to whom he must

have rendered important assistance. His ability to 'find paths' appeared to me almost miraculous." Also Narrative of Thomas Salathiel Martin. MS. in Bancroft Libr., and Rough Times in Rough Places. Micajah McGehee. Century Magazine. Vol. XLI, No. 5, pp. 771-780.

4. Letter dated "California Goldmines Nov. 15th, 1849." In possession of Commander Robert S. Lecky. U.S.C.G. 12th Coast Guard District.

Journal of James M. Hutchings. Entry of Dec. 19, 1849, written at Hangtown, Calif. ". . . When I came here I thought that considerable difficulty would arise for the miners to take care of their gold, when they had succeeded in digging it, and especially after reading in the papers of so much shooting and danger, to men and property. I was certain of having to sleep with my pistol all 'capt and leavelled,' and my knife beneath my head, for necessary protection—but instead, you can leave your purse (your everything, in fact) in your tent without any danger of losing it."

Personal Adventures in Upper and Lower California. 1848-49. Vol. I. William R. Ryan. "I was informed, that, although thefts had occurred, yet, generally speaking, the miners dwelt in no distrust of one another and left thousands of dollars' worth in gold-dust in their tents whilst they were about digging." p. 22.

5. Ibid. p. 311.

6. Alta California, San Francisco. Sept. 2, 1850. Gives general description of this mail service.

7. The news did not appear in the Sacramento Union, Sacramento, Calif., until Mar. 5, 1859.

8. The Golden Rock Water Company was incorporated Feb. 27, 1856. Articles of incorporation are missing from the files in the Sonora Hall of Records but the index shows the date.

9. See p. 195 and p. 202.

10. "A miners' inch of water varies with different localities to such an extent that it may be said to constitute an arbitrary quantity." Gold Mines and Mining in California. Pub. by George Spaulding & Co., San Francisco. 1885. p. 87.

11. Alta California. April 6, 1860.

12. Union Democrat, Sonora, Calif. Jan. 6, 1955. "Ninety Years Ago" column.

13. Adventures of William T. Ballou. MS in binder. Bancroft Library.

14. These merchants apparently included A. Gamble and Peter and John Gamble according to Heckendorn and Wilson's Miners' and Business Mens' Directory for the year commencing Jan. 1, 1856.

Alta, California, Sept. 13, 1851, states that Gamble's store in Big Oak Flat was supplied by pack animals.

CHAPTER VII

1. Reminiscences of an Old Soldier. James E. Hunt. He also states that the flat was ". . . better adapted for agricultural purposes than for mining." p. 93.

The remaining information in this chapter is from original sources: interviews, questionnaires and letters, carefully compared and checked.

CHAPTER VIII

1. See Map No. 247 in Maps of the California Gold Region, 1848-1857. Carl I. Wheat. On this map First and Second Garrote are indicated by captions Garota 1 and Garota 2.

2. See pp. 179-180.

3. From a manuscript reminiscence signed "Tennessee and partner," in the Jason Chamberlain carton at Bancroft Library. "I dont know why they call this 2nd Garrote. I dont think a man was ever hung here altho (sic) the historic oak near our house has the reputation of having 8 men hung one morning before breakfast but I know that story to be a lie started by a stage driver to entertain inquisitive passengers."

4. Statement concerning the lynching at Second Garrote, signed by Paul Morris. Typescript in folder at Yosemite Museum Archives. Yosemite, Calif.

CHAPTER IX

1. Mrs. Henry Crocker of Crocker's Station.

2. Miss Haight was wrong. The trees were maples according to John Muir who was certainly qualified to judge.

3. It is difficult to tell from Miss Haight's manuscript whether the young man's name was Arni or Arin as, written in longhand, they look very much alike.

4. Union Democrat, Sonora, Calif. May 1, 1869.

5. Yosemite Book of 1868. J. D. Whitney. p. 99.

"The Hetch Hetchy may be reached easily from Oak Flat by taking the regular Yosemite Trail, by Sprague's ranch and Big Flume, as far as Mr. Hardin's fence, between the South and Middle Forks of the Tuolumne River. Here, at a distance of about 18 miles from Big Oak Flat, the trail runs off to the left, going to Wade's meadows, or Big Meadows as they are called, the distance being about 7 miles. From Wade's ranch the trail crosses the middle fork of the Tuolumne, and goes to the 'Hog Ranch' a distance of 5 miles, then up the divide between the middle fork and the main river, to another little ranch called 'the Canon.' From here, it winds down among rocks, for six miles to the Hetch Hetchy or the Tuolumne Canon."

6. Tuolumne County Records—District Court Index. Y.T.R. Co. vs Jas. Hardin; No. 1421; Book F.

7. It should be noted that the Road Company, in common with most business projects, had financial problems. A great deal of money had been expended on the road itself, but there remained such items as equipment and payroll and working capital. Steady travel and income were not immediate and it became necessary for the new corporation to borrow money. The following brief items in chronological order will tell the story.

June 1, 1875 Notice of mortgage (dated Feb. 17, 1875) to J. M. Hutchins, executed by Chas. B. Cutting President, George E. Sprague Secretary. Reference Vol 1, Book "B" Vol 7, page 785.

May 16, 1878 District Court. J. M. Hutchins Plaintiff, vs Yosemite Turnpike Road Company. defendants L D Gobin, D B Newhall, George E Sprague, Colonel E Drew, and Robert Simmons, sold by Sheriff T M Yancey, to plaintiff for $5000.00 on execution, for judgement amount to $6755 and costs total $7166.05. Road from Chinese Camp to Yosemite Valley. see Book "D" vol 1 page 219.
(It will be noted that J. M. Hutchings' name was misspelled; a common occurrence in those years even in legal matters.)

May 16, 1878 J. M Hutchins made agreement to sell to Big Oak Flat and Yosemite Turnpike Road Company. Ref. Vol 18 page 126 of Deeds.

April 1, 1879 Incorporation of Big Oak Flat and Yosemite Turnpike Road Company (No. 282. Filed June 23, 1879) Capital Stock $25,000. Term 50 years. Trustees, Charles Kasabaum, William C. Priest, George C. Sprague, L. D. Gobin, C. O. Drew. Deeds to the property dated November 1879. Vol. 19, page 607.

8. Information contained in Mining Camps, A Study in American Frontier Government. Charles Howard Shinn. pp. 203-208.

9. Each miner made his own arrastra. A circle was measured out on level ground bordered with a rock wall at least a foot high and paved with large flat rocks. It was probably not less than 12 or 14 feet in diameter. Then an immensely heavy stone called the drag rock, was placed within the circle and tied to the short end of a long sweep that pivoted on an axis placed in the center. The

long end of the sweep extended beyond the outer edge of the circle and was propelled around and around by a mule. Given this extra leverage it was not too difficult for the patient beast to drag the heavy boulder through the broken ore which pickax and wheelbarrow had dumped into the arrastra. After the ore was finely crushed the miner panned it, or used whatever method pleased him best to recover the gold. The arrastra was always near water. The ore would be carried to it.

10. The spelling koo-cha-bee is used in Up and Down California in 1860-1864. William H. Brewer. p. 417.

The spelling kit-chavi is used in In the Heart of the Sierras. James M. Hutchings. p. 428.

11. Article in the Overland Monthly. Nov. 1899. Also affirmed by Celia Crocker Thompson.

CHAPTER X

1. See p. 49 and p. 51.
2. Bits of Travel at Home. Helen Hunt Jackson. pp. 95-96.
3. Article in Galaxy Magazine. Olive Logan.
4. See Appendix II.
5. See p. 263.
6. Throughout many interviews this measurement varied slightly.
7. Discovery of the Yosemite. L. H. Bunnell. p. 321.
8. My First Summer in the Sierra. John Muir. p. 130.
9. Yosemite Book of 1868. J. D. Whitney. p. 51.
   A Guide to the Yosemite Valley — 1871. J. M. Hutchings. p. 101.
10. Life and Letters of John Muir. William Frederic Badé. p. 190.
11. Bunnell, op. cit. p. 316.
12. In the Heart of the Sierras. J. M. Hutchings. pp. 332-333.

CHAPTER XI

1. Up and Down California in 1860-1864. Wm. H. Brewer. Ed. by Francis P. Farquhar. p. 416.
   A Journal of Ramblings Through the High Sierra of California by the University Excursion Party (in 1870). Joseph Le Conte. p. 105.
   Our Trip to the Yosemite Valley and Sierra Nevada Range. L.N.R.R.
2. My First Summer in the Sierra. John Muir. p. 137.

3. Discovery of the Yosemite. Lafayette H. Bunnell. pp. 321-322.
4. Article in Galaxy Magazine. Olive Logan.
5. My First Summer in the Sierra. John Muir. p. 294.
6. Yosemite Book of 1868. J. D. Whitney. p. 51.

CHAPTER XII

1. From Oration of C. H. Randall, publisher of The Sonora Union Democrat, on the occasion of the festivity in Yosemite Valley celebrating the completion of the Big Oak Flat Road. Published in Sonora Union Democrat. Aug. 1, 1874.

2. From Declaration of Intention (to meet on Sept. 19, 1868, for purpose of organizing a road company from Chinese Camp via Big Oak Flat to Yosemite Valley).

3. From Certificate of Formal Organization of Yo Semite Turnpike Road Company. March 19, 1869.

4. Laws and Judicial Decisions, Relating to the Yosemite Valley & Mariposa Big Tree Grove.

5. Report of Commission on Roads in Yosemite National Park. Senate Doc. 155. 1900.

6. Certificate of organization. Coulterville and YoSemite Turnpike Company, 1870.

7. Sonora Union Democrat. Oct. 25, 1873.

8. Article of Incorporation for Coulterville & Yo Semite Turnpike Company 1870. Court House, Mariposa.

9. Laws and Judicial Decisions, Relating to the Yosemite Valley & Mariposa Big Tree Grove.

10. Merced Grove was named by Dr. John T. McLean. Carl P. Russell quotes from a letter written by McLean to the Yosemite National Park Commission in 1899: "It was determined to carry the road [the Coulterville Road] directly through this grove, which was named the Merced Grove by me because of its nearness to the Merced River." One Hundred Years in Yosemite. Carl Parcher Russell. p. 62.

11. Laws and Judicial Decisions. op. cit.

12. Ibid.

13. Ibid.

14. Ibid.

15. Sonora Union Democrat. Oct. 25, 1873.

16. Ibid., Sept. 13, 1873.
17. Ibid., Oct. 25, 1873.
18. Statutes of California, passed at the Twentieth Session of the Legislature, 1873-1874.
19. Undated newspaper article signed "Paul Morris" in scrapbook of Eugene Mecartea. Also from interviews. The Zigzag was finished July 17, 1874.
20. From interview with John V. Ferretti.
21. From article by C. H. Burden, contained in scrapbook of Celia Crocker Thompson.
22. It was J. M. Hutchings who spoke of this viewpoint as Prospect Point. A Guide to the YoSemite Valley—1871. p. 104. On the next page he places the spot called "Standpoint of Silence" on the old Coulterville Trail, on the segment known as the Lower Trail. J. D. Whitney (more scientific than aesthetic), in speaking of the viewpoint at the top of the Zigzag, states: "This point of view has been rather absurdly called the 'Stand-Point of Silence.' " But this difference of opinion really made very little difference as it was practically never called anything but "Oh My! Point."
23. Sonora Union Democrat. July 17, 1874.
24. Ibid., July 25, 1874.
25. Ibid., March 3, 1866.

Chapter XIII

1. In the Heart of the Sierras. J. M. Hutchings. p. 58.
2. Ibid. p. 58.
3. The following is not offered as a proven fact but simply as a possible explanation of Ten-ie-ya's statement that the white men "were so guided" as not to see the Valley proper when it is evident from Leonard's account that they did not have a guide. There is one incident that might be interpreted as a guiding circumstance over which the Indians had control. One day one of Walker's men brought a basket of acorns into camp. Leonard wrote, "These nuts our hunter had got from an Indian who had them on his back travelling as though he was on a journey across the mountains, to the east side. When the Indian seen our hunter he dropped his basket of provision and run for life." Now acorns were known to come from those lower altitudes which the party was trying desperately to reach but could not because the trail was blotted out by snow and must be searched for slowly and with great waste of time. Finding the Indian's tracks

visible on the fresh snowfall must have seemed providential to the tired and rather bewildered party.

Just east of Ribbon (or Virgin's Tears) Creek the Mono Trail divided, one branch leading to Yosemite and the other westward down to Bull Creek. Freshly made tracks in the direction of Bull Creek would focus all attention on the latter route which the Indians wished Walker to take; which was actually where he most wanted to go and was, in the end, where he and his party travelled.

4. From Crane Flat one may travel westerly along the ridgetop without losing altitude, except in one or two shallow saddles, as far as Pilot Peak. The course at first is along Crane Flat Ridge with Tuolumne Grove to the north, then curves around the drainage of Moss Creek containing Merced Grove to Trumbull Ridge; through the saddle at Hazel Green; up and over the south end of Crocker Ridge; thence onto Pilot Ridge as far as Pilot Peak. On maps the ridge appears to continue but, for practical purposes, may be disregarded as there is such a deep and precipitous break in it just here that no traveler, once down, would climb up again.

5. See Appendix 2.

6. Life and Letters of John Muir. Wm. Frederic Badé. p. 216.

7. According to Carl P. Russell this was a horse trail that led from Dudley Station on the Coulterville Road to the cliffs of Merced River gorge where the descent was made by means of Jenkins Hill; thence up Merced River. See One Hundred Years in Yosemite. pp. 52-53.

8. The Cemetery in the Yosemite Valley. Mrs. H. J. Taylor.

9. Badé. op. cit. pp. 207-208.

10. Ibid. pp. 246.

11. Ibid. p. 211.
    This may have been Tom Hutchins, a full-blood Indian who brought the mail in from Coulterville at twenty-five cents per letter.

12. On the Big Oak Flat run the winter mail was brought from Crocker's on snowshoes and (some of the time) arrived once a week. This was in the later '70's and the '80's. Some years the government contract was held by Jeremiah Hodgdon and some indefinite years by John Phelan.

13. Hutchings. op. cit. pp. 355-357.

14. Ibid. p. 351.

15. Yosemite and the Sierra Club. William E. Colby. Concerning the creating of Yosemite National Park and its subsequent history.

Appendix I

It has been amazingly difficult to assemble the following facts about the many stage lines that served this portion of the Southern Mines. The rivalry and competition among the various stage line companies, especially of the '50's and '60's, led to a constant change of schedules, rates, ownership and routes. This account has been pieced together over a period of years and many of the data come from articles and advertisements in the old newspaper files of Stockton, Sonora, Mariposa, etc. There are bound to be omissions but the facts presented (taken from publications current at the time) are probably correct. Only the stage lines of major interest and importance in serving the Big Oak Flat Route to Yosemite Valley are presented.

According to early Stockton papers several stage and express lines operated between that city and the Southern Mines in the early '50s. Adams Express Company had an office in Chinese Camp, serving Big Oak Flat and Coulterville. Reynolds & Co.'s Express operated from Stockton and served Tuolumne and Mariposa Counties by fall of 1850, however, the more remote camps were required to have their own pack-animal expressman to pick up parcels at Chinese Camp.

In the Sonora "Union Democrat" of September 27, 1850, there appeared a notice that the first daily stage line in the Southern Mines was to run between Sonora, Knights Ferry, Chinese Camp and Coulterville. No guarantee was given that the whole trip could be made by stage, but only as far as the road permitted. The journey would then be completed by saddle animals for which there was no extra charge unless the passenger needed a second animal for baggage. The stage left Sonora early in the morning by way of Montezuma and Chinese Camp and, under favorable conditions, arrived in Stockton at two in the afternoon. At this time the Big Oak Flat Road had not been extended beyond Red Flat or Shepley's Flat, a few miles east of Chinese Camp.

The transportation business was profitable and competition immediately began to increase. On June 16, 1855, the Sonora "Union Democrat" carried an announcement by A. J. Snow of Jacksonville that his express would be able to accommodate six passengers and that he was making four regular trips weekly. In this he reminded the traveling public that his express had been the first to run between Jacksonville and the Garrotes and asked for their continued patronage. In the same year his chief competitor, Archy Yochem, put a notice in the Sonora paper that his express would extend its run from Big Oak Flat to Coulterville and Mariposa, leaving Sonora daily, except Tuesdays. Stage stations were generally twelve miles apart. These early conveyances were commonly known as "mud-wagons" and about the only consideration given to a traveler's comfort was a stretch of canvas over the top to protect him somewhat from the scorching sun or downpour of rain. One passenger called her stage "a hard, lumbering, springless, unpainted fiend." This was the hypercritical lady who, upon leaving Stockton via stagecoach, remarked upon the presence of an insane asylum in proximity to the hotel. "Can this have any connection," she demanded bitterly, "with its being the returning point for YoSemite tourists?"

In 1856 the road to Big Oak Flat was widened to accommodate heavy freighters. The middle '50s formed a period of unrest and dissatisfaction in various parts of the diggings. Many miners moved out; then as ditch companies were formed bringing in the necessary water, they swarmed back into the Mother Lode country. The staging business became profitable again. There was such a rush to the Big Oak Flat diggings that it was sometimes necessary to wait two or three days in Chinese Camp to get a seat on the stage. Passengers were often required to walk up Moccasin Hill unless extra horses were added at the base. Generally six horses were needed for this stretch. In 1860 two daily stages entered Big Oak Flat, one from Sonora and one from Stockton, each via Chinese Camp where horses and drivers were changed. There was also a change of horses at Crimea House, then called Mound Springs Station. At the same time a four-wheeled vehicle with a seat along each side served as a stage between Big Oak Flat and Second Garrote, the end of the wagon road.

One of the earlier stage lines was a spring wagon run by M. J. Dooly from Stockton to Sonora via Knight's Ferry and Chinese Camp. Upon Dooly's death it was absorbed by C. H. Sisson.

According to Bancroft's Guide, No. 5, by 1869 tourists en route to Yosemite Valley could buy tickets at C. H. Sisson and Company's office in Stockton whence stages left daily at 6 A.M., except Sundays. The fare was $20.00 including the transfer to Simon Shoup's stage at Chinese Camp. If the traveler started from the latter settlement the fare was only $13.00. No extra charge was made for the horseback trip from Hardin's Mill, the road terminus at that date, on to the Yosemite. At Shoup's Chinese Camp office the traveler might decide which route he wished to take to the valley—Big Oak Flat or Coulterville—and might board the stage so designated. Bancroft's Guide, No. 8, states that the routes were identical to the top of Moccasin Hill (then sometimes known as Rattlesnake Hill) where Mr. and Mrs. Kirkwood (later Mrs. Priest) established a small stopping place in 1855—a modest inn which became historic Priest's Station.

At Kirkwood's the Coulterville stage, having made a change of horses, crossed Rattlesnake Creek and descended southeastward to Coulterville, thence to the terminus of its road where a saddle train met the tourists.

The traveler who chose the Big Oak Flat stage continued on from Kirkwood's after the necessary attention was given to the teams and stopped for the first night at Savory's Hotel in First Garrote (Groveland). At suppertime Mr. Shoup told his women passengers to don riding habits in the morning in order to be ready for the 28-mile saddle trip which would commence at Hardin's the following afternoon. He also hesitantly informed them that those who wished to change to bloomers at Tamarack Flat, well up in the wilderness, for the uncomfortable ride down the cliff to the valley floor would most certainly be given a chance to change back to the modest habit and sidesaddle as soon as they struck level ground.

By the spring of 1870 the staging terminus had moved up the mountain to Hodgdon's and, according to Bancroft's Guide No. 8, there was a charge of $5.00 for the saddle trip to the floor of the valley via J. M. Hutching's mule train. As soon as the road reached his property Jeremiah Hodgdon broke into the staging game, running a small "mud wagon" from Hardin's Mill eastward to his primitive stopping place. By fall of 1870 the road had progressed to Crane Flat where L. T. Gobin had established a comfortable stopping place. This stretch of road was very narrow and steep and a control station was maintained at Hodgdon's. The guidebook referred to this section of the road as "Hardin's Route."

In June of 1871 the Central Pacific Railroad's "Copperopolis Short Line" from Stockton to Milton, Calaveras County, was completed. Passengers and goods could now come as far as Milton by train. Sisson & Co.'s stage line then ran from Milton to Chinese Camp. The rates were, of necessity, lowered. In this same summer of '71 Hodgdon pushed the stage route as far as Tamarack Flat where it was met by J. M. Hutching's string of saddle mules.

In 1872 Hodgdon formed a partnership with Simon Shoup and an arrangement was made whereby Shoup's stage met Hodgdon's at Hardin's Mill three times a week. Hodgdon then took the passengers on to Gentry's where they were met by the saddle train, keeping them firmly at his new hotel all night en route. The Shoup-Hodgdon project was known as the Yo Semite Stage Line and the saddle train was owned and operated by J. M. Hutchings of Yosemite Valley. Hodgdon built a large barn on a tributary of North Crane Creek close to his stage station. James ("Johnny") Hardin finally acquired an interest in the line and continued to run a small stopping place on his flat.

In 1873, in addition to Mr. Shoup's interest in the aforementioned line, he started his tri-weekly "Sonora to Garrote Stage Line," according to the Sonora "Union Democrat," October 25, 1873. Thence, until July 17, 1874, travel down the cliff was by mule train and the journey from Chinese Camp to the Valley floor was generally known as either "Hutching's Route" or "The Big Oak Flat Route."

Shoup and Hodgdon were still partners in '78. The Sonora "Union Democrat" for April 13th of that year wrote, "Mr. Shoup and Jerry Hodgdon are below fixing preliminaries for their line of stages which we understand are in readiness now to connect with Olive and Co.'s line from Stockton." On November 9, 1878, the Sonora "Union Democrat" stated that Hodgdon had been awarded the government mail contract to Yosemite, deliveries to be made three times a week six months out of the year and once a week during the winter and spring. Interviews established that he made his winter trips on snowshoes.

In 1879 Hodgdon sold out to Charles Kassabaum and John D. Meyer of Groveland but kept an interest in the business. He and his son Thomas remained as drivers for a short period. After almost two years Kassabaum and Meyer dissolved their partnership. Mr. Meyer then gave full time to his cattle raising and Mr. Kassabaum afterward became a director in a later stage line.

In the '70's the "Nevada Stage Company" moved a large portion of their equipment and many of their drivers from Nevada into California. This is a development in staging seldom mentioned by historians, but as late as the early '80's, stages bearing the sign "Nevada Stage Co." ran into the Yosemite Valley over the Big Oak Flat Road. This interstate transfer has been corroborated by interviews. The owners of this line are given as Parker, Pease and Cluggage and their "Yosemite Run" operated from Milton to the Valley via Chinese Camp. In 1881 an advertising booklet put out by the Nevada Stage Company states: "A stage meets the train at Milton at 9:35 A.M.; stops for lunch at Copperopolis; arrives at Priest's Station at 6:00 P.M. for dinner and the night's stop. Leaves Priest's early in the morning via Big Oak Flat and arrives in Yosemite Valley at 5:00 P.M. The round trip amounts to $35.00." Six horses were generally used and at times, when snow still lay on the higher elevations, snowshoes for the animals were added.

Travel to the Yosemite was on the increase and "Jerry" Hodgdon's stopping place became far too inadequate and primitive, especially for women travelers. When John Shine of Sonora became manager of the Nevada Stage Line he appealed to Henry Crocker to build a stage station and pleasing stopping place on his property between the South Fork of the Tuolumne and the road, and a few miles below Hodgdon's Meadows. By the spring of 1881 Mr. Crocker's 15 structures were almost completed. The stage company was indeed proud of its attractive stopping place and only the overflow went to Hodgdon's, whose primary interest had always been cattle raising.

On March 1, 1886, the Great Sierra Stage Company was incorporated, having purchased the "Yosemite Run" of the Nevada Stage Company. Its directors were William C. Priest, of Big Oak Flat, Colwell Owens Drew and Charles Kassabaum of Groveland, Henry R. Crocker and Thomas H. Beals whose property lay in the Santa Maria voting precinct above the settlements. John Shine of Sonora became the company's superintendent and manager. The Great Sierra Stage Line ran stages from Milton to Yosemite Valley via Copperopolis, O'Byrne's Ferry and Chinese Camp. By this time the road was completed to the Valley floor, and tourists were no longer required to change to horse or mule back for the final descent. The stages were no longer of the mud wagon type and more attention was given to the comforts of the traveler.

Among the company's best remembered drivers, many of whom drove for the Nevada Stage Co., were Martin Burrell, Rice Markley, William Carlton, Joseph Ridgeway, John, Dennis and Andrew Shine, "Al" Harkness, Donald McLean, Adam Thomayer, Ned McGowen, Joseph Mulligan, Messrs. Mott and Stoddard, Joseph Johns, Archie McLean, Tom, Jack and Bill Gibbons, Clark Stringham, Samuel Smith, Billy Walton, Billy Hendricks, George Townsend, Thomas Hodgdon, Thomas Jackson who married Margaret Solinsky of Chinese Camp, and William Hodges, distinguished by a scar on his head from a bullet fired by the bandit Vasquez.

After an indefinite period the line was purchased by Capt. W. A. Nevills, a wealthy mining man of the county, and was known as Nevills and Guerins. By 1902 the line was sold to D. A. Lumsden, Saul and Paul Morris of Chinese Camp, and was entitled The Big Oak Flat-Yosemite Stage Co. Nevills became their manager.

In 1897 the construction of the Sierra Railroad was begun, joining Oakdale with Jamestown and Sonora. Chinese Station, a short distance from the town, served Chinese Camp. Yosemite passengers no longer used the Copperopolis Short Line unless they intended also to visit the Calaveras Grove of Big Trees.

In 1902 an advertising booklet was circulated, stating that Paul Morris of Chinese Camp was then the company's General Manager. From him and other sources we have gathered that later the firm was managed by Paul Morris, "Dave" Lumsden remaining in the company, at least for a time. Meanwhile Saul Morris managed the large Morris Brothers' store in Chinese Camp.

In the early 1900's this company owned thirty well-built "Henderson" stages equipped with thorough braces. Concord stages were never used on the route above Chinese Camp. Some three hundred horses were cared for by twenty hostlers along the road and the company's thirty drivers were carefully chosen. Several horse-shoers, road bosses and other personnel were also employed and repair work was done at Egling's shop in Chinese Camp. This was the peak of staging to Yosemite. In 1914 the stage company added to their toll rate sign: "Automobiles defined, vehicle not used with horses." As more and more automobiles entered the Valley the Morris brothers foresaw the end of their profitable business and closed out the run.

For over fifty years the number of accidents was amazingly low. During the last decade the Morris brothers attributed this to detailed inspection of the road before each spring opening of the upper stretches to guard against washed-out bridges, fallen trees and dislodged boulders; and also to a most careful selection of drivers for their skill and discretion. The safety of the passengers was a matter of personal pride to the owners of the line.

Between 1869 and 1915 toll gates were placed in sequence at Sprague's Ranch, Hardin's Mill, Crane Flat and Colfax Springs. For several years before the road was purchased by Tuolumne County, the toll gate stood at the crossing of the South Fork of the Tuolumne River; at present the location of a modern inn, "The Cliff House." The sign read:

BIG OAK FLAT AND YOSEMITE TURNPIKE ROAD COMPANY

Paul Morris, President
Robert Simmons, Road Supt.

George A. Sprague
Secretary-Treasurer

* * * * * * * * *

Franchise granted, Feb. 20, 1869 by State of Calif. to run 50 years.

* * * * * * * * *

RATES OF TOLL

Each passenger each way to Yosemite Valley	$1.00
" " " " in private vehicle or stage	$1.00
" " " " " automobile	$1.00
" " " " on horseback	$1.00
Freight teams each way, 2 animals	$2.00
each additional animal	.50
Loose horses or cattle—each	.10
Loose sheep or goats, each	.05
Bicycle, one passenger	.50

Rates of Toll to Crocker's

Each passenger each way in stage or vehicle 50
   "   "   "   "   " automobile 50
Freight teams each way, 2 animals each way $1.50
                   " additional animal 25
Foot travelers, each way 25
Bicycle each way 50

Terms

Automobile defined, vehicle not used with horses

Directors

Paul Morris, C. O. Drew, Geo. Sprague, E. T. Gobin, Robt. Simmons, Dan Corcoran.
Attorney, John B. Curtin, Sonora, California
Main office: Priest Hotel, Big Oak Flat, California
Rates of Toll Set by Board of Supervisors of Tuolumne
and Mariposa Counties.

Appendix II

As this is a more or less staggering compendium of related facts about the Yosemite National Park not to be found elsewhere between one set of covers, a thumbnail sketch of the available trails by which a man might, in the first decade after its discovery, make his way to and around Yosemite is pertinent.

Most important were the various ramifications of the Mono Trail: Coming west, this much-used Indian thoroughfare left the Mono Lake country; came through Bloody Canyon (which has its beginning in the Mono Pass immediately south of Mount Gibbs); through Tuolumne Meadows; split and went either side of Lake Tenaya. Shortly after the two sections separated, a branch trail forked from the section which led south of the lake and headed south of Yosemite, passing north of Cathedral Peak and south of Half Dome, crossing Little Yosemite Creek about 1½ miles above Nevada Fall, continued southwest, crossing Illillouette and Bridal Veil Creeks. Near the latter, two sheep herders, Westfall and Ostrander, had their cabins and, in 1869, Charles E. Peregoy built his "Mountain View House," used mainly as a noon stop by travelers. The trail forked here and a branch descended sharply nearly 3,000 feet, via what was later Inspiration Point, to the lower end of the Valley floor. This was the descent by which the discoverers entered, having worked their way eastward from the western portion of this trail. Reaching this fork near Bridal Veil Creek the westbound traveler who did not wish to go down into Yosemite might cross a divide; go south down Alder Creek; leaving it, go six miles farther south downhill to Galen Clark's ranch; thence over a high ridge and down Chowchilla Creek southwest to White and Hatch's; thence about 12 miles to the "Mariposa Estate," owned by John Charles Fremont.

This was later roughly the course of the Mann brothers' trail.

Getting back to Lake Tenaya and the trails that had split to go north and south of it: At the west end of the lake they met again and the reunited trail kept north of Yosemite, crossing Yosemite Creek about two miles above the falls; went southwest over a divide to a point just east of Ribbon (or Virgin's Tears) Creek where it again divided. The southern fork proceeded to what was later Gentry's Station and descended the cliff just west of El Capitan along a route which (being widened, graded and much improved) became approximately the "Zigzag," the last lap of the Big Oak Flat Road to the floor of the Valley. The northern fork crossed Cascade Creek; thence through Tamarack Flat. Thence they kept on the ridge northeast of North Crane Creek; thence down to what was later Hodgdon's from whence on northwest it assumed, in mining days, the name "Big Oak Flat Trail" and later "Big Oak Flat Road."

At Crane Flat a branch broke away to travel westward along the backbone of Crane Flat Ridge and Pilot Peak Ridge; finally dipping into Bull Creek at or near Anderson Flat; thence on to the San Joaquin Valley. This was close to and the inspiration for the course of the Coulterville Free Trail.

According to Bunnell (*Discovery of the Yosemite*, p. 321) most of the Indian trails were originally unfit for pack animals. Forward-looking men soon began to widen and blaze them so they could be recognized even with snow on the ground. Some were toll trails, made for profit. Some were not. The year 1856 saw much activity along this line. The brothers, Houston and Milton Mann, a livery stable firm from Mariposa, slashed out a trail which followed the south fork of the Merced River, crossing it at what is now Wawona (old Clark's Ranch) and forming a saddle trail from Mariposa to Yosemite. Hutchings (*In the Heart of the Sierras*, p. 98) states that it was completed as a toll trail in August, 1856. Whitney stated (in *The Yosemite Book*, p. 19) that the trail led from "White & Hatches" to Yosemite and was later purchased by the County of Mariposa for $200 and made toll free. It was more difficult but afforded the best views.

In the same year George Washington Coulter, Lafayette Bunnell and others cleared a path from Bull Creek (which was already connected with Coulterville by a crude road) via Hazel Green eastward to Crane Flat. It appears on maps of the time as "The Coulterville Free Trail." Bunnell wrote (in *Discovery of the Yosemite*, pp. 315-316): "In locating the Coulterville trail little or no aid was afforded me by the Indian trails that existed at that time; for horses had not seemingly been taken into the valley on the north side, and the foot trails used by the Indians left no traces in the loose granite soil of the higher ridges, but what were soon obliterated by the wash from the melting snow. Where trails were found, they had been purposely run over ground impassable to horses, and they were, consequently, unavailable for our use."

In the next year, 1857, the western part of the Mono Trail (leading through Big Oak Flat) was cleared and blazed by Tom McGee, following very closely in the original foot trail. Some of these blazes are still visible. They were so placed as only to be seen on the right-hand side of the trail no matter in which direction one passed. The earlier blazes — for instance those of Tom McGee — are simple slashes made with a hand ax. Later the cavalry made large and definite "T's." One of these is still prominent on the cliff-side trail beyond the log barrier at Gentry's.

The combined Coulterville and Big Oak Flat Trail, after striking the Valley floor, proceeded, somewhat as does the modern north-side highway but closer to the river, to a point near the Three Brothers where the small stream called Eagle Creek flows into the river. Here, on the sand and gravel washed in by the creek, the pack trains forded and made their way up the south side of the Valley to where the habitations were beginning to be constructed.

After 1870 a low-level saddle trail was opened through the Merced Canyon and called "Hite's Cove Route."

This, with the addition through the years of a ferry and sundry bridges, was the picture until, in 1874, the Coulterville and the Big Oak Flat Roads made their respective entries into the Valley.

So much for the pre-road trails. Over them the Indians and then the early settlers came to Yosemite.

BIBLIOGRAPHY

PUBLICATIONS

Alley, B. F. *History of Tuolumne County*. Privately printed in San Francisco, 1882. In Stanford University, Palo Alto, California.

Badé, William Frederic. *John Muir in Yosemite*, a pamphlet reprinted from Natural History, Vol. XX, No. 2, pp. 124-141, 1920.

———. *The Life and Letters of John Muir*. Houghton Mifflin Co., Boston and New York. 1923.

Bancroft, A. L. & Co., Tourists' Guide, Yosemite, 1870, 1871, 1872, 1873.

Bancroft, Hubert Howe. *History of California*, San Francisco. A. L. Bancroft & Company, 1886-1890.

———. Guide for Travelers by Railroad, Stage, and Steam Navigation in the Pacific States, May, 1872. In Bancroft Library, University of California, Berkeley, California.

Bancroft, H. H. & Co., Guide No. 5, Nov. 1869.

———. Guide No. 8, Feb. 1870.

———. Guide No. 52, Oct. 1873.

———Bancroft's Hand-Book Almanac for the Pacific States, 1863. Ed. by Wm. H. Knight.

———. Bancroft's Hand-Book Almanac for the Pacific States. 1864. Ed. by Wm. H. Knight.

Bidwell, John. A Journey to California. (Diary written on Overland Trail in 1841). Pamphlet printed at Weston or Liberty, Mo., 1842. Only known copy at Bancroft Library, University of California, Berkeley, Calif.

Bookwalter, John W. *Scenes in California and the Sandwich Islands*. Republic Printing Co., Springfield, Ohio. 1874.

Brewer, William H. *Up and Down California in 1860-1864*, The Journal of William Brewer. Ed. by Francis P. Farquhar. University of California Press, Berkeley and Los Angeles, 1949.

Browne, J. Ross (aided by a corps of assistants). *Resources of the Pacific Slope*. D. Appleton & Co., New York, N. Y., 1869.

Bryant, Edwin. *What I Saw in California*. D. Appleton & Co., New York, N. Y., 1848.

Bunnell, Lafayette Houghton, M.D. *Discovery of the Yosemite and the Indian War of 1851*. Reprint by G. W. Gerlicher, Los Angeles, 1892.

Business Directory of the Pacific States and Territories for 1878. Pub. by L. M. McKenney, San Francisco, 1878.

California Associated Cyciing Club Touring Guide and Road Book. San Francisco, 1898.

California State Business Directory, 1875-76. San Francisco: D. M. Bishop & Co.

Canfield, Chauncey L. *The Diary of a '49er*. Morgan, Shepard Co., San Francisco and New York, 1906.

Carson, James H. *Life in California*—together with a description of the Great Tulare Valley. Stockton, the office of the San Joaquin Republican. 2nd edition. 1852. Containing the map of the Southern Mines by C. D. Gibbes.

Chapman, Chas. E. *A History of California—The Spanish Period*. The Macmillan Co., New York, 1949.

Childs, George W. *Recollections of General Grant*. Philadelphia: Collins Printing House. 1890.

Clark, Galen. *The Yosemite Valley Illustrated with Photographs by George Fiske*. Yosemite Valley. 1911.

Cleland, Robert Glass. *Cattle on a Thousand Hills*. The Huntington Library, San Marino, Calif., 1941.

Coppeé, Henry *Life and Services of General U. S. Grant*. Chicago: The Western News Co. New York: Richardson & Co., 1868.

Cox, Isaac. *The Annals of Trinity County*. Printed for Harold C. Holmes by John Henry Nash of the University of Oregon. Eugene, Oregon, 1940.

Crofutt, George A. *Transcontinental Tourists' Guide*. New York, 1871.

Daughters of the American Revolution, California Branch. Records of the families of the California Pioneers. Vol. 6, 1942. At the California State Library, Sacramento, Calif.

Davis, William Heath. *Sixty Years in California*. San Francisco. A. J. Leary, Publisher. 1889.

Elias, Solomon Philip. *Stories of the Stanislaus*. Privately printed. Modesto, California, 1924.

Farquhar, Francis P. Jedediah Smith and the First Crossing of the Sierra Nevada. Published in the Sierra Club Bulletin, Vol. 28, No. 3, June, 1943.

Frémont, Brevet Col. John Charles. *The Exploring Expedition of the Rocky Mountains, Oregon and California*. Buffalo: George H. Derby & Co., 1851.

——*Memoirs of My Life*. Including the narartive, *Five Journeys of Western Exploration*. In 2 Vols. Chicago and New York: Belford, Clarke & Company. 1887.

Grant, Ulysses S. *Personal Memoirs and Memories of U. S. Grant.* Vol. I. Charles L. Webster & Co., 1885.

——Portions of a letter to his wife, the former Julia Dent, dated Benicia, Calif., Aug. 20, 1852. Contained in *Stories of the Stanislaus* by Sol. P. Elias who was allowed to use it by the courtesy of Major U. S. Grant, III, grandson of the former president.

Grover's Narrative. Story of an Indian fight in Yosemite. Obtained apparently by Mrs. A. E. Chandler of Santa Cruz, then successively in possession of Galen Clark and George Fiske. At his death it came into possession of the Yosemite National Park officials. Has been published by Carl P. Russell in California Historical Society Quarterly for March, 1926.

Gudde, Erwin G. *California Place Names.* University of California Press, Berkeley and Los Angeles, California, 1949.

Guinn, J. M. *Historical and Biographical Record of Sacramento Valley, California.* Containing information of Wm. Knight. Chicago: Chapman Publishing Co., 1906.

Harlan, Jacob Wright. *California '46 to '88.* San Francisco, 1888.

Heckendorn & Wilson. Miners and Business Men's Directory for the Year Commencing January 1, 1856. Columbia, California. The Clipper Office. In poss. Calif. Hist. Society, San Francisco, California.

History of the Counties of Merced, Stanislaus, Calaveras, Tuolumne, and Mariposa, California. Chicago: The Lewis Publishing Co., 1892.

History of San Joaquin Co., California. Oakland, California: Thompson & West, 1879.

History of San Joaquin Co., California. Pen Pictures from the Garden of the World. Chicago: The Lewis Publishing Co., 1888.

History of Stanislaus Co., California. San Francisco: Wallace Elliott & Co., 1881.

Hittell, John S. *The Resources of California.* San Francisco: A. Roman & Co. New York: W. J. Middleton, 1863.

Hittell, Theodore H. *History of California.* Vol. 3. San Francisco: H. J. Stone & Co., 1897.

Holmes, Roberta Evelyn. *The Southern Mines of California.* San Francisco: Grabhorn Press, 1930.

Hungerford, Edward. *Wells Fargo Advancing the American Frontier.* New York: Random House, 1949.

Hutchings, James Mason. *Scenes of Wonder and Curiosity in California, a tourists' guide to the Yo-Semite Valley.* New York and San Francisco: A. Roman & Co., 1871.

————. *In the Heart of the Sierras.* Oakland, California: Pacific Publishing House, 1886.

Jackson, Helen Hunt (writing under initials "H. H."). *Bits of Travel at Home.* Boston: Roberts Bros. Cambridge: John Wilson & Son, 1878.

Jackson, Joseph Henry. *Bad Company.* New York: Harcourt, Brace and Co., 1939.

Kells, Charles E. *California from its First Discovery by the Spaniards to the Present Time with a Brief Descripiton of the Gold Mines.* By a traveler. New York, 1848. In Huntington Libr., San Marino, California.

Keyes, Erasmus D., Bvt. Brig. Gen. U. S. Army. *From West Point to California.* Biobooks, Joseph A. Sullivan, No. 24. Oakland, California, 1950.

Kuykendall, Ralph S. *Early History of Yosemite Valley, California.* Article in the Grizzly Bear, June, 1919. Reprinted by the Government Printing Office, 1919.

Lange, Herbert O. *History of Tuolumne County, California.* Vol. 1. San Francisco: B. F. Alley, 1882.

Langley, Henry G. *The Pacific Coast Business Directory for 1871-73.* San Francisco, 1873.

Laws and Judicial Decisions Relating to the Yosemite Valley and Mariposa Big Tree Grove. San Francisco: Cubery & Co., Book and Job Printers, 414 Market St., just below Sansome, 1874.

Le Conte, Joseph. *A Journal of Ramblings through the High Sierra of California, by the University Excursion Party* (in 1870). San Francisco: Francis and Valentine, 517 Clay Street, 1875. A reprint in The Sierra Club, San Francisco, 1930.

Leonard, Zenas. *Leonard's Narrative: Adventures of Zenas Leonard, Fur Trader and Trapper, 1831-36.* (Reprinted from rare original of 1839.) Ed. W. F. Wagner. Cleveland, 1904.

Logan, Olive. Article in Galaxy Magazine, Oct. 1870. In poss. Yosemite National Park Museum.

L.N.R.R. "Our Trip to the Yosemite Valley and Sierra Nevada Range." 1883. At California State Libr., Sacramento, California.

Mason, J. D. *History of Amador County.*

McKeeby, Lemuel Clarke. "Memoirs," Calif. Hist. Soc. Quarterly, April & July, 1924.

Mitchell, Annie R. "Major James D. Savage and the Tularenos." Calif. Hist. Society Quarterly, Dec., 1949., p. 323.

Morgan, Dale L., and Wheat, Carl I. *Jedediah Smith and His Maps of the American West.* San Francisco: Calif. Hist. Society, 1954.

Morley, Griswold S. *The Covered Bridges of California.* University of California Press, Berkeley, California, 1938.

Muir, John. *My First Summer in the Sierra.* Boston and New York: Houghton, Mifflin Co.; Cambridge: The Riverside Press, 1911.

——. *The Mountains of California.* Vol. 2. Boston and New York: Houghton, Mifflin Co., 1916.

Nordhoff, Charles. *California: for Health, Pleasure and Residence.* New York: Harper & Brothers, Publishers, Franklin Square, 1875.

Parkinson, Jessie Heaton. *Adventuring in California Yesterday, Today and the Day Before Yesterday.* With Memoirs of Bret Harte's Tennessee's Partner. San Francisco: Harr Wagner Pub. Co., 1921.

Phelps, Charles A. *Life and Public Service of General Ulysses S. Grant.* Boston: Lee & Shepard, 1868.

Remlap, L. T. *The Life of General U. S. Grant and his Tour Around the World.* (1879.) San Francisco: A. Roman, 1885.

Robinson, Alfred. *Life in California Before the Conquest.* Reprint from the first edition published in New York in 1846. Ed. with notes and foreword by Thomas C. Russell. San Francisco: The Private Press of Thomas C. Russell, 1925.

Ruppel, Margaret Gaylord. *El Rancheria del Rio Estanislaus.* Pasadena, California: Castle Press, 1946.

Russell, Carl Parcher. *Early Years in Yosemite.* Calif. Hist. Soc. Quart., Vol. 5, No. 4, Dec. 1926.

——. *One Hundred Years in Yosemite.* Stanford Univ. Press, Palo Alto, California, 1931.

Ryan, William Redmond. *Personal Adventures in Upper and Lower California in 1848-9* With the Author's Experience at the Mines. In two volumes, London, William Shoberl, Publisher, 20 Great Marlborough Street, 1850.

Shinn, Charles Howard. *Mining Camps, a Study in American Frontier Government.* Introduction by Joseph Henry Jackson. Alfred A. Knopf, New York, 1948. A reprint from the edition of 1884.

Sierra Railroad, The Story of a Short Line. Issued June 20, 1948, for the Sierra

Railroad Excursion of the California-Nevada Railroad Historical Society. The Western Railroader, Vol. 11, No. 8, Number 104.

Sierra Railway Company of California. A booklet entitled "Yosemite Valley via line of the Sierra Railway Company of California." 1898.

Statutes of California, passed at the First Session of the Legislature. Begun the 15th Day of Dec. 1849, and ended the 22nd Day of April, 1850, at the City of Pueblo De San José. San José: J. Winchester, State Printer, 1850.

Statutes of California, passed at the Nineteenth Session of the Legislature. 1871-72. Sacramento: T. A. Springer, State Printer, 1872.

Statutes of California, passed at the Twentieth Session of the Legislature. 1873-1874. Sacramento: G. H. Springer, State Printer, 1874.

Sullivan, Maurice S. *The Travels of Jedediah Strong Smith—1738-1831.* A Documentary Outline Including the Journal of the Great American Pathfinder. The Fine Arts Press, Santa Ana, California, 1934.

Taylor, Ray W. *Hetch Hetchy, Story of the San Francisco Water Supply.* San Francisco: Ricardo J. Orozco, Pub., 1926.

Thompson & West. *History of San Joaquin County.* Oakland, California, 1879.

Tinkham, George Henry. *History of Stanislaus County.* Los Angeles Historic Record Co., 1921.

Tuolumne County, Fifty Years of Progress, 1885-1936. Issued by the "Sonora Banner" of Sonora, California. In poss. of Stanford Univ. Libr., Palo Alto, California.

Tuolumne County, An Exposition of its Resources and Possibilities. Issued by "Sonora Union-Democrat." 1909. In poss. Stanford Univ. Libr., Palo Alto, California.

Turrill, Charles B. *California Notes.* San Francisco: Edward Bosqui & Co., 1876.

Vick's Floral Guide. Privately Printed. Rochester, New York, 1876.

Walsh, Henry L., S.J. *Hallowed Were the Gold Dust Trails.* Santa Clara, California: University of Santa Clara Press, 1946.

Western Shore Gazetteer and Commercial Directory for the State of California, Yolo County. One volume being devoted to each county of the State. Compiled and published annually by C. P. Sprague & H. W. Atwell, Woodland, Yolo County, 1870.

Whipple-Haslam, Mrs. Lee. *Early Days in California,* a Pamphlet. Jamestown, California, 1925.

Whitney, J. D., State Geologist. Geological Survey of California. *The Yosemite Book.* Pub. by authority of the Legislature. New York: Julius Bien, 1868.

——.*The Yosemite Guide Book*. Pub. by authority of the Legislature. Cambridge: University Press: Welch, Bigelow & Co., 1874.

Winther, Oscar Osburn. *Express and Stage Coach Days in California*. Stanford Univ. Press, Palo Alto, California, 1936.

Wood, Richard Coke. *Tales of the Old Calaveras*. Pub. by the Calaveras Californian, Angels Camp, 1949.

Wood, Stanley. *Over the Range to the Golden Gate*. Chicago: R. R. Donnelley & Sons, 1889.

Woods, Rev. James. *Recollections of Pioneer Work in California*. Printed by Joseph Winterburn & Co., San Francisco, 1878.

Yosemite Valley, via the Big Oak Flat Road, an advertising booklet. San Francisco, Alta California print, 529 California street, 1881.

MANUSCRIPTS

Abrams, William Penn. MS Diary, Feb., 1849-May, 1850. Written on a journey to California by the Chagres Route and items in the Southern Mines. Recounts seeing Yosemite Valley in Oct., 1849. Bancroft Libr.

Anderson, P. "A Visit to Yosemite Valley," a letter written in 1892 in the Danish language, recently translated. Typescript in poss. Jessie Plowman, Alameda, California.

Archives of California; Departmental State Papers. Naturalization. Tomo XX, One reference slip from. Referring to date of naturalization of Peter Lassen.

Ballou, Wm. T., Adventures of. MS in Binder, Bancroft Libr., University of California. Berkeley, Calif.

"Black Binder" containing facts about early settlers. Calif. State Libr., Sacramento, California.

Brewer, William H. Pocket Daily Journal for the year 1863. Bancroft Libr., Univ. of Calif. Berkeley, California.

Buzzell, Willard Joseph, known facts about. Contained in "Black Binder of Early Pioneers." California State Library, Sacramento, California.

California Battalion, Muster role of Capt. Richard Owen's Company (A) of California Battalion, U. S. forces, commanded by Lieut. Col. John Charles Fremont. From the 7th day of October, 1846. In Calif. State Library, Sacramento, Calif.

Case, Katherine Norton. Reminiscence of a Trip to Yosemite in 1905, MS in poss. Irene D. Paden, Alameda, California.

Chamberlain, Jason Palmer. MS diaries, 1851-1903. In Bancroft Libr., University of California, Berkeley, California.

———. MS. Reminiscence of his Life and that of his Partner, James A. Chaffee, after Leaving Boston for California. Signed "Tennessee and Partner." In Bancroft Libr., University of California, Berkeley, California.

Clark, Galen. MS. "A Plea for Yosemite." In Yosemite National Park Archives. Yosemite, California.

Cutting, Daniel. MS. Diary of year 1852. Written in Southern Mines of California. Incomplete. In poss. Helen Stratton of Chinese Camp, a granddaughter.

Dakin, Henry R. MS. Reminiscences of boyhood days in Knights Ferry in poss. Irene D. Paden, Alameda, California.

Dudley, Hosea E. MS Diary — 1849. Including details of his stay in Stockton, Knights Ferry and Sullivan's Diggings, California. Courtesy of W. D. Mc-Lean, Coulterville, Calif.

Eccleston, Robert. MS Journal of Expedition against the Indians of California. Begins Feb. 12, 1851. In Bancroft Library, Univ. of Calif., Berkeley, California.

Fletcher, Elton. A History of the French Camp Settlement to 1853, a seminar report. College of the Pacific, Stockton, Calif.

Golden Rock Water Company, account book of. Dated 1864. In poss. Margaret E. Schlichtmann, San Leandro, Calif.

Haight, Sarah. MS Diary kept during a trip to Yosemite, beginning May 20, 1858. In California State Libr., Sacramento, California.

Hayes, Wilton R. Overland Diary — 1855. At Bancroft Libr., Univ. of California, Berkeley, California.

Hunt, James E. "Reminiscences of an Old Soldier." Typescript at California State Libr., Sacramento, California.

Hutchings, James Mason. MS. Diary including trip across the plains, 1849. A copy by his daughter, Gertrude Hutchings Mills, in Yosemite Museum archives. Yosemite, California.

———. Letter to "esteemed friend" dated "Old Dry Diggings, City commonly called Hangtown," Dec. 19, 1849. Printed in a New Orleans newspaper. Name and date unknown. Signed "California Correspondence." In Yosemite Museum Archives.

Hutchins, Dexter H. Letters to his wife, dated Stockton 1853-54. MSS in poss. Warren White, College of the Pacific, Stockton, California.

Kingston, Betty. The Story of the Stanislaus. A seminar paper. College of the Pacific. Stockton, California.

Kirtland, Harriet J. A Journal of a trip through the Southern Mines, May 13 to June 3, 1857. Typescript in poss. Calif. State Libr., Sacramento, California.

Knight, Thomas. MS. Recollections. References to Willard J. Buzzell and James Savage in a postscript, following the signature. Bancroft Library.

Knight, William, Known facts about. Contained in "Black Binder of Early Pioneers." Calif. State Libr., Sacramento, California.

Landsburg, Mrs. Statement concerning Sacramento and general customs of miners. MS in poss. Frank Whitlock, Chico, California.

Locke, David Morrell. MS diary written for the most part in San Francisco, 1849. (Longhand copy by Henry R. Dakin, Santa Cruz.) Original destroyed. Copy in poss. Irene D. Paden, Alameda, California.

Locke, Elbridge Gerry. MS diary written for the most part in Knights Ferry, 1853. Microfilm at Bancroft Libr., University of California, Berkeley, California.

Maben, John R. Letter to his wife, Sarah. Dated "California Gold Mines, Nov. 15, 1849." In poss. Comdr. Robert S. Lecky. U. S. Coast Guard. 12th Coast Guard District.

Morris, Paul. Statement concerning the Hanging at Second Garrote. Typescript in folder at Yosemite Museum Archives. Yosemite, California.

Newman, John. Scrapbook (made from a ledger) containing receipts for bills of goods purchased from San Francisco firms in the year 1865-1866. In possession of John Newman, Sonora, California.

Plummer, Charles. MS Diary of 1850. A portion deals with Indians of the Stanislaus River. In Huntington Libr., San Marino, California.

Prindle, Samuel Linus. Diary. Mar., 1849-Apr., 1850. Typescript. Orig. in possession of Everett V. Pringle. Bancroft Library.

Reynolds, Mattie V. Facts about Knights Ferry and David M. Locke, told by his son, Alex Locke, at Scott's Valley. Sept. 18, 1939. Typescript at Bancroft Libr., University of California, Berkeley, California.

, Robert. Letter to wife headed Sonora, California, May 1850. (No surname given.) MS at Huntington Library, San Marino, California.

Scrapbook of California Counties. Santa Cruz to Yuba. Set. W. Vol. 5. At Bancroft Library, University of California, Berkeley, California.

Scrapbook of California Counties. Solano to Stanislaus. At Bancroft Library, University of California, Berkeley, California.

Smith, David S. Narrative of. Compiled by Mrs. H. P. Buckland. Contained in Gold Rush Diary of Byron N. McKinstry, 1850-52, edited with foreword by Bruce L. McKinstry, Riverside, Illinois. In poss. of the latter.

Sprague, G. E. Testimony in the Court Proceedings: Coulterville & Yosemite Turnpike Co., appellant vs the State of California, respondent (No. 18277) Oct. 1893. In Yosemite National Park Archives.

Solinsky, William. Written statement concerning Chinese Camp and his father, C. W. H. Solinsky. In poss. Edward Solinsky, Hobart Bldg., San Francisco, California.

Taylor, Mrs. H. J. The Cemetery in Yosemite Valley. A photostat of typescript, in Calif. State Libr., Sacramento, California.

Todd, Alexander H. Statement. Found in binder of miscellaneous statements at Bancroft Library, Univ. of Calif., Berkeley, California.

Wiggins, W. L. Letter to Thomas O. Larkin, contained in Larkin Documents for the History of California. Vol. 2, Pt. 1, p. 172.

LETTERS, QUESTIONNAIRES AND INTERVIEWS

Bacon, Annie. Interviews on Chinese Camp. Given in Alameda, California.

Baugh, Mrs. Samuel. Interviews concerning Knights Ferry.

Brabazon, Mr. and Mrs. Lynn Owen. Concerning old families of Moccasin, California, and the bridges over the Tuolumne River at Jacksonville. Interviews and questionnaires.

Brennan, Mrs. Daniel Nolan. Interviews and letters concerning Twenty Six Mile Station and Twenty Eight Mile Station on the old Sonora Road.

Browder, Bertha Bolter. Letter and interview concerning Keystone, Tuolumne County, given in Waterford, California.

Byrne, Mattie Lumsden. Letter concerning facts about Tuolumne County.

Cassaretto, Lula Longfellow. Letter and interview concerning Deer Flat, Tuolumne County, given in Piedmont, California.

Cobden, Harry A. Letter from San Francisco concerning Big Oak Flat.

Corcoran, Edwin. Interview concerning history of Deer Flat, Tuolumne County, California, given in Deer Flat.

Curtin, Robert A. Letters and interviews concerning history of Tuolumne County, given in San Rafael, California.

Dakin, Isaac. Interviews concerning Knights Ferry given in Santa Cruz.

Dakin, Wilbur. Interviews concerning history of Knights Ferry given in Alameda, California.

Della-Vedowa, Harriet Orcutt. Interview concerning history of Jacksonville, Tuolumne County, given in Oakland, California.

De Ferrari, Fred. Interviews concerning history of Groveland and Deer Flat, Tuolumne County.

Degnan, Lawrence. Interview concerning early days in Yosemite Valley given in Yosemite Valley.

De Martini, John. Interviews concerning history of Groveland and Deer Flat, Tuolumne County, California, given in Groveland, California.

De Paoli, Clotilda Repetto. Letters and interviews concerning history of Big Oak Flat.

Egling, Mr. and Mrs. George. Letters and interviews concerning history of Chinese Camp and the Tong war. Given in San Jose, California.

Egling, Howard. Letters concerning Chinese Camp and the Tong war. From his home in Le Grande.

Ernst, Emil F. Forester, Yosemite Nat'l Park. Letter containing information on the saddle trail from the north rim of the valley.

Ferretti, John V. Interviews concerning history of Tuolumne County and, in particular, of the "Dead Giant" at Tuolumne Grove of Big Trees. Given in Alameda, California.

Fisher, Eunice Watson. Interviews concerning history of Big Oak Flat and Yosemite Valley, given in Big Oak Flat, California.

Freir, Elizabeth Bacon. Interview on Chinese Camp, Tuolumne County, California, given in Alameda, California.

Goss, Helen Rocca. Letters concerning her father, Andrew Rocca, and the Golden Rock Water Company of Tuolumne County, from her home in Montgomery, Alabama.

Gray, John. Interview concerning history of Deer Flat, Tuolumne County, California, given at Deer Flat.

Harper, Charles. Interviews concerning Big Oak Flat, Tuolumne County, California, given in Big Oak Flat, California.

Harper, Edwin. Letters and interviews concerning Big Oak Flat, Tuolumne County, California, given in Big Oak Flat, California.

Hineman, Don. Letter from Sonora concerning Tuolumne County.

Hopkins, Edwin Doel. Statement regarding activities of Troop M, 14th Cavalry, in Yosemite Nat'l Park. Dated, San Rafael, 1952.

Hughes, Thomas. Interviews concerning Moccasin, Tuolumne County, California, given in Moccasin, Tuolumne, California.

Jones, Eugene. Interview concerning Groveland, Tuolumne County, California, given in Groveland, California.

Kennedy, Helen Weber. Letter and interviews on the life of Charles Marie Weber and beginnings of Stockton, April, 1953.

Lavaroni, Mrs. Jocunda Boitano. Interview concerning the Boitano adobe, given in Groveland, California.

Leidig, Charles. Interviews concerning early life in Yosemite Valley, given in Hayward, California.

May, Ellen Harper. Letters and interviews concerning Tuolumne County, given in Big Oak Flat, California.

McLean, W. D. Interview on Indians of Tuolumne and Mariposa Counties, given in Coulterville, California.

Mecartea, Austin. Interviews on Chinese Camp and Big Oak Flat, Tuolumne County, California, given in Big Oak Flat, California.

Mecartea, Eugene. Letters and interviews concerning Chinese Camp and Big Oak Flat, Tuolumne County, California, given in Big Oak Flat, California.

Mills, Gertrude Hutchings. Letter and interview concerning early Yosemite Valley in Tuolumne Meadows, Yosemite Nat'l Park, California.

Mogan, Nora Carlon. Interviews concerning Groveland and Yosemite Valley given on old Carlon Ranch, Groveland.

Molanda, Peter. Interviews concerning Crocker's Station, given at the site of Crocker's Station, Tuolumne County, California.

Morris, Paul. Interview concerning Big Oak Flat Road given at "Cliff House" on South Fork of Tuolumne River, Tuolumne County, California.

Morris, Saul. Letters and interviews concerning Chinese Camp, Tuolumne County, California, given in Stockton, California.

Osborne, Wesley. Letters and interviews concerning Groveland and the Golden Rock Water Company, given at Sugar Pine Ranch, Groveland, California.

Peregoy, C. F. Interview concerning Peregoy Meadows, given at his home in Lafayette, California.

Phelan, Catherine (Kitty) Munn. Interview concerning Moccasin and Jacksonville, Tuolumne County, California, given in San Mateo, California.

Reid, Anna Jones. Letters and interviews concerning Groveland, California.

Reynolds, Henrietta. Interview concerning the cache of Hudson's Bay Company's weapons uncovered in 1856 at Stockton, California.

Ryan, John. Letter concerning Tuolumne County from his home in Berkeley, California.

Sandner, Maria Ferretti. Interview concerning Moccasin Creek, Tuolumne County, California, given in her home at Moccasin, California.

Schmidt, Charles. Interviews concerning the freight route, Second Garrote, and the Golden Rock Water Company, Tuolumne County, California, given in Second Garrote, California.

Schmidt, Fred. Same.

Sell, William. Interview concerning locations of early day sites in Yosemite Valley, given in his ranch at Ahwahnee, California.

Simmons, Robert. Interview concerning the Big Oak Flat Road, given in Big Oak Flat, California.

Sims, Robert. Interview concerning Chinese Camp, Crimea House and Six Bit Gulch, given in Chinese Camp, California.

Solinsky, Edward. Interview concerning his grandfather, C. W. H. Solinsky, given at his office in San Francisco, California.

Stratton, Helen Cutting. Interviews and questionnaire concerning Chinese Camp, given in Chinese Camp, Tuolumne County, California.

Speer, William. Letter concerning Tuolumne County, from Sonora, California.

Thompson, Celia Crocker. Many letters, photographs and interviews concerning the Big Oak Flat Road, given in Lodi, California.

Tulloch, David. Interviews and questionnaire concerning Knights Ferry, given in Oakdale, California.

Vail, Sylvia Repetto. Interviews concerning Big Oak Flat, Tuolumne County, given in Big Oak Flat, California.

Voyle, George. Interviews concerning Knights Ferry, given in Visalia, California.

Williams, Mrs. H. L. Interviews and questionnaire concerning Knights Ferry.

Willms, Raymond. Interview concerning Knights Ferry.

Wilson, William Henry. Interview concerning Big Oak Flat Road, given in Tuolumne City, California.

Yates, Alice Phelan. Letters concerning Noisy Flat and the Phelan family.

PERIODICALS

Ballou's Pictorial Magazine. Boston, Mass. August, 1855.

California Historical Society Quarterly. San Francisco, Calif. Jan. 1923. *Early Days in Yosemite"* by Ansel F. Hall; Apr. & July, 1924; Mar. 1926; Dec. 1926; Dec. 1949.

Galaxy Magazine. October, 1870. Article by Olive Logan. Yosemite Museum Archives, Yosemite, California.

Gleason's Pictorial Drawing-Room Companion. Boston, Mass. Jan. 21, Feb. 18, 1854.

Grizzly Bear. June, 1919.

Harper's Weekly, New York. July 20, 1872.

Illustrated London News. No. 662. Vol. XXIV (beginning January 7, 1854). Jan. 21, 1854. Page 63.

Knights Ferry, Stanislaus Index. Feb. 1, Feb. 28, 1862.

Mariposa Gazette, Mariposa, California. June 8, 1867; March 13, 1875.

Oakdale Leader. Feb. 16, 1924. May 22, 1930.

Overland Monthly, San Francisco. Bret Harte Memorial number. Sept. 1902.

Pioneer, The. Monthly magazine. Pub. by the Pioneer Publishing Co., San Francisco. Vol. XIII, No. 5, May 15, 1898.

Sacramento Union, Sacramento, California. Mar. 5, 1859.

San Francisco Alta California. Jan. 17, 1850; Sept. 13, Nov. 17, Nov. 24, Dec. 19, 1851; March 14, 1852; Jan. 18, Oct. 17, Oct. 30, Nov. 24, 1853; Mar. 22, Aug. 6, 1856; May 25, 1857; June 18, 1858; Apr. 1, Apr. 6, 1860; Jan. 1, Jan. 8, Jan. 17, 1862; Oct. 8, 1863.

San Francisco Bulletin. Oct. 8, 1855; May 7, May 17; June 9, 1856; June 27, 1857; Apr. 1, 1868; May 28, 1869.

San Francisco Chronicle. Apr. 18, Apr. 21, 1906; Apr. 12, 1910; Sept. 22, Oct. 15, 1912.

San Francisco Examiner. Oct. 15, 1912; April 19, May 9, 1925.

San Joaquin Republican. Jan. 11, 1862.

Sierra Club Bulletin. Vol. 36, No. 5, April, 1939; May, 1951.

Sonora American Flag. Sept. 18, Nov. 6, 1862.

Sonora Banner. Nov. 11, Nov. 24, 1911; June 17, 1937; June 17, 1941; June 3, June 26, 1952.

Sonora Herald. July 27, 1850; Oct. 18, 1853; July 28, 1866; July 6, 1867.

Sonora Tuolumne Independent. July 11, July 18, 1874; May 29, 1886; Nov. 23, Dec. 5, 1911; Jan. 7, 1916.

Sonora Union Democrat. Sept. 27, 1850; June 16, Oct. 13, Oct. 18, 1855; Aug. 26, Aug. 30, 1856; Mar. 13, 1858; Mar. 3, July 11, 1866; Mar. 8, 1868; Mar. 27, 1869; Aug. 13, 1870; July 11, 1871; July 13, 1872; May 10, May 24, May 31, Aug. 9, Aug. 16, Sept. 13, Sept. 20, Oct. 18, Oct. 25, Nov. 22, Dec. 20, 1873; Feb. 7, Apr. 11, May 9, June 20, July 17, July 25, Aug. 1, Dec. 19, 1874; Jan. 16, May 29, 1875; Apr. 13, July 13, Nov. 9, 1878; Aug. 7, 1909; June 29, 1912; June 18, 1932; Jan. 6, 1955.

Stanislaus News, Modesto, California. Jan. 22, 1875.

Stockton Argus. Nov. 7, Nov. 27, 1850.

Stockton Daily Beacon. June 18, 1864.

Stockton Daily Independent. Jan. 1, 1863; Nov. 7, Dec. 26, 1874; Feb. 2, Feb. 11, Feb. 24, Mar. 8, 1894.

Stockton Journal. Aug. 24, Nov. 6, 1850; Mar. 12, 1852.

Stockton Prospector. Dec. 9, 1911.

Stockton Record. Feb. 2, 1935; Apr. 7, 1952.

Stockton San Joaquin Republican. July 1, July 14, Sept. 7, 1855.

Yosemite Nature Notes. Pub. by Yosemite Natural History Association, Yosemite, California, Vol. XXIX, No. 7. July, 1950.

DOCUMENTS

Beauvais, A. B. Report: U. S. Deputy Mineralogy Surveyor, 1873. In General Land Office, Dept. of the Interior, San Francisco, California.

Bergin, William E. Major Gen. U.S.A. Letter (contents taken from documents) from the office of the Adjutant General. Concerning the military assignments of Ulysses S. Grant while in California, between 1851 and 1854. In poss. Margaret E. Schlichtmann, San Leandro, California.

Big Oak Flat Road. A report, dated Feb. 8, 1900, of the Commission on Roads in Yosemite National Park. Senate Doc. No. 155, 56th Congress, 1st Session.

Chinese Camp. MS. Notice of a meeting held at Chinese Camp, Sept. 19, 1868, to organize the Yo Semite Turnpike Road Company and to elect officers. In Bancroft Library, University of California, Berkeley, California.

Chinese Camp. MS. Notice of a meeting held at Chinese Camp, March 19, 1869, in which the Yo Semite Turnpike Road Company was organized and (different) officers elected. In poss. Dr. D. Deakins, Murphys, California.

Coulterville Road. A Report, dated Dec. 4, 1899, of the Commission on Roads in Yosemite National Park. Senate Doc. No. 155, 56th Congress, 1st Session. Feb. 8, 1900.

>   (We are indebted to the courtesy of Ed. Whitmore of Modesto,
>   California, for the use of the following documents pertaining
>   to Knights Ferry.)

Knights Ferry. Bond for $5000 in connection with the ferry known as Knight's ferry and also with Keeler's ferry, filed Oct. 11, 1856, and signed by the four partners, John C. Dent, Lewis Dent, George W. Dent and D. M. Locke.

Knights Ferry. Petition to the Board of Supervisors of Stanislaus Co., begun Aug. 1, 1856; filed Oct. 13, 1856, requesting a license for Thos. W. Lane and others to erect a toll bridge or build a suitable ferry at the (then) present crossing at Knights Ferry. Signed by Palmer and Allen, merchants, and 70 others.

Knights Ferry. Statement that, on Nov. 1, 1856, all the ferry franchise appertaining to Knight's and Keeler's ferries was sold to "Mr. D. M. Lock." Signed "Dent & Bro."

Knights Ferry. Notice that the undersigned intends to apply to the Board of Supervisors of Stanislaus County for a license to build a bridge across the Stanislaus River immediately above the Stanislaus Mills. Dated December 4, 1856. Signed D. M. Locke.

Knights Ferry. Petition of D. M. Locke, who represents that he is the sole owner of Knight's ferry on the Stanislaus River, to the Board of Supervisors of Stanislaus County for permission to build a toll bridge immediately above the Stanislaus Mills. Undated.

Knights Ferry. Bond to the amount of $5000 signed by four men: Palmer and Allen, Lewis McGlauflin and John C. Dent as bondsmen for S. M. Locke in building the toll bridge at Knights Ferry. February 27, 1858.

Knights Ferry. Article of Incorporation for "The Stanislaus Bridge and Ferry Company." Value $48,000. Consisting of Knights Ferry bridge, Two Mile Bar Bridge and Keeler's Ferry. August 4, 1858. D. M. Locke, Pres.

Knights Ferry. Petition to the Board of Supervisors of Stanislaus County for an increase in the toll rate over the bridge at Knights Ferry. Signed D. M. Locke. Dated August 9, 1858.

Knights Ferry. The first annual report of the Stanislaus Bridge & Ferry Co., organized Aug. 1, 1858, at Knights Ferry. Stock $48,000, the whole amt. actually paid in and free from debt. Tolls for the 5 months $6444.00. Expenses 1731.62. Dividends made 4712.38. [Signed] D. M. Locke, Pres. G. J. Slocum, Sec. Dated Jan. 3, 1859.

Knights Ferry. An act of the Board of Supervisors of Stanislaus County granting to "The Stanislaus Bridge and Ferry Company" the right to construct and maintain a bridge across the Stanislaus River, and fixing the rates of toll to be charged when completed. Filed May 5, 1862. Signed A. B. Andeman, Clerk.

Knights Ferry. Misc. Documents in possession of Mr. and Mrs. Roy De Graffenreid, Knights Ferry, California.

Knights Ferry. Certificate of sale containing the name "O'Byrne." Signed Geo. W.

Branch. Dated Mar. 15, 1864. In possession of Mr. Ed. Whitmore, Modesto, Calif.

Sonora. Articles of Incorporation. No. 48, Tuolumne County records. Golden Rock Water Company. February 27, 1856. At Court House, Sonora.

Sonora. Notice of intention to build a toll road. Filed October 17, 1868. MS at Bancroft Library, Berkeley, California.

Sonora. Articles of incorporation. No. 319, Tuolumne County records, Sonora, California. For the Great Sierra Stage Company. Filed March 15, 1886.

Sprague, George. Testimony in the court proceedings: Coulterville & Yosemite Turnpike Co., appellant, vs The State of California, respondent (No. 18227) Oct. 1893. In Yosemite Park Archives.

Wood, Richard G. (for Dallas Irvine, Chief Archivist War Records Branch). Letter (contents taken from documents of the National Archive and Records Service. Washington, D. C. July 25, 1952. In poss. Margaret E. Schlichtmann, San Leandro, California.

MAPS

1848.   Topographical Sketch of the Gold and Quicksilver District of California. In Bancroft Libr., University of California, Berkeley, California.

1848.   A Correct Map of the Bay of San Francisco and the Gold Region. Contained in *Maps of the California Gold Region*, 1848-1857, Map No. 247. Carl I. Wheat, Grabhorn Press, San Francisco, 1942.

——.   Ibid., Map No. 161.

——.   Ibid., Map No. 162.

1849.   Sketch of General Riley's Route through the Mining Districts, July-August, 1849. Bancroft Libr., University of California, Berkeley, California.

1849.   Map of California, Oregon and Texas and the Territories adjoining the Route. J. H. Colton, publisher. New York, 1849. Courtesy of Harold C. Holmes, Oakland, California.

1849.   MS Map of Stockton surveyed for the proprietor, Charles M. Weber, June, 1849, by Bvt. Major Richard P. Hammond. Original in poss. Helen Weber Kennedy, Stockton, California. Copy in Haggin Memorial Museum, Stockton, California.

1850.   Map of the Gold Region of California. J. Disturnell, publisher. New York, 1850. Courtesy of Harold C. Holmes, Oakland, California.

1852.   Map of the Southern Mines. C. D. Gibbes. 1852. Lith. of Quirot & Co., corner California & Mongy Sts., San Francisco. Contained in Life in California, James H. Carson, Stockton, 1852. 2nd edition.

1855.   The Silas Wilcox Map. County Line Dividing Stanislaus and Tuolumne Counties. Courtesy of Ed. Whitmore, Modesto, California.

1861.   Map of the City of Stockton and Environs with additions and corrections to March, 1861, by Duncan Beaumont, E.E. Pub. by Kierski & Bro., San Francisco. In Haggin Museum, Stockton, California.

1863.   Map of a portion of the Sierra Nevada adjacent to the Yosemite Valley, from surveys made by Charles F. Hoffman and J. T. Gardner. Contained in *The Yosemite Book*, J. D. Whitney, State Geologist, 1868.

——.   Plan of Knights Ferry, California. Townsite 2A 12a. Presented to the office of the County Surveyor of Stanislaus Co. by Herman Miller of the Judge Hewel estate, Jan. 20, 1924. Courthouse, Modesto, California.

1865.   Map of the Yosemite Valley from surveys made by order of the Commissioners to manage the Yosemite Valley and the Mariposa Big Tree Grove. Drawn by J. T. Gardner. Contained in *The Yosemite Book*, J. D. Whitney, 1868.

——.   A sectional Outline of the Golden Rock Ditch, Tuolumne Co., California. Undated. Courtesy of Mr. John O'Hara, Sonora, California.

1870.   Map of San Joaquin County compiled from U. S. surveys. Declared official map of county by the supervisors, July 6, 1870. Copy at Haggin Museum, Stockton, California.

——.   Bird's Eye View of the City of Stockton in 1870. Drawn by Augustus Koch. Lith. Britton & Ray, San Francisco, Calif.

1872.   Map of the Routes from San Francisco to the Yosemite Valley prepared to accompany the pocket edition of the Yosemite Guide Book, State Geological Survey, 1872.

1874.   Map of the Yosemite Valley prepared to accompany the pocket edition of the Yosemite Guide Book, State Geological Survey, 1874.

1879.   Map of the principal quartz and gravel mines, Tuolumne Co., California. Taken from government surveys and mining records by J. P. Dart, mining engineer, Sonora, California, August, 1879. Lith. A. L. Bancroft & Co., San Francisco. In poss. Margaret E. Schlichtmann, San Leandro, California.

No   Maps of Land Holdings (large scale) covering country from French Camp,
date.   San Joaquin Co., to Eugene, Stanislaus Co., California. Pub. by Budd and Widdows, Stockton, California.

Hand-drawn maps of the Big Oak Flat Road and Environs. By long-time residents. In poss. Margaret E. Schlichtmann.

Curtin, Robert A.
Map of Cloudman-Keystone Area
Map of Chinese Camp
Map of Upper Big Oak Flat Road

Dakin, Wilbur Jameson
Rough map of Knights Ferry as it was in 1875 (from memory)

De Paoli, Clotilda
Map of Big Oak Flat

Egling, George
Map of Chinese Camp

Harper, Edwin
Map of Big Oak Flat

Morris, Saul
Map of Crimea House and Site of Tong War
Map of Six Bit Gulch and Chinese Camp

Thompson, Celia Crocker
Map of the Upper Big Oak Flat Road.

Index